ESSEX BOY

ESSEX BOY LAST MAN STANDING

STEVE 'NIPPER' ELLIS
WITH BERNARD O'MAHONEY

MAINSTREAM
PUBLISHING

EDINBURGH AND LONDON

First published in Great Britain in 2009 by
MAINSTREAM PUBLISHING COMPANY
(EDINBURGH) LTD
7 Albany Street
Edinburgh EH1 3UG

ISBN 9781845964993

A catalogue record for this book is available
from the British Library

Typeset in Badhouse and Palatino

Printed in Great Britain by
CPI Mackays, Chatham ME5 8TD

INTRODUCTION

- -

Everybody's heard of the Essex Boys firm. They controlled much of the drugs trade in the south-east of England during the 1990s but their lucrative operation was eventually closed down when Patrick Tate, Tony Tucker and Craig Rolfe, the gang's key members, were rendered redundant after being shot through the head. One minute they were sitting in their Range Rover conspiring to flood the county with class-A drugs, the next they were lying in a morgue with their plans and heads in tatters. The police described the crime as 'a senseless slaughter'. I chose to call it fucking justice. News of the three men's demise was the best Christmas present that I and many others have ever had. Tate, Tucker and Rolfe were simply bullies who had got their comeuppance.

There are, of course, those that disagree with me. They try to portray the deceased as decent guys but they undoubtedly have no idea what they were really like. According to one particular hanger-on, they were misunderstood men who treated their friends like brothers; 'They lived like kings' apparently, and 'partied like animals'. The trio were undoubtedly misunderstood. In fact, their heads were so messed up with drugs they didn't have a clue what they were saying or doing, never mind other people being able to fathom out their madness. I have to concede that their friends were treated well, but only by the NHS when they had made their way to hospital after being beaten or stabbed by those bastards. God only knows what planet those so-called kings were supposed to be from because here, on terra firma, I was not aware of any kingdom that they ruled. And as for partied like animals? Yes, OK, I will give them that one, but only because they were animals. How else can dumb animals behave other than like dumb animals?

That may sound harsh, but don't be fooled by all that mythical bollocks about villains not hurting women and kids and looking after their own. The three murdered men didn't care who they hurt and they only looked after themselves. They were more than happy to beat, slash, stab or murder people who dared to interfere in their drug-dealing empire. Even that's not entirely true because they were, in fact, happy to beat, slash, stab or murder people simply because they didn't like the look of them.

That's why I found myself sitting in my car near Pat Tate's bungalow with a loaded gun in my hand one night. Over the previous two weeks, the Essex Boys firm had beaten me, threatened my family, trashed my home and stolen all my possessions. After all that, they were still telling people that they were going to catch me and subject me to a long and painful death. Why? I don't even think they knew the answer to that question. I was supposed to be their mate, one of the boys, in the firm. What a fucking joke. I am grateful that I was not their enemy.

I can clearly remember the night it all came to a head. In fact, it's unlikely that I will ever be able to forget it. I told myself that I'd had enough of their violence and threats; I was not prepared to take their shit any more. It was time for them to experience fear; I had decided that those three morons must die in a hail of bullets . . .

17 November 1994. I have spent the evening driving around looking for Tate, Tucker and Rolfe in their usual haunts but they are nowhere to be seen. I end up driving past Rolfe's home in Chafford Hundred but his vehicle is not in the drive. Tucker's car is also missing from outside his home. I know that if their cars are not there, then they will be absent too, so I drive over to Basildon to look for Tate. The sight of his black Porsche parked outside his bungalow in Gordon Road sends my heart racing and my adrenalin flowing. They are celebrating Tony Tucker's birthday tonight by throwing a party at a snooker hall in Dagenham. I can imagine Tate in the bungalow, no doubt admiring his steroid-

bloated frame in some mirror, preparing to join in with the celebrations. Vain fuck! I have not put any planning into what I intend to do next and so I tell myself that instead of aiming for any particular part of his enormous body, I will just empty the gun I have in my hand into him as he steps out of the front door. My heart is pounding; so much so that it feels as if it's going to burst through my shirt.

In an effort to remain composed, I pray to a god that I don't even believe in. As my breathing moderates itself I notice a light being switched on in a bedroom and I can see the silhouette of a slightly built woman moving across the room. 'Shit, shit, shit,' I hiss through clenched teeth, as I punch the centre of the steering wheel. Tate's long-suffering girlfriend, Sarah, is in the bungalow and no doubt she has their son Jordan with her. I know that I have to abandon my last-minute plan to blow Tate away as he walks out of his home. There is now a possibility that Sarah and their child may come through the door with him and I would not dream of putting either of them at risk. I start the engine of my car and roar off down the street. Common sense tells me to keep on driving but I know that if I allow Tate to live then I am going to die, it really is that simple. I have no choice. I have to go through with this.

I have a pump-action shotgun hidden not too far away from Tate's home and I am beginning to think that I may need it. If one gun fails me, then Tate will undoubtedly pounce on me and I will suffer an unimaginable death. I make my way to the outskirts of Basildon, where I retrieve the weapon that I have hidden in a friend's garden shed. The six-shot pump has been cut down and fits nicely into my jacket. I feel more confident now. I believe that I can end Tate's miserable life and, in doing so, end my own personal misery. I get into my car and head back into Basildon. Pulling over by a railway bridge, I check that my weapons are loaded. I secrete the guns in my jacket and exit my vehicle. I am worried Sarah may see my face; she knows me and may be willing to assist the police if I kill Tate. I haven't had time to get a balaclava and so I tear one of the sleeves from my jumper and, using a knife, cut two eye holes in it. Tate would hate me if he knew what was coming. He likes to think of himself as flash, a bit of a wide boy. Getting shot is bad enough, but he would find getting shot by a badly dressed assassin extremely humiliating. I laugh to myself. Even my balaclava is a fake. Fuck him! I have given up worrying about what Pat Tate thinks. Tonight he is going to die.

I scale a fence and make my way down a steep railway embankment and onto the tracks. It's pitch black and I stumble more than once as I make my way to the rear of Tate's home. After climbing the railway embankment I crash through a thorn bush and vault a panel fence. I have landed in Tate's garden. Fearing I may have made too much noise, I run for cover towards his back door. Crouching down, I check the handgun once more and try to remain focused and calm. The back of the bungalow is lit up; the kitchen window is to my right, a bedroom window to my left. In the middle of these is a frosted glass window that I know is the bathroom. I am beginning to have reservations about carrying out my grisly task, but I know I cannot go back now. 'Do it, Nipper, just fucking do it,' I keep telling myself. I inhale deeply three times, pull on my makeshift balaclava and get to my feet. The bathroom light is on and Tate is moving about behind the glass. I cannot physically see him; I just know that the shadow of the hulk-like frame can only be Tate's because no other human being I have ever known is that big. I pick up a brick and hurl it at the bathroom window, which explodes upon impact. I am standing less than three feet from the gaping hole in the window when Tate peers out. The expression on his face confirms the fear I believe he is now experiencing. Our eyes meet. I aim the gun at his face and squeeze the trigger. Tate calls out, 'No, no,' and I say to myself, 'Yes, oh yes.'

The trigger of my gun 'clicks' and the fucking thing fails to fire. Realising he has been given a stay of execution, Tate turns to run and I lean through the broken window. 'Click'. The gun fails me a second time and so I pull the trigger again. A deafening explosion fills my ears; the bullet finds its target and Tate begins to scream, 'Get the police, get the police. I've been shot.' His fear fills me with a perverse sense of power and I crave to end his worthless life. I had been in Tate's bungalow on many occasions in the past and so I am aware of the layout. As Tate flees from the bathroom he turns right and I know that he has entered the kitchen. I run around to the side window of that room and attempt to shoot him once more but the gun fails to fire for a third time.

Tate is looking directly at me and continues screaming, begging Sarah to call the police. As I point the gun at him again, he runs out of the kitchen and heads towards the front of the property. I assume that he is going to exit via the front door and so I stand facing it, legs apart in a firing position, waiting to blast him with the pump-action shotgun that I have taken from my coat. I can hear both Sarah and Tate screaming now. He is shouting down a telephone, 'Police, Police, get here fucking quick. I've been shot and the gunman is still outside.'

I could burst into the bungalow and finish Tate off but I assume that Sarah is comforting him and therefore I would be putting her in danger. My only option is to save myself and leave the scene before the police arrive. I run through the back garden, clamber over the fence and hurl myself backwards into a thorn bush. Half running, half falling, I make my way down the railway embankment and then jog away along the tracks and into the darkness. As I climb the railway embankment to get back onto the road I can hear the wail of sirens as the emergency services approach Tate's home. Gasping for breath but determined not to be apprehended I sprint to my car, jump in and speed away. I have no idea where Tate has been shot; I am gutted that he hasn't taken one in the head. I just hope the bastard will not survive, wherever I have hit him.

How did I end up in this situation and what in God's name had caused it? Tucker and Rolfe would now try to kill me to avenge their mate. I had only one option left open to me; I would have to shoot them, too.

My life was a fucking mess and it was a mess I could not begin to unravel. I had taken on the most powerful firm in Essex alone and I was going to have to live with that fact, or die trying to defend myself. If only I could have turned back the hands of time, I would never have had anything to do with these people but, as they say, shit in one hand and wish in the other; see which one gets filled first. I had to stop wishing. I was just going to have to deal with the nightmare that I was living. Fortunately, my life had equipped me with enough experience to deal with almost any situation.

CHAPTER ONE

- -

I was born on a day that is synonymous with peace and love. 28 August 1965. It was the day that human rights activist Dr Martin Luther King had taken a crowd of nearly 25,000 people to the steps of the state capital of Montgomery, Alabama, to highlight injustices against black people. Dr King's dream of racial harmony has, in the main, thankfully become a reality and the naked hatred that he so strongly opposed is all but gone. At the same time as Dr King and his supporters marched through the streets of Alabama, I was being born on the other side of the world into an environment that was also awash with love. My father's love knew no bounds. In fact it was made available to any willing female that crossed his path, regardless of their appearance, size, creed or colour. As for peace, hand on heart, I can honestly say that there has unfortunately been very little of it in my life. Wars yes, most definitely wars aplenty.

I was born in Rochford village, a well-to-do suburb of Southend-on-Sea in Essex. The actress Amanda Topping was also born there on the very same day. Topping went on to star in TV programmes such as *The Outer Limits, The X-Files* and *Stargate SG-1*. I, too, went on to make an appearance on TV, but I have to be humble and admit that it was only a brief one-off on the BBC's *Crimewatch*. However, unlike Topping, I have performed on several occasions in front of live audiences. Sadly, those watching me were not theatre buffs, they were jurors at my numerous trials. Rather wisely, Topping's family left Rochford for Canada when she was just three years old. I have often thought that if only there could have been a mix-up at the hospital, then I could have been on that plane and spared all the grief that I have had to endure.

ESSEX BOY

A small row of shops and well-kept homes with tidy gardens provide for the village's 7,600 inhabitants. Most of them commute to work in the nearby towns of Southend, Basildon and Chelmsford. Until the early 1980s, the largest employer in Rochford was the Lesney factory, which manufactured the famous Matchbox miniature die-cast model cars, but even that's gone now. It's fair to say that not a lot goes on in Rochford.

My father's name was Syd and my mother's name was Lynne. Syd was an Essex boy through and through; born in Westcliffe-on-Sea, he has spent the majority of his life breaking the law and women's hearts. Approved school, Borstal training, prison, blondes, brunettes and redheads; you name it, my dad will have sampled it. I can recall him being imprisoned for five years when I was a very young boy. My mother was so distraught following his incarceration that I honestly thought I would never see him again. Armed with a cosh, he had been approaching the cashier's kiosk at a petrol garage when the police, who had been lying in wait for him, swooped after a tip-off. Like most criminals, my father had evaded capture far more often than he was caught and would spend his ill-gotten gains on the finest threads, the finest wine and, of course, the finest women. In fact, women were his weakness; his every waking moment was spent pursuing them. My mother must have had the patience of a saint to put up with his bad behaviour.

They had met after my mother had the misfortune to encounter my father one evening after he had been seriously assaulted. At the time, she lived just up the road from my father and happened to come across him staggering down the street covered in blood. Four men had attacked and beaten him after they found out that he had been sleeping with a friend's wife. His jaw and nose had been broken and his teeth had cut through his tongue, so my mother helped him back to her home to administer first aid. My father repaid her in kind and nine months later I was born. They later had two more children together, my sisters Natalie and Lyndsey. When I was just four, my mother announced that she could no longer stand my father's philandering and they separated. I don't suppose theirs was ever a love match made in heaven. My sisters and I stayed with my mother while my father left England to tour the world.

Three years later, my father returned from his travels to announce that he was going to remarry; not my mother, thankfully, but some other not-so-lucky lady named Marie that he had met in France. This relationship produced my half-sister Sophie, who left these shores with her mother approximately eight years later. I have not seen or heard of them since. Unsurprisingly, my father's insatiable love life later provided me with two other half-sisters, Dawn and Sophie-Sydney.

While my father was busy populating the planet, I was blissfully ignorant of his chaotic lifestyle and attempting to enjoy my childhood. Like all young boys, I idolised my mother and whatever words of wisdom she bestowed upon me I accepted as the gospel truth. For reasons known only to my mother, she decided to become a strict vegetarian and so I blindly followed suit, believing that it was in my best interests. The only problem was I hated vegetables and so I ended up starving myself. As my weight plummeted, my mother grew so concerned for my health that she used to make shepherd's pie with meat in it and tell me that it had in fact been made with soya beans. At the age of 11, I was so thin that I became quite ill. The lack of nutrients in my body caused me to be anaemic and I am told that this triggered an awful disease, which nearly claimed my life. I was so frail that one day I found myself unable to walk from one end of our garden path to the other without stopping for breath. Fearing I was about to suffer some sort of attack, my mother rushed me to the accident and emergency department at Southend Hospital.

I can remember being taken into a side room where, for reasons never explained to me, a nurse inserted her lubricated and gloved finger into my anus. I could not quite believe what happened next. (No, my father didn't end up marrying the nurse!) I was suddenly surrounded by concerned-looking orderlies who strapped me to the bed and whisked me away at speed to a children's ward. I was then informed that a specialist was on his way to examine me. I was troubled by the haste of those around me; it was as if time was not on my side. I don't recall what the specialist told me but I do remember that the expression on his face didn't fill me with confidence. I knew that something was very wrong and for some reason I became desperate to see my father, so I asked my mother if she would contact him. Begrudgingly, she agreed to do so. I was kept in overnight, and the following morning I was transferred by ambulance to St Bartholomew's Children's Hospital in London. It was there that my mother explained to me that I had leukaemia.

This disease is, in layman's terms, cancer of the blood or bone marrow. I was told that a rapid increase of immature blood cells in my bone marrow had made it unable to produce healthy blood cells. These malignant cells had then spilled over into my bloodstream and spread to other organs in my body. I didn't have a clue what it all meant, I just knew that it was serious and so I resigned myself to the fact that I would be staying for a long time at the hospital. This may sound bizarre but I actually began to enjoy my stay at St Bartholomew's. My father became part of my life once more and was visiting me regularly. Both he and my other numerous visitors always brought me sweets and toys, and nobody dared tell me off, regardless of what I said or did. I was being spoilt and enjoying every minute of it.

Kempton Ward, where I was housed, was full of children like me who were suffering from various types of life-threatening diseases. I can recall that one day my father brought me a Scalextric car-racing game. Two of the children on my ward, Raymond and Barnaby, were playing with me and because I was losing I began acting like a spoilt brat, shouting and being generally disruptive. The nurses, who had previously witnessed my bad behaviour on more than one occasion, decided to put me in a side room, away from the other children, as punishment. The following morning I was made to apologise profusely to them before being moved back on to the ward.

I can remember looking to my right, towards Barnaby's bed space, and seeing the staff remove his tiny, thin body. Two nurses laid his corpse out on a trolley and covered it with a bed sheet before wheeling him out of the ward. To this day, I don't know if Barnaby died in his sleep or if he suffered some sort of organ failure. Cancer claimed my other friend, Raymond, three weeks later. I don't think I really understood death at such a tender age but it was undoubtedly all around me.

The chemotherapy that I underwent caused all my hair to fall out. It was a horrible experience that made me feel extremely weak and unwell.

Every now and again minor celebrities and footballers would visit the ward and they would always say how brave we all were. To be perfectly honest, not one of us on the ward could work out what they were on about. We all used to ask, 'What is brave about lying in bed, receiving treatment for a disease that we had no choice in having?' 'Unlucky', in my opinion, would have been a more appropriate word. After three months of intensive treatment, I was told by a doctor with a beaming smile that I was well enough to go home. I thought that I would be returning to school and some form of normality but it turned out to be a living hell. All the other children at school mocked me by saying that I resembled the *Beano* comic book character 'Plug'. Some felt the need to either slap my head or trip me over. With my bald head and tombstone teeth, I accept that I must have looked a sorry sight. In a well-meaning effort to alleviate the campaign of bullying against me, my mother purchased a nylon wig for me, which prompted my tormentors to throw food at it or use it as a frisbee. Disillusioned but undefeated, my mother arranged an appointment for me to get some cosmetic relief at the dentist, but this resulted in me being fitted with a steel brace that had more than enough wire in it to fence off fucking Hyde Park. I looked and felt ridiculous; I was every arsehole and bully's dream.

At Christmas, a well-meaning teacher decided to put me centre stage in the school play to deliver a solitary line. The idea was that it would boost my confidence. On making a rather grand entrance down a flight of multi-coloured steps, I was supposed to say, 'I have travelled to the four corners of the world,' but my buck teeth and nerves resulted in me mumbling, 'I have travelled to the four corners of the weald.' The audience erupted with laughter and I fled the stage in tears. Later that night, I placed a chair against my bedroom door to prevent family members from entering and after ripping out my brace I began scraping and hacking at my front teeth with a heavy-duty file. Grinning in a blood-spattered mirror, I was genuinely pleased with the result until the following morning. The nerve endings in my teeth had been cut and were exposed, causing me extreme pain every time that I inhaled. My gums and upper lip were swollen where the coarse file had torn at the flesh and, after rinsing the blood from my mouth, I could see that my teeth were uneven, cracked and chipped. I told my parents, teachers and a bemused dentist that I had fallen over and smashed my mouth on a kerbstone, but I don't think any of them believed me.

The bullies loved my latest look because it provided them with an abundance of fresh material for their repertoire of hate, bile and ridicule. My mother didn't help with the torment that I faced. Instead of being normal, doing what others did and buying a dog for a family pet, she arrived home with a fucking goat, the symbol of Satan. My fellow pupils' mothers would meet them at the school gates wearing floral dresses with Lassie-type dogs on leads. My mother would arrive dressed up like a car crash with the goat on a rope. I was so embarrassed I used to hide in the bike sheds until the other children and their parents had dispersed. Don't get me wrong, I love my mother, but if my father had taken her to a wife-swapping party, I am in no doubt that he would have come home with a box of the host's unwanted bric-a-brac.

A few months after returning to school, the bullying unexpectedly and abruptly ended, but it was replaced by a far more challenging problem. I was diagnosed with testicular cancer. I had been in the bath one evening when I realised that I would require a wheelbarrow to transport one of my testicles around if it grew much larger. I reluctantly asked my mother to examine my genitals and after doing so she rushed me once more to the now familiar accident and emergency department at Southend Hospital. Later that night, I was back among my dying friends in St Bartholomew's. My nylon wig was placed on my bedside table, now redundant among a ward full of bald patients, but a constant reminder of the bullying that I had suffered at school. I was dreading having to undergo any sort of chemo- or radiation therapy and after pleading with my mother to intervene she promised me that I would be spared the ordeal. The doctors said that it was an understandable but foolish decision, but my mother was adamant that she would rather let me fight the disease naturally. The hospital staff conceded that they could not force me to have what could prove to be life-saving treatment, but my father said that he could, and he would.

The following morning, he instructed a firm of solicitors to make an emergency application to 'save my life' at the High Court in London. My mother argued that I was very weak and had suffered enough, but when a specialist told the court that my chances of survival without the treatment were virtually non-existent I was made a ward of the court. This meant that any important decisions regarding my welfare would be made by a third party working for the courts rather than by my parents. The very next day, I was taken to a room and laid on a table. Heavy lead shields were put into position to protect the unaffected parts of my body and a powerful radiation machine began to 'cook' the offending testicle. This process took approximately five or ten minutes and, at the end of it, all I wanted to do was sleep. When I awoke later that night, my father was sitting next to my bed looking extremely serious and morose. 'I have some bad news, Steven,' he said holding my hand. 'The doctors have informed me that you may never be able to have children.' I was still a child myself and so couldn't appreciate just what was so bad about this news. I can remember looking back at my father and thinking: why would I want to have bloody children anyway? My mother looked equally devastated when she came to visit me, but at least she brought me a new toy and sweets to soften the blow of the 'devastating news'. For the next three months, I underwent more radiation treatment and was administered numerous drugs, which made me feel more ill than the disease I was stricken with. If I ate, I threw up, and on the rare occasions that I managed to keep food down, I suffered from chronic diarrhoea. My weight plummeted and once more I found that I had little or no strength. Those that came to visit me were visibly shocked by my appearance but again, unlike many of the other children on my ward, I managed to pull through.

When I was eventually discharged from the hospital, I elected to stay at home rather than face the school bullies. My mother did encourage me to attend but I think she worked out that I had previously been tormented and so allowed me to remain at home. While I had been in hospital my mother had formed a relationship with a very decent man named John Winter and shortly after I was discharged from the hospital they married. I really liked John; he was a kind, considerate, well-meaning man who treated me as if I were his own son. Sadly, he passed away in 2000. He had been suffering from a peptic ulcer, which is an extremely painful but treatable disorder. Unfortunately, John's ulcer eroded one of his blood vessels, which caused gastrointestinal bleeding from which he died. Soon after my mother's wedding, my father announced that he had also met a woman and intended to marry for the third time. Fortunately for my father, although possibly less so for Beverley, his bride, the number three turned out to be lucky and they remain married to this day. I must admit that the very thought of watching *The Jeremy Kyle Show* these days fills me with horror. I half expect that every mystery father they say is waiting in the wings to meet a long-lost offspring will be mine.

My absence from school attracted the attention of the local authority and they threatened all sorts of legal action against my mother if I did not attend. My mother's pleas for understanding fell on deaf ears and so, with a heavy heart, she was forced to pack me off to school each morning. Once I was out of her sight I would make my way to the local church and hang around the graveyard or, if it was raining, I would seek shelter and warmth in the local launderette. I wasn't a ghoul or some sort of morbid weirdo; I chose to hide among the dead simply because I couldn't be seen from the road and few people ever ventured into the church grounds. Even if they did, they were so preoccupied thinking about their dearly departed that they rarely even noticed me.

At the age of 15, I left school without any qualifications or indeed much basic education. Hands up, I admit that I wasn't the brightest bulb in the box, but I had done something few other kids my age had ever done: I had stared death in the face twice and walked away to tell the tale. As I grew older, the knowledge that I had survived such an ordeal, not once but twice, gave me great confidence and a strong belief in myself. If I was strong enough to cheat death, I knew that I had the inner strength to face any adversity, and so I vowed that nobody would ever get away with bullying or intimidating me again.

The first job I had after leaving school was cutting cheese into blocks, for which I was paid the princely sum of 50p an hour. I suppose that potential employers regarded me as thick and so it was a case of doing what I was given rather than choosing a career. I wasn't cutting cheese for long. A friend of the family offered me a job rubbing down cars prior to their being re-sprayed and I gladly accepted. The hours were long, the work repetitive and exhausting, and so after just a few weeks I walked out.

My illness, appearance and reluctance to attend school had alienated me from other children and so I didn't have any true friends to speak of. I would roam the streets alone, gazing into shop windows thinking of all the things that I could buy if I had money, but I no longer had a job and, therefore, there was no chance of me obtaining any. It then occurred to me that if I did my shopping when the stores and shops were closed, money would not have to exchange hands.

The first place I ever broke into was Oxfam. In my defence I didn't commit the crime for my own benefit. I had been walking past the shop one day with my father when he pointed to two vases in the window and said that he liked them. I didn't have the money to buy them for him, so I decided to break in and steal them instead. That night I tipped all of my father's tools out of a canvas holdall, jumped onto my bike and headed for the Oxfam shop. After parking near my intended target, I checked that the road was clear before jogging across and into the Oxfam shop doorway. People had left bin liners full of old clothing at the door and so I tore one open, took a jumper out and went in search of a house brick. I soon found one of a suitable size, wrapped it in the jumper and smashed the glass pane in the shop door. While I was doing this a man walked past, so I dropped the jumper and went after him. 'Excuse me. Have you got the time, please?' I asked. The man looked at me as if I were something disgusting that he had just stood in and continued to walk away. Fuck him, I thought, before running back to the shop.

I climbed through the broken window and put the vases into my holdall. I glanced across the road to ensure that nobody was coming and noticed that a man was trying to steal my bike. I clambered back through the window and ran towards the would-be thief but he saw me coming and made off in the opposite direction. Muttering something about fucking crooks and nothing being safe unless it's nailed down, I climbed back into the shop.

Behind the counter I found a large glass cabinet, which was locked, so I picked up a bowl and threw it as hard as I could in an effort to smash my way into it. The bowl hit the cabinet, bounced off and narrowly missed my head before smashing on the floor. I knew that I was making too much noise and so I picked up 75p off the top of the till, put a can of crazy foam in my holdall and made good my escape.

After successfully committing such a petty crime, there was only one way that my criminal career could go and that was up. Soon I was carrying out burglaries at off-licences, builders' merchants and post offices. If I couldn't get my hands on hard cash when committing a burglary, I would take anything that I thought I could sell later. One time I filled two black bin liners with cigarettes and hid them under a shed at a local bowling club. I asked around to see if anybody was interested in purchasing the goods that I had stolen and one local entrepreneur agreed to buy the lot. As I walked away from the bowling club with the cigarettes, a police car happened to pull up alongside me and so I ran. As I made good my escape, one bag burst open, spilling all of the boxes of cigarettes out onto the road and so I dropped it and continued to flee. Glancing over my shoulder, I could see that a police officer was in pursuit and so I turned down an alleyway only to be confronted by a wrought-iron gate with a sign that read 'Beware of the Dogs'. I had always been terrified of dogs and so rather than risk being chewed I gave myself up to the gasping officer who had pursued me. I was promptly arrested and charged with theft.

I don't know if a passer-by had stopped and picked up the boxes of cigarettes that I had dropped, but they certainly disappeared while I was in police custody. The charge sheet that I was given stated that I had stolen 50 boxes of cigarettes when I knew I had in fact stolen nearly 200. You can't trust anybody these days! I hope they choked on them.

Staring out of my bedroom window at the rain one evening, I decided that I would venture out to a local bar to play pool. I didn't usually play the game and I have no idea why I felt such a sudden inexplicable urge to begin, but something inside told me that I should do so. Looking back, it was probably boredom; people do the funniest things when the mind is idle. The only thing that prevented me from curing my craving was the fact that I didn't have any money. Close to my home was a corner shop that I had considered robbing for quite some time. Fondling one of my father's old pool cues, I told myself that there was no time like the present, and so I tore the sleeve off my jumper, cut two eye holes in it and selected a large knife from the kitchen drawer. I had no intention of cutting or stabbing anybody; the blade was going to be used merely as a tool of persuasion. When I went downstairs, I hid the knife by the front door, pulled my makeshift balaclava onto my arm, put on my coat and went to leave the house. As I was walking through the front door, I picked up the knife and pushed it up my sleeve in an effort to secrete it. At that very moment, my father walked up the garden path.

'What are you doing with that?' he asked.

'I'm going to make a cash withdrawal. See you later,' I replied.

When my father saw my mother, he told her what he had seen and what I had said to him. 'That boy is stupid going out with a knife,' he said rather philosophically. 'He'll get himself into trouble.'

Standing outside the corner shop, I adjusted my home-made balaclava and looked up and down the street to ensure that no have-a-go heroes were in the vicinity. Moments later I burst through the shop door. The lady behind the counter began to scream. I ordered her to open the till but my words fell on deaf ears; she continued screaming and ran from one end of the counter to the other. I chased her back and forth, shouting, 'Open the fucking till. Open the fucking till,' but she was clearly not listening, nor was she prepared to comply with my demands. When she began to call out, 'Peter, Peter,' I panicked, as I assumed that somebody else was in the rear of the shop. A dog began to bark and seemingly from nowhere a heavily built male appeared from behind the counter. I had no intention of getting involved in a fist fight and so I turned and ran out of the door.

When the police arrived at the shop, the lady gave them a detailed description of the miniature robber, and triumphant officers were knocking at my front door within minutes. At the age of eighteen, I was still only five feet tall, which is why I was given the nickname 'Nipper'. Doctors had explained that the treatment I had received for leukaemia may have affected my development and so there was no guarantee that I would ever grow any taller. Fortunately, they were wrong and I did gain six inches over the next few years. Unfortunately, in the meantime I was the most distinct-looking teenager in the Southend area.

My mother invited the police into the house and as soon as they set eyes on me I was arrested for attempted armed robbery. I asked if I could fetch my coat before departing for the cells and as one of the officers escorted me upstairs I heard my mother say to his colleague, 'Oh yes, Steven did go out with a knife about that time. His father was really unhappy about it.' My escort looked at me and smiled.

I knew that there was no point in denying the offence and so I simply said, 'It wasn't worth it, was it?'

The officer laughed and replied, 'It never is, son. It never is.'

When I was interviewed about the offence, I made a full and frank confession before being charged with attempted robbery. The following day I appeared in court and was remanded in custody to Her Majesty's Prison (HMP) at Ashford, in Kent, to await trial. This may sound somewhat bizarre to many people but, like my stay in hospital, I actually found myself enjoying the experience. For the first time in my life I wasn't being bullied, I had like-minded friends and everything I needed was provided for me. When I appeared in court for sentencing, the judge ordered that I should serve two years and three months' imprisonment. I was 18 years of age. I certainly didn't need to invest in a pair of sunglasses because my future was looking far from bright.

The morning after I was sentenced, I was transferred to HMP Chelmsford, home to lots of young men from the Southend area. The first face I recognised when I entered the jail belonged to a man named Malcolm Walsh, from Leigh-on-Sea. I had occasionally attended school with Malcolm but I wouldn't have described us as friends. Because we did recognise each other, Malcolm and I exchanged pleasantries and after a few brief conversations found that we had a lot in common. That is, we both made what little money we earned from committing crime. In the weeks and months that followed, our friendship grew and we spent a lot of time together. I was released from prison two months before Malcolm. On the morning I walked to freedom, we had both vowed to keep in touch but, apart from exchanging letters for the first two weeks, neither of us bothered to keep our promise. Three months later, I bumped into Malcolm at a pub called The Carlton, in Leigh-on-Sea. It was a chance meeting but we soon rekindled our prison friendship and became partners in crime. Malcolm and I earned a dishonest living committing burglaries, an occupation I now concede is vile. Like all criminals, we tried to justify our immorality by telling ourselves that, despite the fact that we were breaking the law, we were not all bad. For instance, we had pledged never to break into people's homes, but breaking into their businesses and stealing their cars was deemed acceptable. We never stopped to think that the people whose homes we spared could have been the very same people who owned the businesses that we looted. The money that I made from our unscrupulous activities brought me relative happiness, but Malcolm was described by those who knew him as 'the most miserable bastard in the world' because he never did smile. I have no idea why he was so emotionless but he possessed only one facial expression: serious. Looking back, we were an odd couple because unlike miserable Malcolm I was always laughing and joking with people.

One New Year's Eve, I had argued with my father about something trivial. I cannot now recall the root cause of our dispute but I did end up sleeping at Malcolm's flat that night. As revellers welcomed in the New Year, two armed, masked men burst into a petrol station in Leigh-on-Sea. Brandishing their weapons, they ordered the staff to open the safe and made off with an unknown quantity of cash. Later that night, through an acquaintance, I was asked to dispose of a briefcase that the robbers had used. The following morning, Malcolm drove me to a landfill site and I threw the briefcase, which was full of papers from the garage safe, into a pond. We stood watching and waiting for the briefcase to sink but the fucking thing floated out to the middle of the pond with the grace of a swan. Bricks, rocks and even a huge paving slab failed to sink the briefcase and so we eventually gave up trying and drove back to Malcolm's flat. Unbeknown to Malcolm and me, one of the men working at the landfill site had been watching us. He had taken a note of Malcolm's number plate and, after we'd left, he had retrieved the briefcase from the pond using a mechanical digger, then phoned the police.

Malcolm knew instinctively that something was untoward, as he kept saying to me that he thought we were going to be raided. When we arrived back at his flat, he announced that he and his girlfriend were going away the following morning for a few days. The next day, as he prepared to leave, the front door of the flat was kicked in. I guessed that it was the police because the postman, Malcolm's only other regular visitor, had an irritating habit of rattling the letterbox rather than knocking or kicking the front door off its hinges. Before I managed to crawl out of bed, my room was filled with menacing faces, who ordered me to raise my hands above my head and sit up. A pair of handcuffs was snapped onto my wrists and I was informed that I was under arrest for armed robbery. I was ordered to get dressed and, after doing so, I asked if I could get my shoes out of the kitchen. One of the officers told me to remain where I was while he fetched my shoes but when he went to open the kitchen door Malcolm's Rottweiler began to snarl and bark at him.

'Is your dog dangerous?' the officer asked.

'No, my dog has never bitten anybody. He would run a mile if you shouted at him,' I replied.

Feeling reassured, the officer ignored the snarling dog and attempted to walk into the kitchen. The Rottweiler immediately launched itself at the officer and sank his teeth into his arm. Screaming for help, the policeman stumbled back out of the kitchen and slammed the door.

'I thought you said your dog doesn't bite,' he shouted.

'He doesn't,' I replied, 'but that's not my dog.'

Red-faced, the officer, who wasn't seriously hurt, soon established that I was not Malcolm and de-arrested me. Moments later, raised voices and a barrage of expletives indicated that the policeman's colleagues had finally located Malcolm. They were in the process of arresting him in another room and so my savaged guard went to join them, leaving me alone. When the police left with Malcolm, I must admit that I was surprised that I too hadn't been arrested. Not that I had had anything to do with the robbery; I just thought that police procedure would have demanded it, in case I disposed of any incriminating evidence on Malcolm's behalf. Revelling in my good fortune I settled down to watch the morning TV talk shows but just as the results of yet another paternity test were going to be announced, two policemen entered the flat via the remains of the front door. 'Steven Ellis, I am arresting you on suspicion of armed robbery,' one said. I was allowed to fetch my own shoes from the kitchen before being put into a police car and taken to the local station.

As soon as my cell door slammed shut I heard Malcolm calling from an adjacent cell, 'Is that you, Steve? Is that you?' Over the next hour we discussed our predicament in whispers through our cell doors and it was agreed that I would not ask for bail if charged. Our thinking was that so long as the police got either one of us for the robbery then they would be satisfied and not pursue the other. I had a previous robbery conviction following my bungled attempt to hold up a local convenience store with a knife. If I said nothing when questioned and didn't ask for bail afterwards, the police might think I had accepted my fate and look more favourably upon any bail application that Malcolm might make. After spending three or four weeks on remand, I could then make my own bail application to the court and, as they didn't have much, if any, evidence linking me to the robbery, it would likely be granted.

Our plan initially worked like a well-oiled machine but, like all machines, it did eventually break down. Malcolm had been granted bail immediately by the police and I was remanded in custody to HMP Chelmsford to await trial. Three weeks later, and just five days before Christmas, my solicitor made my application for bail but, to my horror, the magistrates rejected it and I was returned to my prison cell.

CHAPTER TWO

There was very little festive spirit in HMP Chelmsford that Christmas.
Visits from my family served only as a reminder of the seasonal goodwill and cheer that I was missing. However, I was not alone. The alcohol-fuelled festive celebrations around Essex, and the pitched battles that ensued in the pubs and on the streets, brought numerous new faces into the prison. This fresh intake of inmates brought with them much needed illegal contraband and news of events from beyond the prison walls. It was refreshing, to say the least, to have new blood in our midst. Among the new arrivals one man stood out from the rest. I can only describe him as being a tanned, muscle-bound man mountain. His name was Patrick Terence Tate and, according to the other inmates, he was a legend in the Essex underworld.

In December 1988 Tate had been dining with his partner, Sarah Saunders, at a restaurant called the Happy Eater in Basildon. The Happy Eater was a fast-food outlet specialising in flipped burgers and American-style fries rather than gourmet delights. Tate had popped in there to help satisfy his enormous appetite after a night of particularly heavy clubbing, which had been fuelled by a cocktail of drugs. After consuming enough food for three men, the bill arrived and Tate reasoned, in his unreasonable manner, that he was being overcharged.

'Fucking rob me?' he screamed, as he gripped the cashier by the throat. 'I will show you how to fucking rob people.' Tossing the trembling man to one side, Tate had then ransacked the till and made off with approximately £150. Less than 24 hours later, both Tate and Sarah Saunders had been arrested for robbery. Tate quite rightly told the police that Sarah had had no involvement in what he called his 'dispute with the restaurant staff', and so she was released without charge. Tate, on the other hand, was charged with robbery and taken to Billericay Magistrates Court, where the police recommended that he should be kept in prison until his trial because of the severity of the offence. Tate, being the man he was, had made other plans.

When the magistrate asked Tate to stand up to hear his fate, he hit one guard full in the face with the back of his left hand, and pushed the other onto the floor. Vaulting the dock, Tate raced towards the exit doors but several police officers stood in his way in an attempt to stop him. The sheer size of Tate sent two of them sprawling as he collided with the human wall and another was punched so hard he was rendered unconscious before he even hit the floor. Outside the court entrance a high-powered motorbike awaited Tate's arrival. Its engine purred as the driver kept nervously glancing over his shoulder, but as soon as Tate mounted the machine it roared into life and disappeared down Billericay High Street in a cloud of blue exhaust smoke. A few days later, Tate surfaced in Spain where he planned to work alongside costa del crooks, smuggling cannabis from Morocco into mainland Europe.

Initially, Tate was welcomed with open arms by the expats but after a few weekends of witnessing Tate's drug-induced bad behaviour his potential partners began to avoid him. Likewise the Spanish authorities, who were prepared to suffer the presence of British fugitives, would not tolerate having local people terrorised by them. Eventually, both the police and the British criminal fraternity in residence made it clear to Tate that he was not welcome and would have to leave. Unable to understand why others were not prepared to have fun and run amok, Tate went in search of amusement across the border in Gibraltar where he was promptly arrested by British police officers. Three days later, Tate waved goodbye to his place of exile in the sun after being deported to languish in a cell on D Wing of HMP Chelmsford.

Prison life is the ultimate head fuck; the days are long and unbelievably monotonous. You wake up at 0700 hrs and have breakfast at 0800 hrs. Lunch is served at 1300 hrs and tea at 1600 hrs. An hour or so later, you're allowed out of your cell for a piss and then you're generally locked up again until the following morning. If you're lucky, you are given a job sewing mail bags or carrying out some other equally tedious task. If you're very lucky, you get a job with the cleaners, in the kitchen or as a gym orderly. Employment in any of the latter departments not only gets you out of your cell more often, it opens a window of opportunity for you to have small perks and get involved in wheeling and dealing contraband. Those who work in the kitchen sell food and the ingredients inmates use to make alcohol. Cleaners sell spare clothing and additional bedding, and those that work in the gym offer the most important product of all – lines of communication.

Often inmates involved in the same case are put onto different wings within a prison, to prevent them from manufacturing stories for use in their defence. Others are separated because one inmate may be intent on giving evidence against another. Prisons have just one gymnasium and, therefore, all inmates do, at some stage, come into contact with the gym orderlies. Case papers, handwritten notes, verbal messages, threats or even physical violence can be dished out to inmates for a fee by those working in the gymnasium. As soon as Tate arrived in Chelmsford prison, he was given a job as a gym orderly. Normally, inmates join a long queue for consideration for this prestigious post but Tate's physique and domineering presence ensured that he wasn't subjected to, what he considered to be, such a pointless process. One inmate did complain about Tate's appointment being unfair but he later retracted the allegation in a letter of apology from the hospital wing. Apparently, he saw the folly of his protest after falling backwards down a flight of stairs.

I worked as a cleaner on the wing and this job provided me with the opportunity to attend the gym regularly, as I was rarely locked in my cell. Since I took a genuine interest in a training regime, fitness fanatic Tate took an interest in me. At that time in his life Patrick Tate was an incredibly thoughtful and genuinely nice guy. A bit boisterous perhaps, without doubt hyperactive, but regardless of these failings Tate would do anything for anybody that he liked. One of my duties as a wing cleaner was to take a trolley containing inmates' possessions to and from the prison reception area. Tate immediately recognised that my job was a business opportunity and gave me contraband to smuggle from one area of the prison to another.

When parcels are posted in to prisoners from their friends and families, they are checked by security and if any banned items are found they are kept with the prisoners' property in reception until they are due to be released. Tate arranged to have a packet of hacksaw blades posted in to him, which were immediately seized by security and placed in his property. Tate then asked me to steal the blades from his property box in reception and smuggle them onto the wing.

'What the fuck are you going to do with them? Saw through the bars and escape?' I asked as I handed them over to Tate.

'No, you will find out soon enough,' Tate replied, laughing. The following morning, Tate informed a senior prison officer that he knew hacksaw blades had been hidden on the wing and were going to be used in an escape bid by inmates. The entire prison was immediately locked down and searched. Eventually, the blades were found in a store cupboard and Tate was hailed as some sort of hero by the prison staff. It was a feather in Tate's cap and, as a reward for his 'honesty and assistance', he was made a 'trustie' by the prison officers.

Unfortunately for me, during the search for the blades, officers had found 180 fresh raw eggs that I had stolen from the kitchen and hidden in my cell. They were not for my sole consumption; bodybuilders in the jail used to pay good money for them as they are high in protein. As Tate enjoyed his hero status, I was led away to the solitary confinement block after being charged with theft. The following morning, the inmate who brought my breakfast to my cell told me that Tate had said that I had to plead 'not guilty' to the charge of theft.

'Don't ask questions. Just trust Tate and you will be OK,' the man said. 'He is going to be in court soon for robbery and escaping from custody to Spain. As he knows that he'll lose his trustie status when he's sentenced Tate has said that he'll say the eggs were his.'

'Tell Tate thanks, but I will plead guilty as I stole them,' I replied.

It was hardly the crime of the century but Tate's offer was an extremely generous one and very much appreciated. Tate considered my reluctance to accept an easy way out of my predicament as the mark of an honourable man and one that he could trust. I think that incident, albeit trivial, did bring us together as friends and undoubtedly a bond was formed. I didn't know it at the time, but Tate was allowed to read inmates' confidential files when a certain prison officer was on duty. The officer, who felt intimidated by Tate, would turn a blind eye while he would slip into the landing office and read up on anybody he had suspicions about. I was told that after I had refused Tate's offer to take the blame for me, that he had read my file just in case I was an informant and part of some elaborate plot to befriend him and learn his darkest secrets. There was nothing on my file to indicate that I had ever co-operated with the authorities and so his fears were proved to be unfounded. Once established as firm friends, Tate and I would spend most of the day together training in the gym. I was initially concerned that I was neglecting my prison duties and would lose my job but Tate told me not to worry as he would square everything with the staff. True to his word, Tate made it clear to all concerned that if he and I were allowed to train when we wanted and for as long as we wanted, he wouldn't be disruptive, something nobody in their right mind would want.

In March 1991, I appeared at Chelmsford Crown Court charged with armed robbery. I pleaded 'not guilty' but accepted that I was guilty of handling stolen goods, namely the briefcase and its contents that Malcolm and I had tried to dispose of at the landfill site. There was a lot of hand-wringing and muttering but eventually the prosecution accepted my plea and dropped the robbery charge. For possessing stolen goods I was sentenced to three months' imprisonment but I had spent longer than that in custody awaiting trial and so I was released immediately. Despite the euphoria I felt at being a free man once more, I vowed never to forget my friend Tate and so within days of my release I was back at the prison visiting him.

I would take Tate anything that he needed and assist his girlfriend Sarah in any way that I was asked. When I wasn't attending to my friend's needs or chaperoning Sarah, I was out and about in the Essex badlands committing crime with Malcolm. He, too, had eventually stood trial for the alleged robbery but after mimicking me and pleading guilty to handling stolen goods, he had spent only a few weeks in custody. While I had been marking time in HMP Chelmsford Malcolm had been busy relieving local businesses of their hard-earned cash and stock. The work required two men and so in my absence he had recruited an up-and-coming wannabe gangster named Damon Alvin. Everybody who came into contact with Alvin was wary of him because he would do practically anything to win a dispute. For instance, at the tender age of ten he had been arrested for arson after a building had been burned down. Apparently the owner of the torched house had somehow upset Alvin and he had vowed to pay him back.

Alvin occasionally attended Our Lady of Lourdes Catholic School in Leigh-on-Sea, and one of his closest friends there was Malcolm's younger brother Kevin. Alvin would often visit the Walsh's family home and it was there that he had become acquainted with Malcolm. Despite Alvin's being just eleven years of age at the time and Malcolm seven years his senior, members of the Walsh family have described the pair as inseparable. Three years after his arrest for arson, the smouldering embers of Alvin's criminal career were reignited when, under Malcolm's guidance, he chose burglary as a profession. It was a trade that Malcolm taught Alvin both quickly and well. Aged 15, Alvin had announced to his long-suffering parents that he was not only leaving school but home as well because he said he was bored. Owing to the antisocial hours that Malcolm and Alvin were forced to work, Malcolm decided that it would be beneficial if Alvin moved into his home. The pair were soon breaking into other people's property more often than morning was breaking to signal the dawn of a new day. They would burgle two or three industrial units or shops per night and spend their days selling the goods they had stolen to villains throughout Essex. As Alvin's bank balance swelled, so too did his ego. Anybody foolish enough to displease him was punished with a merciless beating. On one occasion, he stabbed an off-duty soldier three times simply because he had made a comment about the West Ham United Football Club hat that Alvin was wearing. In another incident,

Alvin struck an elderly man in the face after he had complained about litter being thrown into his garden. The man told police that Alvin had hit him with a pickaxe handle and the force with which he had hit the ground had broken his ankle.

A few months later, Alvin and four others were arrested after two men had been found: one having been punched, kicked and beaten with sticks as he lay on the ground, and the other stabbed. Alvin was not some sort of Neanderthal man who dragged his knuckles around the streets of Southend beating people up at his leisure. On the contrary, Alvin was known to be a clever, cunning and devious individual. He would seek out the weak or defenceless members of society to use or assault, simply because he wanted to create the impression that he was a force to be reckoned with. I cannot say for certain why I disliked Alvin so much because he never said anything he shouldn't have to me. There was, however, undoubtedly something about him that made me feel uncomfortable in his presence. He was forever asking questions about people I knew or places I went: questions no person, other than someone with an ulterior motive, would bother to ask. Another thing I disliked about him was the fact that the only thing that appeared to matter in Damon Alvin's life was Damon Alvin. He was a selfish bastard. I was never rude to Alvin because, after all, he was Malcolm's friend, but I never went out of my way to make him feel welcome either.

The night before the famous annual Derby horse race, Malcolm planned to break into a bookmaker's shop near Southend and make off with all of the punters' bets. The bookie's safe had been concreted into the floor of the office and its rear secured with bolts to the wall of the room. Malcolm had worked out that if he smashed through the wall from the outside, he could then quite easily access the back of the safe and remove the money. Fortunately for Malcolm, the part of the wall that the safe was behind was conveniently hidden by a shed. As the task in hand appeared to be a relatively easy one, Malcolm had initially decided to commit the crime alone, but after experiencing difficulty getting through the wall and into the safe he telephoned two associates to assist him. Even with two pairs of extra hands, the safe proved to be more secure than Malcolm had imagined, so he telephoned me. When I arrived, we busied ourselves smashing the concrete that held the stubborn safe in place. As we toiled away Malcolm's lookout hammered on the rear door of the bookmaker's and an accomplice opened it.

'A police car has just turned around at the top of the road,' the lookout said.

'Close that fucking door, you idiot. We don't need a running commentary of what's going on in the street, and don't bother us again unless the police are taking an interest in us,' I shouted. I looked at Malcolm and shook my head. 'No wonder you rang me for help. These clowns are hardly the A-Team, are they?'

Five minutes later, a police car screeched to a halt at the front of the bookmaker's and a second vehicle blocked the rear entrance of the premises. We later learned that a vigilant member of the public had been looking out of their window and noticed that the back door of the bookmaker's had been opened and immediately telephoned the police. The very man who had been hired to be a lookout for us had actually been the person who had alerted a member of the public to our presence.

Trapped inside the building, we did our best to hide but the police smashed the front door open and sent in two dogs that soon found and savaged us into submission. When we appeared in court, I was sentenced to three months' imprisonment and Malcolm and his bungling buddies were given non-custodial sentences. To be honest, I was seething because I had only been invited to take part in the job when it was in progress, and even then it was only because the other men were incapable of completing it. My anger was short-lived because, ten days later, Malcolm joined me at HMP Chelmsford after he, too, was sentenced to three months' imprisonment, but in his case it was for fighting.

Upon my arrival I was disappointed to learn that my friend Tate was no longer in the prison. I was told that he had been moved to HMP Swaleside on the Isle of Sheppey, in Kent. Neither Malcolm nor I were particularly bothered about our predicament as we knew it would only be a matter of weeks before we were free once more. Unfortunately for Malcolm, while serving those few short weeks, his father, who had been suffering from cancer, passed away. 'Totally devastated' are the only two words that accurately describe the effect his father's death had on Malcolm. The prison staff became so concerned for his mental health that they moved me into his cell to try and cheer him up. I am no psychiatrist, so I thought the best plan of action would be for me to be myself and not dwell on his sad loss. I have always been a bit of a bookworm and so I decided that I would read to Malcolm in the hope of getting his mind of things. I chose *Killing for Company*, the ghost-written autobiography of serial killer Dennis Nielsen. Upon reflection, it probably wasn't a wise choice and my late night recitals, detailing death and human suffering, did little to mend my friend's broken heart.

When I was released from Chelmsford prison, Tate wrote to me asking if I would bring Malcolm to visit him at HMP Swaleside. I have no idea why Tate wanted to meet Malcolm; I think it was just curiosity because I had often talked about him. Kenneth Noye, the infamous Brinks Mat gold thief, was at Swaleside and Tate was telling Malcolm and me how well they had been getting on. Noye, according to Tate, was a reserved, polite, no-nonsense man, the type of guy who he would love to do business with. Malcolm and I just thought that Tate was talking the talk and trying to impress us but, upon reflection, whatever Tate thought or said, regardless of how improbable or bizarre it may have sounded, Patrick Tate firmly believed it and would make it happen.

As well as trying to forge friendships in the underworld, Tate was busying himself trying to settle old scores with people that he claimed had upset him. A man I shall call Peter Mills had been sentenced to ten years' imprisonment for robbing a jeweller's shop in Essex. He too was in HMP Swaleside and happened to be in the visiting room on the same day as me, Malcolm and Tate. Mills's visitor was a man I shall call Simon Gold, who had allegedly been riding the motorbike that Tate had leapt on the back of to escape from Billericay Magistrates Court. Both Mills and Gold have since claimed that Tate informed the police that they were involved in various offences in exchange for immunity from prosecution. Mills is adamant that Tate was his accomplice when he robbed the jeweller's. They had initially got away with the crime but, when Tate had been arrested in relation to an unconnected matter, Mills had immediately been taken into custody and the jewellery recovered. Tate kept glaring over at Mills and Gold, saying that he was going to do them, but he didn't approach the men while Malcolm and I were there. At the time, I did not believe that Tate would even dream of informing on other criminals but so many stories and allegations have arisen since then, from credible people, that they are very hard to dismiss.

When Tate was released from prison in 1994, he did his personal best to keep himself out of trouble. He appeared totally devoted to Sarah and I suppose, in his own troubled mind, he really did believe that he was going to manage to go straight. Sadly, Tate's life was one never-ending contradiction; his brain knew what was right and what was best for him, but his heart loved the excitement of being a criminal and craved all that was bad for him. Three days after being released, Tate arrived at my home and insisted that we go out for the evening. There were absolutely no drugs involved, nor were drugs mentioned; it was simply two friends meeting up for a quiet night out. Sarah, the best thing to ever happen to Tate in my opinion, would not tolerate him taking that shit and so Tate was refusing to touch it. As we sat in a bar sipping lemonade, Tate told me that Sarah was pregnant and there was not enough room for all three of them in her home. Tate knew that I had a large three-bedroom flat in Grand Parade, Leigh-on-Sea, and so he asked if he could stay with me until he could secure a larger property for himself, Sarah and their child. 'Sarah will remain where she is for now. It's only me that needs a room,' Tate said.

'No problem,' I replied without hesitation. 'I am happy for you and it's a pleasure to be able to help you both.'

As soon as Tate moved into my home he began thinking of ways to earn the money that he would need to support his family. Being told what to do in return for a pittance of a wage was not an existence that Tate could give genuine consideration to, and so, within a couple of weeks, he had abandoned any notion of earning an honest living. We were both soon immersed in credit card scams, distributing counterfeit money, robbing drug dealers and selling cannabis. Tate had met a man in prison, who I shall call James, and he happened to be on the ascendancy in the ever-thriving drugs trade.

Tate had kept in touch with James since his release and he knew that he was regularly supplied with large amounts of cannabis. It was decided that, when the time was right, Tate and I were going to rob James's supplier. We arranged a meeting with James and put our proposal to him. Initially, he was reluctant to play any part in our plan but when Tate began to lose his temper over his interpretation of a snub, James quickly reconsidered and agreed that, when he was due to pick up his next shipment of drugs, he would let us know. When the call came, less than a week later, Tate told me that James was on his way to Kent to purchase 80 kilos of cannabis and we were going to intercept it. An hour later, Tate and I were parking our car in a quiet Kent suburb and walking towards a large, well-kept house.

Not in the habit of knocking on doors, Tate ran and hurled his enormous frame at the front door and emerged on the other side roaring at the occupants, 'Stay fucking seated. Stay fucking seated.' Following Tate through the splintered remains of the front door, I entered the lounge waving a gun around and saw that three terrified men were cowering on the settee.

'On the floor now, arseholes, and keep your hands above your head,' I barked.

When the men complied, I set about tying them up with nylon rope, but Tate grabbed the largest man by the head, dragged him from the floor and began punching him mercilessly. Blood splashed the walls as blow after blow rained down upon the man's face.

'You fucking cunt,' Tate shouted, 'you had better tell me where the gear is or you are going to die.'

His face a mask of blood, the man could barely speak with fear and so Tate began to strangle him. I thought it highly unlikely that Tate's vice-like grip around his already crushed windpipe would permit the man to speak, so I suggested to Tate that he be allowed to breathe. When Tate had relaxed his grip a little, I could see that the man's swollen head had turned blue and his bulging eyes were barely able to focus, but he did manage to tell Tate that the cannabis was in two vehicles parked outside the house. A crushing blow to the middle of the man's chest emptied his lungs of oxygen and he was left struggling to answer Tate's final question about the whereabouts of the keys. Pointing a bloodstained shaking hand, the man indicated that his car keys were in a jacket hanging on the door.

Having retrieved the keys Tate turned his attention towards the other men, one of whom was crying.

'Fucking keys. Give me the other fucking set of keys, you slags, or I'll shoot you all,' Tate roared.

The men quickly complied with Tate's request and, moments after gate-crashing the social gathering, we were striding back through a hole in the wall where the front door had once stood. Tate opened the boot of both vehicles to ensure the drugs were on board and then like an excited child he began to shriek because he had found not only the cannabis but a bag containing £50,000 in cash.

'Eighty fucking kilos, Nipper, and a wedge of cash, not a bad night's work, eh?' Tate said. 'I will have to take a bit of additional expenses to get my clothes dry cleaned though. One of those bastards has bled all over me,' he added laughing.

We drove both of the vehicles back to where we had parked ours and transferred the cash and drugs into our boot. Laughing and joking about the fear we had instilled in our victims, we headed back over the QE2 Bridge and home into Essex. I was paid £60,000 for that night's work; Tate paid himself £60,000 and James, who had reluctantly assisted us with setting up the job, was paid the same. I was more than happy earning £60,000 for three hours' work and, as an added bonus, Tate never did ask for my contribution towards his dry-cleaning bill.

Our other business interests were not as lucrative as robbing drug dealers but they did provide us with a steady income. Tate would purchase high-quality forged £50 notes for £12.50 each and together we would descend upon a town and spend £1,000 worth in chain stores, which have a policy of giving cash refunds on returned goods. Having made our purchases we would then travel to a neighbouring town and, receipt in hand, return the goods for genuine banknotes. Throughout the day we would also use an array of brand-new credit cards that one of Tate's cohorts had stolen from the Royal Mail sorting office. Apparently, credit cards and other such valuable items are stored in a secure cage prior to delivery and Tate's friend had the job of handing them out to the postmen. Tate claimed that for every ten credit cards due to be delivered in south-east Essex, at least two would end up in his wallet.

Tate had another lucrative business but he insisted this was 'strictly sole trader only'. To be honest, even if Tate had offered me a partnership in this particular venture, I would have declined because he was hiring out young prostitutes to depraved and desperate clients. His staff-recruiting methods were simple but effective. Tate would book appointments with working girls at massage parlours or their homes and, after putting the product through its paces, demand that they work for him. Few argued. All eventually complied. Patrick Tate could be a very persuasive man.

In September 1994, Tate met a man named Tony Tucker and his sidekick Craig Rolfe at a cafe in Southend. Tate had gone into the cafe with a man named Shaun Miller, who also happened to know Tucker and Rolfe. The men were introduced by Miller, and Tucker immediately warmed to Tate. Weighing 18 stone and standing 6 ft 2 in. tall, Tate was the type of man that Tucker would deem 'useful'. When Tucker invited Tate to meet him and Rolfe for a drink at a nightclub in Southend later that night, he readily accepted. As soon as Tate returned to my flat that day he talked excitedly about his new friends. He urged me to go to the club with him to meet them but I declined the offer as I was already tired of hearing about just how great Rolfe and Tucker were. The name Rolfe meant nothing to me but I had heard of Tucker because he was involved in the running of a Basildon nightclub named Raquel's. That club had started hosting rave nights that were run by a promotions team that I knew, which had previously held them at a smaller venue in Southend. The good people of Southend generally only visit Basildon for court appearances or funerals; they certainly do not go there to socialise. However, because this particularly popular promotions team moved their rave nights to Raquel's, to accommodate their ever-increasing customer base, many of the Southend 'in crowd' followed them. Tucker, who ran the security at Raquel's with a man named Bernard O'Mahoney, became friendly with some of these people and eventually began socialising with them in the nightclubs along Southend seafront.

It was in these clubs that I had first heard stories about him and the vicious door firm that he controlled. Anybody foolish enough to cause trouble in premises looked after by Tucker's firm was given unimaginable beatings. At Raquel's, in Basildon, revellers were often slashed with knives, kicked senseless or hurled down three flights of concrete stairs. One man was permanently blinded and another beaten with sticks and doused in petrol. Tucker insisted that all the door staff who worked for him must comply with the age-old adage that the customer is always right.

'If they insist on causing trouble, let them have it, but make sure that they won't ever feel like asking for it again,' he would say.

When Tate returned home early the following morning from his meeting with Tucker, he woke me up and rambled on about earning more money than he could ever spend.

'Tucker runs nightclub doors and we will be able to get people to sell gear in his clubs,' Tate said with his usual enthusiasm where money was involved.

'Yes, great. Fucking marvellous. Save it until I wake up, eh?' I replied, burying my head back under the sheets.

From that day onwards, Tate spoke little of anything else other than Tony Tucker and their money-making schemes and plans. It was hard not to notice that Tucker had made a huge impression on Tate. The following weekend, at Tate's behest, we travelled to Epping Country Club to meet his new friend.

Epping Country Club was, at that time, the page-three girl and premiership footballers' playground. Queues of wannabes, B-list celebrities and East End gangsters snaked around a large car park waiting to get in. When we arrived, Tate marched to the front of the queue with me in his wake and, after shaking hands with the door staff, entered the club. We found Tucker standing near the bar surrounded by a group of blonde Essex girls who tottered on their high heels, giggling insanely at his every word. Tucker, like Tate, was a huge man and had a very intimidating aura; it was almost as if you could smell violence when you were around the two of them. Tucker shook my hand firmly and called over a friend who he introduced as Craig Rolfe. He wasn't as tall as

Tucker but he had clearly been abusing steroids as he was stuffed into a jacket that no longer quite fitted him. 'Sneaky', that's how I would best describe Rolfe; there was just something about him that wasn't quite right. He tended to sneer when he spoke, as if he was somehow mocking you. I know I may sound paranoid for making assumptions about people I had only just met, but that doesn't mean that they were not out to get me. After shaking my hand Rolfe turned his back on me to talk to the girls in Tucker's entourage; a classic display of ignorance, in my opinion.

When the club closed, we all went back to a house in Chafford Hundred, which I assumed was Tucker's. A large bag of cocaine was emptied onto a glass coffee table, and Rolfe immediately began to hoover the drug up his nose. Tucker told us that he was not very happy with a man named Jimmy Joel, who had allegedly burgled the home of a woman who had recently been diagnosed with cancer. He produced two syringes, one of which was full of pure heroin and another that contained a potion that he called 'pink champagne'; a cocktail of steroids and cocaine.

'Top that up,' Tucker said to Rolfe as he handed him the syringe full of heroin.

Rolfe rolled up his sleeve, slapped his arm several times and after sticking the needle into a vein he withdrew a quantity of his own blood. Rolfe then shook the syringe, drew more blood and shook the syringe again until his blood and the heroin mixed to resemble the pink champagne.

'The cunt who burgled that woman's house is going to get this,' Tucker said, holding the syringe full of heroin and Rolfe's blood. I thought it was all talk designed to impress Tate, but the following night Tucker rang and asked us to meet him.

'That guy I am after is going to Epping Country Club tonight,' Tucker said. 'Do you want to come up there with me?'

Tate answered for us both and as we were getting into Tucker's car a few hours later he handed me a revolver.

'What the fuck do I want that for?' I asked Tate.

'It might be needed, so just hang on to it,' he replied.

The atmosphere in the car on the way to the country club was very menacing. Tucker was talking about the best way of disposing of Joel's body and Tate was getting visibly excited about the various ways in which they could kill him; none were pleasant. Tucker eventually finalised a plan whereby Joel would be lured to Rolfe's vehicle and offered a syringe full of pink champagne. To allay any fears that Joel may have, Rolfe would inject himself first and would then offer Joel an identical syringe. Identical in appearance only, that is, because unlike Rolfe's syringe Joel's would contain the pure heroin mixed with Rolfe's blood, which would kill him within seconds. To ensure Joel complied with Rolfe's request, Tucker and Tate decided that I should sit in the back of the car and if there were any problems I was to threaten the man with the gun.

'And what happens if he still doesn't do as he is told?' I asked.

'Then shoot the cunt twice in the back of the head,' Tucker replied.

With the benefit of hindsight I can see just how ludicrous it was to even suggest doing such a thing but that night in that car, immersed in an atmosphere of pure evil, I am in no doubt that I would have done it.

Before we arrived at the club, a former football hooligan turned bouncer named Carlton Leach, and approximately 20 of his friends, had spotted the man we were intending to kill. Leach, another recently recruited friend of Tucker's, had approached Joel but he had seen him coming and fled. Tucker and Tate were incensed to learn that Leach had scared Joel away and after a few minutes of incoherent ranting we all got back into the car and returned to the house that I believed was Tucker's. Another large bag of cocaine was poured onto the glass coffee table and Rolfe immediately buried his nose in it. Tucker produced a bag of syringes and injected himself with a cocktail of drugs.

'Have a go, Pat, it's the bollocks. You'll love it,' Tucker said as he offered Tate a syringe.

Tate looked at the syringe and then at me, as if seeking my approval.

'Don't be fucking daft, Pat, think of Sarah,' I said but he just shrugged his shoulders and plunged the needle into his arm.

That stupid act, that moment, signalled the end for my friend. Tate loved the buzz that the cocktail of drugs gave him and his constant use of it from that night onwards changed him from a friend into a fiend. As the powerful drugs took a hold of Tate he seemed to lapse into a semi-conscious state. He began mumbling about Rolfe being incapable of murdering the man that Tucker wanted dead.

'Some fucking mate you are, you cunt,' Tate sneered.

'Oh bollocks, Pat. I am the man,' Rolfe replied, in an effort to make light of the abuse being aimed at him.

Tate's facial expression made it clear that he was not joking with Rolfe and when he demanded I give him the revolver the room fell silent.

'The fucking gun, Nipper. Give me the fucking gun,' he shouted.

Rolfe leapt to his feet and ran to the nearest exit, which happened to be an open window. Laughing insanely Tate grabbed the gun from me, cocked it and staggered to the window to shoot Rolfe. Before Tate could take aim and fire, Tucker had grabbed his arm and wrestled the gun from him. Both men fell to the floor giggling like fools, totally out of their minds on drugs. I got up and walked out of the house in disgust.

As I closed the front door behind me Rolfe began screaming from the garage roof, 'No, Pat. No, please don't.' When Rolfe looked down and saw that it was me and not Tate leaving the house, he begged me to go and ask Tate not to shoot him.

'Ask him yourself, you fucking idiot,' I replied, before walking away.

Later that day, Tate was dropped off at my flat in a terrible state. He could tell by my face that I wasn't impressed with his antics.

'What the fuck did you do that shit for?' I asked him.

'I know, I know. I won't ever do it again. Please don't tell Sarah because if she ever finds out she will dump me,' he replied.

Sarah had recently given birth to Tate's son Jordan, and I knew that she would have undoubtedly ended their relationship if she knew what he had done and so I agreed that I would not tell anybody. Unfortunately for Tate, he was a walking advertisement for his own bad behaviour and habits, and it was only a matter of time before everybody would become painfully aware of his uncontrollable drug addiction.

CHAPTER THREE

I am not sure why Tate turned into the Jekyll and Hyde figure that he became. He was such a nice guy when I first met him but, once he had an audience of people he wanted to impress, he would take drugs to give him confidence and turn into the monster they expected him to be. I am not sure that many of Tate's numerous 'friends' ever did get to know the real Patrick Tate. When I was in prison, he would tell me all about his youth and times that clearly meant a lot to him. His family had lived in St Neots, a relatively crime-free picturesque town in Cambridgeshire. While roaming the streets one day, Tate had found a leather pouch containing £300 on the roof of a parked car. A policeman who had been entrusted to look after the money for his colleagues' Christmas party had put the pouch on the roof of his car while securing the vehicle and then forgotten to retrieve it. Tate told me that he had no idea that the cash belonged to the police but he had decided to celebrate his good fortune by throwing his own Christmas party.

'It was a lot of money in those days, I bought a record player and leather jackets for me and my mates,' he said. 'I took cab rides into Cambridge, ate at the best restaurants and still had enough left for a night on the town.' A jealous friend rang the police and told them that Tate had stolen the money and when he was taken into custody they convinced him to come clean, not only about the £300 but about every other misdemeanour that he had ever committed.

From what Tate told me there were no serious offences. He said he had confessed to trivial matters such as stealing a rubber from Woolworths and breaking a window once while playing football. Tate was adamant that he couldn't tell them about any serious crimes simply because he had never committed any. If you choose to become a criminal, there are two things that you must never, ever do: upset the police and upset the police. Tate had stolen their Christmas party money and, therefore, Tate was going to pay.

When he appeared in court, he was sent to an approved school in Grimsby. I have had the misfortune to visit Grimsby and can, therefore, say with some authority that sending him to that town would have been punishment enough, but the added misery of the approved school was, I would say, excessive. Tate told me that, in his opinion, it was the time he spent in that approved school that turned him into a 'proper' criminal.

'The other kids in there taught me how to break into cars, where I could sell stolen goods and what I should or shouldn't say if I was ever caught,' Tate said.

When he was released and returned home, Tate ventured out into the wider community to employ his new skills. The school he attended was constantly writing to his mother, Marie, enquiring about items that had gone missing from their premises. Tate once gave his younger brother Russell a bicycle as a present but when he went out into the street to ride it, a group of boys set about him and snatched the bike back, claiming it was theirs. When he left school, Tate managed to get a job as a butcher's apprentice. He married a local girl named Donna and saved up to buy a car. His mother thought that he had finally settled down, but one evening Tate was involved in a police chase that ended 70 miles away in Chelmsford. He lost his job as a result of being convicted of such a reckless crime and almost overnight his life became a whirlwind of drugs, booze, girls and bodybuilding; little wonder his wife divorced him.

As I sat in the flat one day, listening to Tate talking to Tucker on the phone about killing Jimmy Joel, I honestly felt sorry for him. Tate had no problem with Joel, he didn't even know him, but he was ranting about torturing and killing him just to impress Tucker. It was pathetic.

'Why the fuck are you getting involved?' I asked him when he put the phone down.

'Because Tucker's my mate and that slag has taken a liberty,' Tate replied.

I couldn't argue. I was no better. I had been prepared to shoot the guy in the head and I had never even met him.

It was the drugs, the fucking drugs, they were ruining us all. The next time Tate and I met Tucker he was still talking about how he desperately wanted to murder Joel and how he had now put several of his minions to work in an effort to lure him to a suitable place of execution. After a few days, Tucker received word that Joel had unwittingly agreed to meet a man he believed to be a trusted friend at a service station near Chelmsford. Almost drunk on feelings of joy, Tucker quickly recruited a gang numbering 20 men who then set off in a convoy of cars to the meeting place with murder in mind. I was in a vehicle with Carlton Leach, Tucker and Tate. We were all tooled up with various blades and weapons capable of causing horrific injuries. The acidic smell of industrial ammonia hung heavy in the vehicle because somebody had failed to secure the lid on one of the many bottles in the boot.

'Squirt', as bottles of ammonia were more commonly known, was the weapon of choice in those days. One sharp 'squirt' of the container holding the noxious fluid would send an almost invisible spray into the face of an opponent. Even if the ammonia failed to hit the eyes, which would temporarily blind the victim, the fumes the fluid produced still affected their eyesight and restricted breathing. The natural reaction for anybody receiving an eye injury is to close their eyes and raise their hands to the face. This rendered the victim defenceless and the attacker could continue the assault without fear of being assaulted themselves. Nobody in Tucker's firm went anywhere without their squirt.

When we arrived at the service station, Joel stood alone in the middle of a large car park. Like vultures circling their prey, the convoy of cars swept around Joel, effectively trying to block any escape route that he may have had. As our vehicle screeched to a halt, Tucker leapt out and pulled a butcher's meat cleaver from his jacket.

'Come here, you mug cunt,' he shouted.

Taking the only sensible option open to him, Joel turned and ran for his life. Fortunately, a few of Tucker's fuller-figured friends had not yet disembarked from their vehicle and Joel was able to make good his escape.

'Come back and fucking fight me,' Tucker bellowed after him.

To everybody's surprise Joel stopped running, turned and shouted, 'I will fight you anytime you want, but tell your mates to get in their cars and leave us two alone.'

All eyes fell on Tucker, who should have been the man he was always claiming to be, and fought Joel. Instead, he raised the meat cleaver above his head and ran towards Joel screaming threats and obscenities. Joel simply turned and ran in the opposite direction. Everybody present knew that Tucker had embarrassed himself; one or two even walked away, vowing never to back him again.

Two weeks later, Tucker was in the changing room of Jimmy Connor's gym when Joel walked in to the reception area. The changing room door was open and Tucker looked up at Joel as he greeted the receptionist. Expecting trouble, Joel put his back firmly against the wall and continued his conversation but kept one eye fixed firmly on Tucker. When Tucker had finished dressing, he picked up his holdall and walked straight towards Joel. Two or three paces before he reached the man that he had recently threatened to kill; Tucker bowed his head and walked by, staring at the floor.

As one episode of madness ended, Tate and Tucker were about to send yet another careering into our chaotic lives. Malcolm Walsh had told me that he had met a man from Canning Town in the East End of London who had £240,000 worth of stolen traveller's cheques for sale. He asked me if I knew of anybody who might be interested in purchasing them and so I said that I would ask Tate. Never one to miss an opportunity Tate contacted Tucker, who agreed to pay £60,000 for the cheques on the condition that he was given a sample first. The following morning, myself, Tate, Malcolm and a man I shall call Nick travelled to the East End to meet the man and pick up the sample, to ensure they were genuine. The cheques came in books of quite high value and so the man we met insisted that one of us remain with him until Tucker had examined the sample and returned it.

Malcolm agreed to stay with the man while the rest of us drove to Tucker's house with the book of cheques. When we arrived, Carlton Leach was with Tucker. I thought that he was just paying a social visit but, after Tucker had made a phone call and verified that the cheques were genuine, Leach announced that he was returning to London with us. I looked at Tate to register my disapproval but he just shrugged his shoulders. I immediately sensed that something was not quite right but I kept my suspicions to myself.

As we pulled up in a pub car park in Canning Town to meet the man, Tate turned around to me and said, 'There's been a change of plan, Nipper. We're going to rob this guy.'

'Oh for fuck's sake. You can't rob him. He's a friend of Malcolm's,' I replied.

Tate glared at me and said that he could do whatever he wanted and if anybody tried to stop him they would die.

'Fuck you,' I said. 'I want no part of this slag trick. I am staying in the car.'

Tate seemed to think that I was joking because he kept looking at me and laughing.

'Nipper, do you want to give your mate Malcolm the bad news or shall I?' he asked.

Staring straight at Tate I didn't even give him the courtesy of a response. I felt disgusted that he would even contemplate ripping off a man who had taken the time and trouble to visit him in prison. At that moment Tucker and Leach pulled up in a 4x4 and the man selling the traveller's cheques walked out of the pub and into the car park. Tucker and Leach got out of their vehicle and swaggered towards him. As the man extended his hand to greet the duo, Leach grabbed him in a bear hug and Tucker punched him.

'What the fuck is happening, mate?' the shocked man shouted.

As Tucker went to punch the man again he threw his arms up, freeing himself from Leach's grasp, and ran. Leach gave chase, tripped the man up, punched him a few times as he lay on the floor and then pulled him to his feet by his jacket lapels. The man continued to shout and so Leach hit him again but he didn't fall over, he simply shoved Leach backwards with both hands, which sent him sprawling onto the floor.

Before making good his escape, the man called out to Tucker, 'You haven't heard the last of this, you cunt.'

Leach, Tate and Tucker were laughing but everybody in the London underworld knows that you don't fuck with firms out of Canning Town without suffering some sort of comeback.

To save face for the botched robbery, Tucker boasted to his friends and associates that they had taken all £240,000 worth of cheques off the man. Some have since theorised that the robbery was the catalyst for Tucker and Tate being murdered. It may well have been, but I was present that day and I know for a fact that they left east London empty-handed and extremely embarrassed. That night I started receiving threatening phone calls from the Canning Town firm, who were convinced that I had lured Malcolm and his friend to the robbery, but I agreed to meet them alone to prove that I had played no part in anything underhand.

'I am deeply embarrassed by what happened. Malcolm is a true friend; I wouldn't dream of doing anything like that,' I said.

I was told that they would be in touch to arrange the meeting but I didn't hear from them again. I assume that they believed me. Malcolm was less forgiving; he refused to even discuss the episode with me. A few days later, I was shopping in Sainsbury's with my girlfriend. We were queuing at the checkout and I was gazing out of the window. Suddenly Malcolm's car came into view and as he glanced inside the shop our eyes met. I guessed by the expression on his face that he wasn't pleased to see me. Any doubts I may have had were confirmed when he jumped on his brakes, flung his car door open and leapt out. I gave my money and my mobile phone to my girlfriend, told her to abandon her shopping trolley and disappear. I was in no doubt that Malcolm and I were going to fight and I wanted her out of the way. I walked to the main entrance, where I found Malcolm waiting for me.

'We have got something to sort out. Where do you want to do it?' he said. Before I could reply Malcolm suggested that we fight in the car park.

'Fuck off. It's covered by CCTV. I will fight you in the toilets,' I replied.

Malcolm looked me up and down, shook his head and said, 'Fuck you, Steve,' before striding away.

The odd thing is, the next time we met he spoke to me as if the attempted robbery had never taken place. I did try to broach the subject but he simply raised his hand and said that he was not interested. When I saw Tate and Tucker, I asked them to apologise to Malcolm but their attitude to everybody and everything was 'fuck them'. They really had come to believe that they were invincible and nobody would dare to even take them on, let alone defeat them.

One evening we were out in Southend at a nightclub and Tucker asked me to go to Chris Wheatley's house to collect some cocaine for his personal use. Chris had been a member of Tucker's firm for a number of years, running the door of a nightclub called Club Art in Southend. I liked Chris. He was a really decent no-nonsense man who was prepared to stand up to anybody. A young guy named Danny, from Basildon, had been ejected from Hollywood's nightclub, in Romford, by Chris and his uncle, a top Southend face was not happy about it. Threats to shoot Chris, petrol-bomb his home and cripple him followed, but he refused to apologise for ejecting Danny because he believed that he had been in the right. Fortunately for all concerned, Danny was a regular at another of the nightclubs where Tucker provided security, Raquel's, in Basildon, and he got on well with the head doorman. This doorman was also friends with Chris and so he was able to resolve the issue amicably.

When I arrived at Chris's flat, I purchased five grammes of cocaine and approximately twenty Ecstasy pills. I returned to the club and asked Tucker for the money, but he began to shout about him not giving money to anybody.

'Chris works for me. It's my fucking gear. I am not paying for anything,' he bellowed.

'Well, if you aren't paying for the drugs, you aren't getting them,' I replied.

Tucker reluctantly paid me but for the remainder of the evening he moaned constantly about having had to do so. The following evening, we visited Raquel's. It had once been a really violent venue; fleets of ambulances rather than taxis queued up outside when it was closing because the clientele were prone to fucking or fighting each other rather than enjoying themselves. A northerner named Bernard O'Mahoney had taken over the running of security at Raquel's after numerous bloody encounters with the locals had forced his former boss to quit.

In February 1993, O'Mahoney had invited Tucker into Raquel's as a not-so-silent partner. They had agreed that O'Mahoney would fight the firm's battles to secure the door of the club and Tucker would provide all of the illicit drugs that the chemical generation that frequented the venue would require. O'Mahoney soon cleared the local troublemakers from the venue (usually head first via the rear concrete stairs), which in turn attracted promoters keen to put on rave nights. Violence and Ecstasy did not mix and so O'Mahoney's efforts to ban the local hoodlums reaped huge rewards for Tucker's drug-dealing operation. Raquel's went from being a club containing more than 800 snarling, spitting yobs to a club containing more than 800 loved-up pill heads. Tucker was delighted with the arrangement but, to my surprise, O'Mahoney didn't seem too keen on Tucker.

One of the very first things that he said to me when we were introduced was, 'Don't take any notice of anything Tucker tells you and don't get too involved.'

I thought it was an odd thing to say but, from what others later told me, Tucker was aware of O'Mahoney's views and the pair only tolerated each other because they were both earning well out of the club. O'Mahoney led us through the reception area and up two flights of stairs to a dining area where he said we wouldn't be disturbed. After identifying our party to one of the bar staff, O'Mahoney informed us that anything we required would be on the house. I am not sure what was on the diners' menu but, considering all the horror stories that I had heard about the place, I suspected that it would have been broken leg of lamb.

There was a fantastic atmosphere in the club and everybody appeared to be having a good time. As the champagne flowed a group of girls gathered around us and I began to talk to one or two of them. I don't know what it was but I could somehow sense that all was not well with Tucker, who the girls appeared to be ignoring. When a man in his 20s approached the girls and asked them if they were sorted (for drugs), Tucker called him over.

'Have you got any gear for sale?' he asked.

'Sure, mate, what would you like?' the man replied.

Grabbing the man by his throat, Tucker slapped him hard across the face with his free hand and demanded he hand all of his drugs over to him.

'Fuck off, you can't do that to the guy,' I said.

'He's nothing. I can do what I fucking want,' Tucker replied.

Before I could say another word Tucker emptied the trembling man's pockets and shouted at all of the girls present to fuck off. A barmaid activated the panic alarm and the DJ began calling over the PA system, 'Security to the dining area. Security to the dining area.'

Moments later, O'Mahoney and several other doormen appeared, clearly expecting trouble. When O'Mahoney walked over to Tucker, he pointed out the young man whom he had robbed and alleged that he had been causing trouble. Almost immediately the man was apprehended and the last I saw of him he was disappearing from the club via a fire exit. The attention-seeking, jealous and vindictive Tucker that I had seen that night was the real Tucker, but rather naively I believed his actions had been out of character. The Tucker that I thought I knew was always telling me what a good friend I was and offering to do me favours.

'You're like a brother to me,' Tucker would say, but looking back, he used to say the same to everybody.

The longer I spent in Tucker's company, the more O'Mahoney's words of advice made sense. I began to feel uncomfortable at some of Tucker's antics and this led to us arguing on more than one occasion. One night, we all went out to the Café de Paris nightclub in London's West End. I had taken my usual one Ecstasy pill and the others had injected themselves with a cocktail of drugs and were snorting copious amounts of cocaine every few minutes. While out on the dance floor emulating a cripple trying to walk without sticks, I felt somebody pinch my backside. When I turned around, a black male smiled at me. Racial harmony is fine by me, as is brotherly love, but not in the biblical sense, which is where I draw the line. I pushed the man away from me and advised him that he should not return unless he had taken out comprehensive medical insurance.

Out of nowhere a huge hand gripped my shoulder and a deep voice growled, 'Leave it out, son. You don't need the trouble.'

As I turned towards whoever was offering me this advice I came face to face with former British heavyweight champion boxer Gary Mason.

'That geezer pinched my arse. I'm not having that,' I said.

Tucker ran over to my aid, grabbed my admirer and launched him through a fire exit door. When he returned, he simply glared at Mason and told me to ignore him. It has to be said that Gary Mason was doing no more than attempting to prevent trouble, but Tucker did not see it that way. Throughout the rest of the evening he made derogatory remarks to me about Mason and said that he had taken a liberty by interfering with somebody in our circle of friends.

Later that week, Tucker, Tate, Leach and I attended a Luther Vandross concert at the Royal Albert Hall with our girlfriends. Tucker had hired one of the VIP boxes and every few minutes the curtains were drawn so that we could snort cocaine on the balcony. As the drugs began to take effect, the mood became more boisterous and Tucker began leaning out of our box to see who was next door. Tucker was like a kid at Christmas when he saw that it was Gary Mason and a boxing promoter. He spent the rest of the evening gesticulating and mouthing abuse but, to his credit, Mason did not respond. I personally found the whole sorry episode rather embarrassing.

In a rare effort to relax, Tucker, Tate, Rolfe, myself and four girls went to a Chinese restaurant where Tucker claimed to be a regular customer. The staff greeted us warmly and the manager insisted on leading us to a table where he assured us that we wouldn't be disturbed. I formed the impression that the manager was seating us at a table out of the way so that his other customers, rather than us, wouldn't be disturbed. The meal passed off without incident, but when the waiter presented us with a bill for more than £250 Tucker said that he wasn't going to pay. Tate pulled out a thick roll of banknotes from his pocket and offered to pay half but Tucker was adamant.

'Don't be like that. We've had a good night and it's not right to cause trouble with the girls here,' I said.

'Fuck them. I am not paying and neither is anybody else,' Tucker replied. I got up, walked over to the manager and began counting out my money in order to pay the bill. Tucker jumped up from his seat, grabbed the cash and repeated that nobody was going to pay the bill. Everybody in the restaurant had stopped eating and was looking at Tucker.

He thought for a moment and then after producing a coin from his pocket said, 'OK, we will flick a coin for the bill.' He spun the coin high in the air before catching and covering it with both hands. 'Heads or tails?' Tucker asked the manager.

When the manager muttered 'tails', Tucker showed him the coin and shouted out, 'He lost, he lost.' Moments later, we were heading for the door and being sneered at by a group of very unhappy Chinese waiters and their disgusted customers. This incident was typical of Tucker, he was a tight bastard; he would never put his hand in his pocket to pay for anything, although he never did mind dipping his hand in other people's pockets.

A huge outdoor dance event had been arranged at a stately home in Kent and one of the promoters invited us all to attend. Tucker, Tate, Rolfe and I met Leach and a few of his friends at the venue and soon immersed ourselves in the carnival atmosphere. Tucker took up a position near the stage and began handing out packets of Ecstasy pills to his drug runners to sell. As soon as he spotted a drug dealer that was not on his payroll Tucker grabbed him by the throat, slapped his face, stole his cash and drugs and warned him that he would be wise to leave. I am aware of at least four drug dealers that he robbed in a similar fashion that day. Tate and I had wads of fake £20 banknotes, which we used to purchase drink tokens.

A clause in the venue's licence prevented alcohol being sold over the bar, but there was nothing to stop alcohol being exchanged for tokens. The discs were £5 each and so for every one that we purchased we were given £15 in change. Tate and I made approximately £2,000 each at this event. As well as the £15 profit we made from each purchase, we were getting a steady stream of free alcohol when we handed the discs in at the bar. I don't drink but by early evening Tucker and Tate were both drunk and beginning to behave boisterously. I had a water fight with a prostitute named Paula who was accompanying Tate and this attracted the attention of security. When the first two doormen arrived, they began shouting at Paula and me to calm down but when they noticed Tate and Tucker staring at them, they immediately radioed for assistance. By the time their colleagues had arrived, Leach had joined us, wearing a ridiculous pair of leather trousers, with his entourage in tow. I am not sure if it was the sight of Leach in leather trousers that scared the testosterone-filled doormen or if it was the thought of fighting the men who were backing me, but they soon turned and walked away without saying another word.

Another of Tate's prostitutes was a girl in her early 20s named Adele. Despite her tender years, Adele had only recently been released from her third prison sentence before accepting Tate's offer of employment. Her attractive looks and feminine attire masked what was really a ruthless and very violent young girl. One evening she rang Tate and claimed that a customer named Rob, who he had sent, had slept with her but refused to pay the agreed fee. Not only that, but when Adele had threatened to call her boss, Rob had stolen her mobile phone. I found it hard to believe that a man Tate actually knew would do such a thing. It was more than likely that he had had some sort of dispute with Adele and the phone had been taken as a surety, but Tate was having none of it. Ten minutes after receiving Adele's call Tate and I arrived at Rob's front door. Tate rang the bell but before anybody had time to answer it he had demolished the door and was kicking Rob around the lounge.

'The money. The phone. Pay me. Give it to me,' Tate screamed as he attempted to put an impression of Rob's head into the wooden floor.

When we left with the mobile phone, the money Tate claimed was owed and a little extra we had taken for expenses, Rob was left lying motionless in the corner of the lounge with a 28-inch television set on his head. As I walked from Rob's house back into the street, I practically bumped into a police officer who immediately recognised me.

'What are you doing around here, Ellis?' he asked. Before I could answer Tate strode into view and the policeman said, 'Patrick Tate! I thought you were still in prison.'

Images of Rob appearing at the window wearing his television set and calling for help raced through my mind. To humour the policeman, but more importantly to get him away from the vicinity of Rob's house, Tate and I walked along the street chatting briefly with him. At the first opportunity we said goodbye to the officer and walked off down a side street where we waited until we were sure that the policeman had gone. We then made our way back to our vehicle.

The following morning, I got into my car and drove towards my girlfriend's house. As I reached the end of my street I noticed that a police vehicle had pulled out from a side street and appeared to be following me. I immediately rang Tate to warn him that the police may be going to stop me and, if I was correct, the flat could also be about to be raided. As I turned out of the road I lived in, the blue lights and siren on the police car began to flash and howl. Instead of pulling over I waved one hand to indicate to the policeman that I would stop my car further up the road. I had decided to drive to a gym and pull up in the car park where I knew there would be several witnesses to whatever occurred thereafter.

When I eventually stepped out of the car, a police officer handcuffed me and informed that I was under arrest for wounding with intent, robbery and aggravated burglary. I made no reply and was taken to a police station where I found Tate occupying the bench in front of the desk where suspects are processed.

'Fancy seeing you here,' Tate called out. 'Say fuck all, Nipper, the best brief that money can buy is already on his way down here.'

We both denied the allegations and were bailed to reappear at the police station in two weeks so that an identity parade could be arranged. The officer in charge of the case had wanted it to take place much sooner but finding several men of Tate's size and stature at short notice proved to be impossible.

That night we sent people to Rob's house to talk to him about the health issues giving evidence against us would raise, but they were informed by neighbours that he was under police protection at a secret location. Undeterred, we decided to apprehend and educate Rob when he attended the identity parade. Two hours before we were due at the police station Tucker, who had insisted on involving himself, parked his car where he could see everybody that came and went. Tate parked his car near to the police car park entrance and I parked my vehicle adjacent to the exit. Confident that we would be able to trap Rob when he left the police station, Tate and I went inside to take part in what we thought would almost be a formality.

Anybody who met Tate would remember him; he was certainly the biggest man I have ever seen in my life. It wasn't so much his height, it was his sheer body mass. Without hesitation Rob identified Tate as the man who had assaulted him but he failed to pick me out of the line-up. I can only assume that Rob wasn't able to focus after Tate's first punch had landed. Even if he had, I am sure that the television set being wrapped around his head would have played havoc with his memory. When we left the police station, Tucker was waving manically and pointing to a vehicle that was exiting the car park. Realising that the driver was Rob, Tate and I ran to our vehicles and sped after him down the street. Soon we were hurtling along the A12 towards Colchester. Rob by this time was aware that we were following him. I could see his head turning around to look at us in an almost pecking motion and then back to navigate the road ahead. I tried to overtake him but he made a sharp left and disappeared up an exit slip road. Tucker and Tate managed to turn off and continued to pursue Rob into Colchester town centre.

As Tucker and Tate were forced to slow down in the traffic several police cars boxed them in and ordered them from their vehicles. They both denied chasing anybody and said that they were visiting the town for lunch.

'You know that we know the score, so get in your cars, turn around and disappear,' one officer told them.

That same week, Tate, Tucker and I were contacted by Rob's brother-in-law, who asked us to meet him at a local gym. He explained that Rob was truly sorry for ringing the police but he had only done so because he thought that he was going to be killed. As for robbing Adele, it was total nonsense. They had agreed a fee for her services but later she had demanded more and snatched Rob's money from his wallet. Rob had grabbed Adele's mobile phone and simply said that she could have it back when the money that she had stolen had been returned.

'He's terrified, he thinks he's going to die. If he drops the charges and disappears, will you please promise not to look for him?' Rob's brother-in-law pleaded.

Tate pretended to think about the proposal for some time, and after muttering, 'I don't know' several times to himself, he finally agreed to spare Rob's life. Almost weeping with relief Rob's brother-in-law walked out of the gym, leaving Tate and me collapsed in fits of laughter.

CHAPTER FOUR

One afternoon Tate, Tucker and I met up at Jim Connor's gym, Progress House, in Hadleigh. Most of the doormen and bodybuilders around the Southend area used to train there. Tucker had been going to this gym for about ten years, long before he got involved in drugs and the nightclub security industry. He used to train with a guy named William Theobald who, ironically, owned the land where Tucker eventually met his death. William's brother, Peter, discovered the bodies. William once considered Tucker to be his friend and would regularly pick him up from his home to take him training. However, their friendship ended when Tucker left his wife and 'drifted away into other things'.

I had been attending Progress House on and off since leaving prison. It was more than just a gym; the people were friendly there and it was extremely well run. As soon as we met Tate, he gave Tucker and me energy drinks and after we had finished them he fell about laughing saying that they had been spiked with large amounts of the mind-bending drug LSD. 'Don't worry, I'm loaded too,' he said. I hadn't planned to spend my day hallucinating and thinking I was living on fucking Mars, but as the drug took hold I began to see the funny side of Tate's prank. Come to think of it, I began to see the funny side of everything because I was completely off my tits.

I was driving my white BMW 5.35 Alpina, Tucker his black Porsche and Tate was behind the wheel of a brand-new Porsche 928 that he had acquired earlier that day. Tate was extremely proud of the car and the number plate that he had purchased for it: ANO 928 S. Macho banter about our vehicles turned into bravado and boasting and before long we were hurtling around the streets of Southend, racing one another. Driving on the wrong side of the road and jumping red lights at more than 100 mph while high on drugs. It's surprising that nobody was killed.

After defying death for nearly an hour, we screeched to a halt outside a 7/11 convenience store in Hamlet Court Road. We all went in the shop to purchase a drink and as we did so Tate threw a bread roll at me and so I returned fire with a ten-inch birthday cake. Within seconds we were all engaged in a full-scale food fight. The store manager shouted at us to stop and said that he was going to call the police. Tate snatched the phone from the manager's hand, punched it until it smashed and advised the ashen-faced man never to mention the police again. Unbeknown to us the manager had already alerted the police using a panic button and, as Tate continued to lecture the man about the pitfalls of involving them, they burst through the door. As Tucker tried to walk out of the shop one of the officers blocked his path and gripped his arm.

When I saw that the policeman had hold of Tucker, I walked over to him and said, 'Leave it out. You're not going to nick him.'

'And who are you?' the officer replied.

'Never mind who I am. Just let go of him because we are leaving,' I said.

As I was talking to the officer his colleagues were talking to Tate, who offered to give the shopkeeper £100 to cover the cost of any damage. Just as it looked as if a solution to please all had been reached, the officer talking to me pulled out his handcuffs and informed me that I was under arrest. I didn't resist until he tried to put me into his car. I have never assaulted a police officer and despite my long list of convictions I genuinely bear them no ill will. There are good and bad in all walks of life and the police are no different, but I had made my mind up that I wasn't going to be put into the patrol car, even if it meant physically resisting. Nervously eyeing Tate and Tucker, the arresting officer's colleagues realised that they may have a problem if the situation deteriorated and so they pleaded with him to release me.

'Fuck him. If he's going to nick me, let him do it,' I said.

The officer tried to bend my wrist so that I would get into his car but I stood firm and told him that he was wasting his time.

Tucker and Tate were glaring at the officer, who looked to his colleagues in the hope that they would back him up but they were having none of it.

'Consider yourself lucky,' the officer said as he unlocked the handcuffs and freed me.

'There's nothing lucky about it,' I replied. 'You wanted me to get in your car and I refused. Now you want me to go home, I have decided that I want to get into your car.'

Hands up, I was being an arsehole, but I was out of my head on acid and acting the fool. I opened the rear door of the police car and climbed in. Fortunately for everybody concerned, including myself, a fleet of police vehicles converged on the scene and an inspector ordered that I be taken away immediately to the nearest police station.

Tate and Tucker were released without charge but I was detained in the cells overnight. After nine hours in a police cell coming down from my acid trip, I was interviewed by the arresting officer. It was all rather informal; he asked me what I had been drinking to get into such a state and why I had been so keen to be taken into custody.

'I think my drink may have been spiked,' I lied. 'As for wanting to get arrested, the truth is I didn't. I was merely trying to attract your attention so that you wouldn't nick my mate Tucker.'

At the end of the interview, I was released without charge and warned about the dangers of leaving one's drink unattended in pubs and clubs.

That night I was at home with Tate when the phone rang; it was Tucker and he claimed that he was coming around to see us but he couldn't find the flat. Tate and I looked at each other in complete bewilderment as we both knew that Tucker had visited my home on numerous occasions and knew exactly where I lived.

'He is probably out of his head but he will find us eventually,' Tate said. Ten minutes later, Tucker was hammering on my front door and when I opened it he rushed past me into the lounge. Shouting and swearing, Tucker claimed that he had just been involved in a fight with three men and had to abandon his car. Tate and I armed ourselves and asked Tucker to take us back to his vehicle so that we could find the culprits. We all got into Tate's car and drove to a street named The Ridgeway. Tucker told us that he had stopped to ask a man for directions, the man had been rude to him and so he had got out of his vehicle and hit him. Two other men had then attacked Tucker and he claimed that he had knocked one of them out. Fearing he would be overpowered, Tucker said that he had decided to run rather than stand and fight.

When we arrived at the scene of the alleged altercation, Tucker's vehicle was parked at the side of road. It was locked, which I thought was odd if he had really got out of it in haste to fight. The three men he said that he had fought were also suspiciously absent. Tucker got into his vehicle and followed Tate and me back to the flat. I asked Tate what he made of Tucker's story but he didn't reply, he just looked towards the heavens and blew hard.

As soon as we were in the flat Tucker and Tate began snorting cocaine. I asked them not to do it in my home but neither of them took any notice. As the night wore on, I was asked what the police had said to me when I was questioned about the food fight and when I told them the truth they immediately looked at one another.

'Isn't that grassing?' Tucker asked Tate.

'What the fuck are you on about? I have never grassed on anybody in my life,' I replied.

Tucker explained that when I had said I was trying to prevent him from being arrested I had mentioned his name and therefore I was grassing.

'Oh, fuck off. It was a bun fight in a shop, not the Great Train Robbery. They arrested me and haven't even charged me, so how can that be grassing?' I said.

Tucker looked at Tate and after a few moments he conceded that it had all been a bit trivial. I don't know why but I felt that Tucker and Tate had been trying to engineer a situation with me that night. I kept telling myself that Tate was a good friend of mine and wouldn't dream of doing such a thing, but I overlooked the fact that my friend Tate was no more; his mind had been taken over by the shit he was sticking up his nose and in his veins every few hours.

In the early hours of the morning, Tucker said that he had to go home and offered to drop me off at my car, which had been left outside the 7/11 store. Once we were alone in his vehicle I took the opportunity to speak my mind to him. I said rather bluntly that I thought that he was taking the piss out of me, adding rather swiftly that I was not being disrespectful, nor was I being confrontational; I was just saying exactly how I felt.

Tucker pulled over to the side of the road, switched off the engine and said, 'Nipper, I am really worried about you. It's not me that's the problem, it's the drugs that you're taking. They are making you really paranoid. I think the world of you, I would never harm you. You're my brother.'

I was taking one Ecstasy tablet a week, the odd acid trip and an occasional line of cocaine or ketamine, an Amy Winehouse-type habit, but Tucker's words were so sincere I began to believe him and even experienced a twinge of guilt. That night I kept thinking about all that had happened and the following morning I rather foolishly mentioned to Tate that I thought there was something not quite right about Tucker. When Tate asked me what I was implying, I said that I thought Tucker was false, I didn't believe that he wasn't mugging me off, and I didn't believe his story about the three men attacking him. I therefore thought that he was full of shit. Tate didn't reply but I sensed my truthful comments about his hero had somehow upset him.

I have always thought that if the truth hurts people then so be it; you cannot change the truth, so people just have to learn to deal with it. It wasn't my fault that I was having serious doubts about the Mafia don that Tucker was making himself out to be. His partner Anna had recently given him a book about the Krays, which he had left at my flat. I had picked it up out of curiosity and flicked through the pages. I had burst out laughing when I read the inscription that Anna had written on the inside cover. 'Let them hate you just so long as they fear you.' Tucker was so proud of the dedication he had later read it out to Tate and me. As Tate feigned admiration and heaped praise on such deep, meaningful words, I sat cringing. Tucker was on drugs but he had no excuse for being totally deluded. Who in God's name did he think he was?

Tucker had a health food shop in Ilford, which was losing money, and so he told Tate and me that he intended to stage a burglary and take all of the stock before he bankrupted the business. It was agreed that Tucker would take me over to the premises so that I could give him advice about making the burglary appear genuine. After all, I did have a wealth of experience in that particular field. On the way to Ilford, we called into a clothes shop called Zoo, which sold top-of-the-range designer labels. I purchased £2,500 worth of garments and as I unrolled a bundle of banknotes with which to pay, Tucker said that he could do with the cash and gave the assistant a company cheque from his shop. After handing over the cheque and taking the money from me, he walked out of the shop. I knew that the cheque would never be honoured by Tucker because he had told me that he was folding the company, but he didn't think to offer me so much as a drink out of it.

When I mentioned the incident to Tate that evening, he surprised me by saying that I was getting too close to Tucker and I should not trust him. 'He's jealous of our friendship. He keeps hinting that he dislikes you and you shouldn't be trusted. Be careful, Nipper. Be very careful,' Tate said.

I wish that I could go back to those moments when my friend Tate was thinking clearly, free from drugs. I would have kept him away from Tucker and he would still be alive today. Sadly, time marches on; it cannot be stopped and it cannot be turned back. Tate and Tucker were not dissimilar; each an unstoppable force, incapable of being pushed back, marching on and on towards their doom.

A few months earlier, Jimmy Connor's gym had been broken into and Tate had written a letter to Jim claiming that I was responsible. Hand on my heart I wasn't and I have no idea why Tate blamed me, because we were close friends at that time. I suspect that it was because his drug addiction was loosening his grip on reality. Tate had woken me early one morning around the time of the burglary and demanded a gun. I asked him what the problem was but he had refused to tell me. Without my knowledge, Tate had taken a .38 revolver from my bedroom and then asked me to drive him to Jim Connor's gym.

Tate's partner, Sarah Saunders, is Jim's niece and I assumed at the time that there had been some sort of family dispute in which Tate had decided to intervene. When we arrived at the gym, Tate told me to park around the corner and he had then exited the car with the gun. I sat waiting for the sound of gunfire but, after a few minutes, Tate ran back and jumped into the car. As we sped away I noticed that tears were streaming down his face. I didn't say anything and when we arrived back at the flat Tate went into his bedroom.

Some time later, I met Jim who told me that he had been in the gym when he heard somebody knocking loudly on the door. When he had opened it, Tate was standing there gun in hand. Jim had asked Tate what he was up to but instead of answering he had just broken down. Embarrassed rather than alarmed Jim had tried to console Tate but he had simply turned and run away. Nobody will ever know what was on Tate's mind that day. I am not sure that even Tate knew what he was thinking at the time.

Not long after Tate's letter had been delivered to Jim Connor I went to Progress House, left my keys and wallet at reception and went into the changing rooms. Once I had begun training somebody took my keys from reception and had a spare set cut at a local shop. They then returned my original set of keys to reception. The following night I had been out with Malcolm attempting to remove a safe from a supermarket. Unable to cut the back off and get at the contents of the safe, we had manhandled it through a fire door and into our van. Using chisels and cutting equipment at a workshop that we had access to, we eventually managed to prise the safe open only to find that it was empty. I was tired and in a foul mood when Malcolm dropped me off outside my flat at five o'clock the following morning.

Thoughts of sleep were soon forgotten when I saw that my front door was wide open. Calling out to anybody who might have been inside I entered the flat and looked around each room. Whoever had been there had gone, but they had left the distinct smell of cigarette smoke and two dirty glasses in the sink, one of which was broken. I don't know why, but I automatically assumed that I had been burgled by the man who lived directly above me. I armed myself with a hammer, knocked on the man's door and when he answered demanded to know what he had been doing in my home. When the man denied ever setting foot in my property, I grabbed him by the throat and threatened to hit him in the face with the hammer unless he told me the truth. Still the man denied ever being in my home, so I walked back down the stairs mumbling incoherently and cursing the scum that commit burglary.

The following weekend, Tate asked me if I had any amino acid capsules, which bodybuilders take for protein, and so I gave a handful to him.

'These are no good, they are out of date,' he said after inspecting them.

I knew that there was nothing wrong with the capsules and so, when Tate suggested that I should try a couple myself, I agreed, just to prove that they were OK. Unbeknown to me, Tate had emptied the capsules and refilled them with ketamine. I can recall beginning to feel light-headed. The people in the room with me, whose faces became blurred, were laughing at me, but after that everything else is little more than a hazy memory.

I did not know it at the time, but Tate had deliberately drugged me in the hope that he could goad me into murdering a man. As the ketamine capsules began to render me totally incapable of being able to rationalise or think for myself, Tucker and Tate confided in me that one of Tate's cousins and a doorman I'll call Ron Redding had been the men in my flat, waiting for me to come home. It had been their intention, Tate said, to confront me about the burglary at the gym and cut my right hand off as punishment.

Fortunately for me, the safe at the supermarket had kept me out until the early hours of the morning and they had tired of waiting and gone home. Tate leaned forward in his seat, embraced me and then whispered in my ear that I should kill Redding. I was completely out of my mind on the drug and Tate quite easily convinced me that it was a good idea.

I can vaguely remember Tucker holding my video camera and laughing, he kept saying to Tate, 'Be careful what you say. I'm taping him.' They must have been drugged up too because Tate began pulling faces for the camera and was chanting, 'Kill him, Nipper. Kill him.' There was a 2.2 handgun in my flat that one of the firm had used in a shooting. Tucker handed me the weapon and said that if I was a 'proper person' I would shoot Redding. Almost zombie-like, I took the gun from Tucker, got into my car and went in search of the man my so-called friends had urged me to execute.

I knew that Redding worked as a doorman at a pub near Leigh-on-Sea and so I drove up and down the street trying to catch sight of him. I saw Redding's car parked outside the pub and so I pulled up further down the road, but at a place where I could still keep my eye on it. When Redding eventually finished his shift and left the pub, I followed him at a discreet distance. I knew that he lived in Basildon and so I began to try to think of suitable places where I could force his car to stop so that I could get out and shoot him. Without indicating, Redding's car suddenly slewed across the road and pulled up outside a Kentucky Fried Chicken store. I couldn't stop without drawing attention to myself and so I drove past Redding's vehicle and pulled up about 100 yards away.

Five minutes later, Redding's car flashed past me. Catching just a fleeting glimpse of the driver I was unsure if it was in fact Redding at the wheel. Confused by the drugs that I had unwittingly taken I decided to pull alongside the vehicle on a stretch of dual carriageway to see if my intended target was at the wheel. As I looked across at Redding, he looked back to see who the lunatic was who had so obviously been following him. In a blind panic I applied my brakes and let Redding take the lead once more. When Redding pulled up outside his home, I turned into an adjacent road and began checking that the gun was fully loaded.

A short sharp tap at my window startled me and when I looked out Redding's puzzled face was gazing back at me. 'All right, Nipper, what are you up to?' he asked. I knew that Redding would have armed himself with something before approaching my car and so I didn't dare risk pointing the gun at him.

'I'm looking for Henry,' I replied. Redding had a friend named Henry and so he asked me what I wanted him for. 'I don't know but I better go and find him,' I said before starting the car and driving off. The drugs were beginning to wear off by the time I had pulled up outside my flat. Tate had gone to bed and Tucker had left. I couldn't believe that I had planned to shoot Redding, a decent man who to my personal knowledge had never intended to cause me any harm.

My head was pounding because of the drugs Tate had given me and so I went straight to bed. When I awoke later that afternoon and went into the lounge, I saw that my flat was a complete mess. I am an extremely tidy person who likes everything in my home to be in order and so I was absolutely livid. Tate had recently held parties at my flat without my permission or prior knowledge but this mess hadn't been caused by a party; it could only be described as an orgy of destruction.

When I went into the bathroom, I found two naked teenage prostitutes in the shower, used syringes scattered around the floor and empty champagne bottles in the bath. I threw the girls out and after barging into Tate's bedroom began shouting about him taking the piss out of me. Tate, who was barely able to focus on me because he was so drugged up, didn't appear to even realise why I was so upset. When I began to tidy up my flat, I found a bag containing my kettle, a toaster and various other electrical goods. I had no idea why either Tate or Tucker would have put them in the bag. I certainly didn't think that they had planned to steal them. Before I could ask Tate, he left the flat with his two prostitutes in tow.

The following morning I opened the drawer in my bedroom to get some underpants. Hidden among my clothing I found a black leather bag stuffed with drugs and money. I was livid. Tate had hidden his drug stash in my room so if the police raided the house I would be accused of possession. He had not yet returned home and so I walked into his bedroom and packed his meagre possessions into a suitcase and left it by the front door. When he came home and saw the suitcase in the hall, he asked what I was up to.

'You hid drugs in my fucking room. I don't want you or your drugs in my flat. You're a junkie and you don't even know it,' I shouted. Tate looked at the suitcase and back at me before replying.

'I am no fucking junkie. I control the drugs, they don't control me.' Tate said that he had nowhere to go and pleaded with me to let him stay until he had sorted somewhere else out to live and, like a fool, I agreed. As I continued tidying up my flat I found a saucer in the lounge with what appeared to be cocaine on it. Tate had gone back out and so I tipped the powder in the sink and washed the saucer with boiling water. When Tate did arrive home that night, he was incoherent and barely able to stand and so he didn't notice that his drugs had been disposed of.

The following morning, when I got out of bed, Tate had already left the flat. When I entered the lounge, I found a crack pipe and a cocaine-like substance on a saucer so I threw the pipe in the dustbin and washed the saucer. When Tate walked into the flat later that day, he was with his brother Russell. As soon as Tate saw me he began shouting about me throwing away £600 worth of crack cocaine.

'Are you so fucked you don't realise you are taking it? There was less than a gramme of that shit on the saucer,' I said.

I reminded Tate that I thought that he had become a junkie and I didn't want him or his drugs in my flat. Russell stood in the hallway without saying a word but when he took out a cigarette and went to light it I asked him not to do so. When he asked what my problem was, I explained that I did not smoke and therefore I did not like people doing so in my home. Russell put the cigarette in his mouth and asked me what I intended to do if he didn't stop.

Before I could reply, somebody had knocked the door and I went to answer it. A man in a suit began telling me how meaningless my life must be without the particular product that he was selling and so I thanked him for his advice and closed the door. When I went back into the lounge, I saw that Tate and his brother had gone into the garden to smoke. Russell didn't say any more about the subject and so I too chose not to raise it. However, when Russell left my flat, Tate astounded me by saying that if his brother had started fighting with me then he would have joined in on my side. Up, down, happy, angry or depressed, there was no longer any way of telling which Tate I was going to encounter on any given day because of his drug addiction.

Later the same day, Tucker's friend Carlton Leach knocked on my door. Leach claimed that he had been involved in an altercation with a black guy while working on the door at a private party in Battersea, south London. Apparently the man had taken exception to the way Leach had treated him and rather foolishly returned firing a gun. I say 'rather foolishly' because Leach and several members of his door team had soon overpowered the man and beaten him mercilessly. The police were called and after Leach had agreed to make a formal statement against the gunman he was arrested. During the fracas Leach's vehicle had been shot several times and the police impounded it in the hope of gathering further evidence. I wasn't sure why Leach had decided to pour his heart out to me and so I asked him how he thought that I could help.

'It's like this, Nipper. I desperately need a car to get back and forth to work in London,' Leach said.

I had a second-hand red Ford Fiesta 1600 parked outside my home doing nothing, and so I said that he could take that. I had purchased the vehicle for my girlfriend, who was learning to drive. As she wasn't due to take her test for two weeks I assumed that Leach would have returned it by then. The vehicle had not been taxed, so I gave Leach the log book and the money to tax it for me. While we were talking, I mentioned that my friend had just stolen a trailer full of quality leather jackets and he had given me 100 to sell on his behalf. Leach said that he would be able to sell 20 of them for me as a favour for loaning him the car. He picked 20 of the most expensive jackets, loaded them into the Fiesta and disappeared. I never saw the jackets or the vehicle again; I later learned that Tucker sold the car and the jackets the very same day.

At approximately 2200 hrs that night my house phone rang, and when I answered it Donna Garwood, Tucker's 16-year-old mistress, asked me if I had seen him. I wasn't in the mood for doing Tucker or his friends any favours and so I replied, 'No, I have not seen him and nor do I particularly wish to see him. He is probably at home giving his missus one up the arse.' I had never liked Garwood. She thought that she could talk to people how she wanted simply because she was Tucker's bit on the side. I had awoken one morning to find her and Tucker asleep in the spare bedroom of my flat. I automatically assumed that it was his partner and that assumption was reinforced when I used to go to a house I assumed was Tucker's and she was there. Only when Tucker invited me to his real home did I meet his partner, Anna, and discover that the other house was, in fact, Rolfe's.

I am not the type of man that embraces deceit among alleged loved ones; my opinion of Garwood was therefore pretty low. As soon as I had told Garwood where Tucker might be she had slammed the phone down. Early the next morning, I was awoken by somebody hammering on my front door. Still half asleep, I opened it to find Tucker, Rolfe and a man named Peter Cuthbert standing outside. Without saying a word the three men walked into my home and when I asked them what they wanted Tucker made the sign of a gun with his two fingers against his head.

I assumed that he had come to pick up the 2.2 revolver that I had intended to shoot Redding with. I had wiped the weapon clean of all fingerprints since that night and hidden it in a cupboard, so I showed Tucker where it was. As soon as he had picked up the gun he grabbed my throat with his left hand, lifted me off the floor and shoved the weapon into my temple. Spitting phlegm he began screaming at me, 'Fuck my missus up the arse, would you? Fuck my missus up the arse?' After 20 or 30 seconds, Tucker shoved me into my bedroom and threw me on the bed. Sitting astride me he kept jabbing the barrel of the gun into my head and mouth and shouting, 'I am going to show you what this can do.' I could tell by the froth around his mouth and the crazed look in his eyes that he was high on crack cocaine. Tucker suddenly stopped shouting and ordered Rolfe to search the house for jewellery and anything else of value. He then took a butcher's meat cleaver from inside his jacket and asked me if I would prefer to lose one of my hands or one of my feet. I thought that if he was going to sever one of my limbs I would at least survive the ordeal and so I could fucking shoot him. I am left-handed and so I held out my right hand, closed my eyes and waited for the searing pain.

When I had finished silently counting to ten, I realised that Tucker was not going to carry out his threat and so I opened my eyes. Tucker was standing over me, his eyes were bulging and he was grinning like a madman. After snapping out of the trance-like state that he was in Tucker put the meat cleaver back in his jacket, turned and walked away. I jumped off the bed and began shouting, 'What the fuck have I done?'

Cuthbert held me back and repeatedly asked me to calm down but I was incensed. I pushed Cuthbert out of the way and went after Tucker. As he reached the front door he turned quickly, grabbed me by the throat and lifted me off the floor. Slamming me against a wall he pulled out the meat cleaver and threatened to bury it in my head. Cuthbert grabbed Tucker's arm and pleaded with him to calm down.

Fortunately for me, Tucker released his iron grip from my throat and walked out of the door. When my unwelcome guests had all left, I rang Tate to ask him what I was supposed to have done. He told me that Tucker was having a bad day and I should not worry about it. I couldn't work out if Tate was joking or he simply couldn't grasp the enormity of the liberty that Tucker had taken with me. I thanked Tate for his words of wisdom and rang Tucker to ask if he could give me an explanation for his abhorrent behaviour.

Tucker exploded into a rage and began screaming at me, 'Have you sorted it?' When I asked him what it was that I was supposed to sort out, he replied, 'You told Donna that I do my missus up the arse.'

Before I could explain that it was a comment made in jest, Tucker said that he was going to put me on my knees, make me apologise and then shoot me in the head. 'Go and fuck yourself up the arse, you mug,' I said before ending the call.

Tucker's concern for his partner was about as meaningful as Garwood's. In my opinion Tucker couldn't care less about either woman; he just wanted people on tap that he could use to satisfy his own whims and wishes. A good example of this is when I returned home one morning to find three females naked in my bath. After asking who they were and what they thought they were doing, I was informed that they had spent the night in my flat snorting Tate and Tucker's cocaine. I told them to get dressed and I would call a taxi for them. Half an hour later, the three girls left.

The following week Tate, Tucker, Anna and I were enjoying an evening out at a nightclub when the girls who had been in my bath walked in.

When they saw Tate and Tucker, they came over to say hello and one of them said to Anna, 'Hi, you must be Donna.' Tucker's face looked like thunder.

'Her name is Anna, now fuck off,' he said, glaring at the guilty party. When the embarrassed girl walked away, Tucker summoned one of his minions, named 'Ginger Mickey', and whispered in his ear. Ginger Mickey disappeared and returned ten minutes later with a set of car keys, which he handed to Tucker. When Tate enquired what was going on, Tucker explained that Ginger Mickey had grabbed the girl who he was claiming had insulted Anna, and demanded her car keys. When the terrified girl had handed over the keys, Ginger Mickey had told the door staff that Tucker wanted her ejected from the club and they had complied. The car, a Mini Clubman, was driven away by Mickey and crushed at a scrapyard the following morning; the girl had no choice but to accept her loss because she was far too scared to complain.

I am no hard man but I am nobody's fool either. Others may have been intimidated by Tucker and his firm but I wasn't going to forget what he had done to me, nor was I prepared to take any more of his shit. I left the flat immediately and purchased a combat knife. I then went in search of somebody who would sell me a gun.

The first person I approached had an array of firearms for sale but when I mentioned who I may have to shoot he refused to sell me anything.

'I am not protecting that bastard. It would make my day if he got blown away, but I am scared that he will find out I have sold you a gun to shoot him with,' the man explained.

I got much the same response from all the people I approached in Essex. However, I did eventually find a firearms dealer in south London who didn't know Tucker. He sold me a bulletproof vest and initially offered me a sub-machine gun but I couldn't afford it so I settled for a pump-action shotgun and a 2.2 revolver. On my way home, I stopped off at the Bull public house on London Road in Pitsea.

After finding a space at the rear of the car park, I walked into the bushes and began cutting down the barrel and butt of the shotgun. As an ex-prisoner I was acutely aware that if I was caught with firearms I could be returned to custody for up to five years and so I kept one eye on the road as I worked hard to complete my task. Having cut the barrel off, I started work on the butt of the gun. At that moment a police car swept onto the car park and pulled up less than ten feet away from me. I laid flat on my stomach on a bed of nettles and thorns and grimaced as I fixed my eyes firmly on the police vehicle door. After a few minutes of inactivity, I risked looking at the occupants by raising myself up onto my elbows. Two officers were drinking tea from a Thermos flask and eating sandwiches. Despite the rash from nettle stings on my neck and the numerous scratches from thorns on my torso I managed to feel pleased with my situation. Forty-five minutes later, the police officers packed away their flask and sandwich boxes and departed.

When I had finished cutting down the shotgun, I returned to my flat and was horrified to find that all of my clothing and most of my household goods had been stolen. Anything the thieves couldn't carry had been smashed, slashed or broken. Food and a substance that looked like excrement had been smeared all over the carpets and walls; my home had been destroyed. I rang my girlfriend and advised her to avoid any contact with Tucker, Tate and Rolfe's girlfriends. I explained that I was in an extremely dangerous situation and my adversaries would try to use my family and friends in their efforts to find and harm me.

My girlfriend refused to believe that Tate and Rolfe would get involved but I just knew that my friendship with Tate no longer meant anything to him, and Rolfe would follow blindly in any event. After ringing my family and warning them that Tucker and his henchmen may come looking for me, I rang Donna Garwood and asked her what she had said to her moronic boyfriend.

'I told him what you had said about his missus because it was out of order,' she bragged.

Garwood had clearly overlooked the fact that she was having a sordid affair with the partner of the woman she was pretending to be concerned about. I cannot repeat what I said to her but it involved sex and travel and I may have implied that she was a troublemaker. Having completed my rant, I telephoned Tucker and asked if he was responsible for the carnage at my flat. He didn't admit or deny responsibility; he just laughed at me and said that my possessions had been used to furnish a flat that he had acquired for Garwood to move into.

'Tate's taking his favourite prostitute off the game and she is moving in there too,' Tucker said. 'You don't need your stuff anyway, Nipper, because I am going to kill you.'

I cannot see the point in shouting about what you may or may not be going to do; I believe that actions speak much louder than words and so I simply hung up. I went into my flat and secreted myself in a small cupboard under the stairs. I had a clear view of the front door and had decided that as soon as Tucker or anybody else walked into my home I was going to open fire on them with the shotgun.

I spent six hours crouched in that cupboard but I had to abandon my plan in the end because I was suffering from extreme cramp and a lack of sleep. I went into my bedroom and lay down, still clutching my weapons, on what was left of my bed before falling into a deep sleep. I was awoken the following morning by the sound of my phone ringing. When I lifted the receiver and groaned 'Hello', Tate asked me how I was and apologised for Tucker's behaviour.

'Don't worry, Nipper. It's all sorted,' Tate said. 'We're going to Canning Town to sort out a bit of business and then we will come around to see you at midday.'

I told Tate that I would wait in for them and replaced the receiver. As soon as I had done so I put my bulletproof vest on, grabbed my firearms and ran towards the cupboard under the stairs. At the last minute I changed my mind and ran out of the back door and into the garden. I was looking for a suitable shooting position so that I could take them out in quick succession. As I left the garden and walked up an alleyway at the side of my flat I heard the screech of tyres and car doors slamming. I dashed behind a parked car in the street and checked that my weapons were loaded. I could see Tate and Tucker's Porsches abandoned in the middle of the road and I could hear my front door being kicked open. I then heard Tate calling out my name as he searched the flat and Tucker was shouting out to Rolfe to look for me in the back garden. All three of them then met in the street just yards from my hiding place and began discussing their next move.

When they eventually left, I went back into the flat and found a note that Tate had left for me. It read, 'Don't let me lose all respect for you, Nipper. I am trying to help you. Please get in touch.'

I rang Tate and asked him how trying to kill me was ever going to help me.

'You kicked my fucking door in, you prick. I watched you. I was only going to kill Tucker before today but now you're all going to die.'

Tate didn't answer and the line went dead. I ran out of the house and hid in an alleyway opposite my flat. Moments later Tucker's Porsche pulled up and he and Rolfe got out and walked down the alley to the rear of my home. I remained where I was, waiting for Tate to pull up in his vehicle but, after a few minutes, I concluded that he must have gone home. The hour had arrived for Tucker and Rolfe to die.

When I had cut the barrel off my shotgun, I had tied a length of rope to the stock so that I could sling it over my shoulder and hide it under my jacket. As I entered the alleyway, I practised opening my jacket, letting the shotgun fall and then swinging it up from my side into the firing position. Fuck knows what film I had seen such a motion in, but it was extremely slick and effective. In my left hand I clutched the 2.2 revolver, which was loaded and ready to fire.

As I reached the rear of my flat I saw that Rolfe was in the process of stealing my motorbike leathers from the garden shed. I could hear loud banging and thought that Tucker must be in the shed trying to break the padlock off my 750 Suzuki motorcycle but this stopped as I approached. I decided to hide behind a nearby garden gate and wait for the two of them to step into the alleyway where they would have little or no chance of escape. As Tucker walked out of my garden with Rolfe immediately behind him I emerged from my hiding place with a weapon in each hand.

Tucker was visibly shocked and could only manage to utter, 'Nipper. Nipper, you cunt.'

'Fucking Nipper. Fucking Nipper,' I shouted. 'Have some of this, you mug.' I pulled the trigger of the handgun, while aiming at Tucker's head, but it failed to fire.

Rolfe dropped my motorbike leathers and ran. Tucker, to my amazement, fell to the floor and began making a pathetic whimpering noise interspersed with pleas of, 'No, no.' I pulled the trigger again but the gun failed me once more. Tucker realised that he had an opportunity to escape and so got to his feet and ran. As he did so I pulled the trigger again and on this occasion the weapon fired. I have no idea where the bullet went but it failed to find the intended target as Tucker continued to flee the scene. I ran after Tucker and Rolfe and opened fire with the shotgun. They immediately vaulted a hedge and began running through people's gardens in an effort to escape me.

I did manage to unleash two more shots but I was chasing the duo as I did so and my aim was, at best, poor. I have to admit that I was more scared during this encounter than I had been when Tucker had threatened to sever my limb. I had been like a man possessed with murderous intent when I had tried to shoot the bastards and when it was over the extent of my own rage terrified me. I knew it was not over yet, though; I would have to kill them before they caught and killed me.

That night Tucker's business partner, Bernard O'Mahoney, rang me and offered his assistance. He said that Tate and Rolfe had been to Raquel's nightclub, in Basildon, looking for me. Tate had told O'Mahoney that if I did turn up he was to let me in, ring him or Tucker and keep me there until they arrived.

'They are going to top you, Nipper. They are telling everybody that you grassed them up for an incident in a 7/11 store,' O'Mahoney had warned. 'If you want somewhere to lay low, I have people up north you can go to. Alternatively, if you want to stay in Essex I can try and talk to them.'

O'Mahoney offered to meet me but I told him in no uncertain terms that he was too close to those three bastards to trust. I wasn't aware at the time that O'Mahoney's offer of help was genuine. I later learned that he thought no more of the trio than I did, but I was so paranoid through fear that I wouldn't have trusted the good Lord himself if he had appeared and offered to assist me. This was one battle that I was going to have to fight and win alone.

CHAPTER FIVE

Unlike Tucker and Tate, I do my best to carry out any threats that I make and, the following night, I shot Tate at his bungalow in Basildon. The only regrets I have are that the bullet smashed his arm rather than his head and I didn't manage to shoot Tucker and Rolfe too. When Tucker heard about Tate being shot, he hid in his house and telephoned Rolfe to come to his aid.

'He has gone fucking mad and shot Pat. Get yourself over here and bring a gun because I think I'm next,' Tucker whined.

When Rolfe arrived, Tucker made him search the area around his house before he dared venture outside his front door. When Rolfe informed Tucker that I didn't appear to be in the vicinity, they raced to Basildon hospital in Rolfe's car. Sarah Saunders was already at Tate's bedside and she later told me that Tucker had been laughing about me trying to shoot him and Rolfe, and boasted that I would have to be killed for what I had done. I am still alive today, those three are not. Enough said.

The morning after I had shot Tate, my girlfriend was taken to Basildon hospital by two of Tucker's gofers and shown the damage that the bullet had caused. Tate was lying in bed drugged out of his mind, shouting, 'Your fucking boyfriend did this. Tell him if he doesn't give himself up to us, everybody he cares about will pay.'

Trembling with fear, my girlfriend was then taken to the premises in Basildon where Tate's prostitutes operated from. No reason was given to my girlfriend for this visit but she was asked if she was currently employed, the implication being that she could be forced into prostitution if she didn't divulge my whereabouts. Fortunately for her, she was not troubled again after being dropped off near her home.

Later that evening, I was contacted by my friend Malcolm Walsh who told me that Tucker wanted me to know that he intended to kidnap one of my sisters and torture her until I agreed to give myself up. My sisters were aged five and fifteen at that time and I was naturally horrified and incensed. Malcolm apologised for passing such a message on to me but said he had only done so because he thought that considering the state of mind Tucker was in he may well have carried out his threat.

'He was drugged up, saying he was going to cut your sisters' fingers off one by one,' Malcolm said. 'He was almost crying with temper; the guy is a fucking arsehole.'

I purchased a double-barrelled shotgun, drove to my father's home and, after explaining what I had been told, gave him the weapon. My father and I picked my sisters up from school and after packing several suitcases they headed to a hotel in Ipswich. Saying goodbye to them was extremely difficult; I don't mind admitting that I cried. I truly believed that I was going to have to kill Tucker or be killed myself. A grave or a prison cell. My future prospects were hardly mouth-watering.

I knew that Tucker would be going to visit Tate that evening and so I decided to lie in wait and shoot him. I drove to Basildon hospital and put on a ridiculous-looking cheap plastic mackintosh. If I was going to have to lie in bushes or out in the rain for some time, I wanted to at least remain dry.

Vehicles were pulling up at the visitors' entrance and dropping passengers off before driving to the car park, which was some distance away. I thought it unlikely that Tucker would drive himself when he had so many minions at his disposal, and so I decided to stand outside the main entrance of the hospital and shoot him as he got out of his vehicle. I dread to think what I looked like as I marched up and down the concourse growling, spitting and staring at the occupants of every vehicle that pulled up.

'Nipper, Nipper,' a voice called out. 'What the fuck are you up to?' I spun around to find a man I knew named Jason Smythe laughing at me.

Pulling the shotgun from my coat I began saying, 'Tucker, fucking Tony Tucker. I am going to blow his fucking head clean off.' Jason stopped laughing and begged me to put the weapon away.

'What has he done to you? Please go home, Nipper. You're in no state to be out here,' Jason said.

I didn't realise it at the time but Jason was right. I was in such a hyped-up state of anger and frustration that I was actually weeping. Jason told me that the police were looking for me everywhere and I would be wise to get into my car and go before somebody telephoned them. Both Tucker and Rolfe had made formal complaints to the police about me attempting to murder them and Tate had told them that it was me who had shot him. Grassing bastards. They didn't mind bullying and intimidating people, but when they feared for their own safety they had run to the police for protection. Before getting into my car and driving away, I thanked Jason for advising me that I was now wanted not only by Tucker and Tate, but also by the police.

I think that I suffered some form of mental breakdown that night. I was weeping for my family, shouting obscenities that only I could hear and laughing at the images of Tate and Tucker's bullet-riddled bodies that swarmed through my head. The most powerful emotion was fear for my family and so I decided to take a drastic course of action in the hope of saving them. I telephoned Tucker's friend Carlton Leach and asked him to meet me.

'Tucker's going to hurt my sisters if he can't catch and kill me. I know that if he catches me I face a terrible death, so I need your help,' I said.

'What can I do for you?' Leach replied.

'I want you to shoot me. I can't let them hurt my family and I can't face being caught. It's my only option, but I can't do it myself,' I said.

Leach fell silent for a few moments before telling me that he couldn't possibly do such a thing. He said that Tucker was out of order for threatening my family, but all he could do was try to talk him out of it. 'I'll ring him and ask him to leave your family alone. I don't think he will listen but I will try to make him see sense,' Leach said.

About an hour later, Leach rang me back and said that Tucker had given his word that my family would be left alone but I was going to have my arms and legs hacked off.

'Tucker said that he wants to see you in a wheelchair,' Leach said.

'Well, tell Tucker he is a fool, because if he leaves me alive, I will somehow get hold of a gun and blow his big fucking head off.' I replied.

I was still distraught and Leach, to his credit, suggested that I call him back the following morning after he had talked to Tucker face to face rather than over the phone.

'He may listen to me and leave you alone. All I can do is ask,' Leach said.

The following morning, I rang Leach and he invited me to his home. Fearing it was a ruse so that Tucker could catch me, I drove around the streets near to where Leach lived looking for familiar vehicles. When I finally entered Leach's home, I was armed with a pump-action shotgun and my revolver, which were secreted under my plastic mackintosh.

Leach told me that he wanted no part in my dispute with his friends but he didn't want to see either me or them getting hurt. Sitting on the sofa, I looked like a fucking chameleon, my eyes darted from door to door, window to window and room to room. I was still unconvinced that Leach had not lured me to his home so that Tucker could catch me. At one stage I jumped up from the sofa, pulled out my revolver and began looking in the other rooms, checking that the patio doors were locked and searching under the stairs.

Leach sat in the lounge shaking his head in disbelief. 'They have really got to you, haven't they, Nipper? I promise you that this is not a set-up,' he said.

Leach asked me if the gun I had in my hand was the one that I had used to shoot Tate. Rather than admit my guilt to a man I knew had made a statement about a gunman shooting his car up, I just laughed, thanked him for his assistance and left. Later that day I rang Jason, who I had met outside the hospital the night before. I mentioned that I had been to visit Leach and he said that he knew. When I enquired how he could possibly have known, Jason said that Leach had telephoned him and said that, in the state of mind that I was in, I was a liability running around with loaded guns. Jason claimed that he had then been asked by Leach if he could lure me to a quiet location out of town so that I could be 'taken care of'. 'Stay away from them all, Nipper. You're playing roulette with your life,' Jason warned.

I had become so paranoid I didn't even trust Jason and so I decided to ring the root cause of all my problems: Pat Tate. I am not sure what his blood pressure was like before I rang but he was in danger of suffering a heart attack by the time we had finished talking. The call started in a civil manner; I reminded him how friendly we had once been, but when I suggested that drugs had destroyed him he began screaming incoherently down the phone.

'Shut up, you fucking idiot. I am going to come up to that hospital and put one in your head,' I said before hanging up.

Tate was in no doubt that I would carry out my threat, the lump of lead in his arm bore testament to the fact that my word was my bond. Tate immediately rang Tucker and pleaded with him to bring a gun to the hospital for his protection. It wasn't the brightest idea that Tate had ever had. The hospital staff were already tiring of him and his visitors taking illegal drugs and being unnecessarily loud. When a prostitute had been found giving oral sex to Tate, he had been moved to a private room off the general ward. This move had made matters even worse because Tate's guests ignored the official visiting times and partied well into the night, every night.

One morning, while Tate was having the dressing on his wound changed, a nurse making up his bed discovered the loaded gun that Tucker had supplied under his pillow. The police were called immediately and Tate was arrested for possession of a firearm, ammunition and a quantity of various drugs. Since Tate was still on licence from his ten-year sentence for the Happy Eater robbery, he was immediately returned to prison. I spent every hour of every day and night searching for Tucker and his sidekick Rolfe. Only one thought occupied my troubled mind; find the bastards and kill them before they kill me or a member of my family. It was Tucker that I really wanted to execute, but if Rolfe happened to be with him then he could have some lead as well, but ironing him out was not a priority; his death would be nothing more than a bonus.

* * *

Rolfe had recently purchased Tucker's house, as he had put it on the market after moving up the property ladder, courtesy of his lucrative drug-dealing business. It was so lucrative, in fact, that even after moving Tucker could afford to pay Rolfe's mortgage in return for his chauffeuring, drug distribution and general skivvying services. Tucker and Rolfe both lived in the Chafford Hundred area, which was then a new housing development near Essex girls' heaven – the Lakeside shopping centre. They were aware of the vehicle that I drove, so if I was going to ambush them I would have to replace it. I bought an old Volvo from a friend of mine in Southend: it started, it ran, it was cheap; but beyond that there's nothing positive that I can say about it.

Driving towards Tucker's house I passed a large pub on a roundabout called the Sandmartin. As I turned off the roundabout I noticed a black Porsche 928 parked on a grass verge. Glancing at the registration number as I drove past I saw that it was the unmistakable TT9 plate belonging to Tucker. My heart began to race as the adrenalin surged through my body. I had found Tucker's vehicle and knew that he would not be far away. I pulled over and reached for my pump-action shotgun. My task was distasteful but I knew that I would not hesitate to carry it out. I couldn't see anybody sitting in the Porsche and so I got back into my car, drove a further 100 yards and parked.

I knew that when Tucker returned to the vehicle he would have to drive towards me, unless of course he did a three-point turn in the road. That would take time and so either way I would have an opportunity to shoot him. I decided that as he approached me I would stand in the road, blast his windscreen out with the shotgun and then, when he had stopped, I would empty the handgun into his body and head. I sat motionless in my car for ten to fifteen minutes, my eyes fixed on the rear-view mirror. I dared not avert them for a split second just in case my target got into his car unnoticed.

After an hour or so, I began to wonder if Tucker was going to return to his car, so I decided to get out and look for him on foot. I secreted the shotgun in my jacket and walked around the surrounding streets, but he was nowhere to be seen. As I returned to my car I heard Tucker's Porsche roar into life. I ran as fast as I could, jumped into my vehicle and gave chase. My car was no match for Tucker's high-powered machine and soon I was watching in despair as his tail lights disappeared into the distance. Just as I was giving up hope of ever cornering my prey I drove past the Esso service station at the Lakeside shopping centre and saw Tucker's Porsche parked at the pumps.

I circled the garage and could make out a large man at the rear of the vehicle, presumably filling it up with petrol. I couldn't shoot him on the garage forecourt because there were too many cameras and knowing my luck of late I would probably miss, hit a petrol pump and engulf half of Essex in a ball of fucking flame. 'Shit, shit,' I said to myself. 'I'll have to let him have it when he pulls away from the garage.' As the Porsche drove away from the forecourt I pulled in behind it and placed the shotgun on my lap. Initially, heavy traffic allowed me to keep up with the vehicle but as soon as the Porsche hit a long stretch of open road my car was left behind in a cloud of smoke.

The following Saturday night, I put on a baseball cap, a pair of nerd glasses and drove to Tucker's home to await his arrival. I knew that he usually stumbled in just before sunrise but I wanted to secure a good parking position from where I could launch my attack. The last week had really taken its toll on me. I don't mind admitting that I was scared. In fact it was more than that; I was absolutely terrified.

There is no shame in experiencing fear, running from it maybe, but I had not even considered that. My friend Malcolm had become close friends with Damon Alvin since the incident with the traveller's cheques had soured our relations. Alvin, a man like Tucker, who was prone to boasting and exaggerating but was undoubtedly still dangerous, had promised to acquire a live hand grenade for me.

'Shoot Tucker's window out and then toss it in the car. That will solve your problem,' Alvin had said.

I had met Alvin on two occasions to pick the grenade up, but both times he had arrived with guns for sale but no grenade. Alvin kept saying, 'It's coming, it's coming,' but I reminded him that so was fucking Christmas.

Tony Tucker, the so-called 'Diamond Geezer', was living in a cul-de-sac called Diamond Close at the time. I parked at the entrance to it, lowered my seat so that I could see just over the dashboard and settled down for what I thought would be a long night. I could not see out the back of the vehicle because I had packed what few possessions of mine that Tate, Tucker and Rolfe had not smashed or stolen into the car and they were obstructing my view. As I glanced from side mirror to side mirror I could see a pair of headlights approaching from the direction of the nearby shopping centre. My pump-action shotgun and revolver lay loaded on the passenger seat next to me. When the vehicle reached me, it appeared to slow down but it did not stop.

As soon as it had disappeared from view I got out of my car and went to a nearby alleyway for a piss. When I walked back towards the car, a man with an Alsatian dog shone a high-powered torch into my face and asked me what I was doing.

'Take that fucking light out of my face,' I said.

I was not sure if the man was police or a security guard but he had some sort of uniform on. Again the man asked me what I was doing and when I explained that I had stopped for a piss in the alley he went in search of the evidence. Illuminated by a street light I could see that the man was a security guard but that fact gave me little comfort. If he saw the guns on the seat of my car, I was in no doubt that this Sherlock Holmes wannabe would ring the police.

I got into my car, threw a coat over the guns and locked the door. Banging on the window, the guard demanded that I open the door. Trying my best to ignore him, I turned the key in the ignition but the engine refused to start. As I pumped the accelerator the guard ran around to the passenger door and tried to open it. As I stretched across the seat to ensure that it was locked, I accidentally moved the coat and revealed the guns. Instead of doing the sensible thing and running away, the guard ran to the back of my car and opened the hatchback door.

'Seize him, seize him,' the guard shouted as he tried to force his deranged dog into my car.

Fortunately, my personal effects prevented the dog from getting into the vehicle but I knew it wouldn't be long before fucking Sherlock would solve that particular problem. The car was still refusing to start and so I disengaged the handbrake and let it roll down a slight incline. The engine failed me when I first tried to bump start it but at the second attempt it roared into life.

As I pulled away, the guard, who was clearly intent on earning his wages that night, appeared in front of my car brandishing a scaffold pole. I accelerated rather than slowing down. I was wanted by the police for three attempted murders and numerous firearm offences and so I reasoned that running over an overenthusiastic security guard wouldn't make much difference to any sentence that the courts were going to impose upon me. Bang! The sound of the windscreen exploding made me jump back in my seat. I looked up expecting to see the have-a-go hero sprawled across my bonnet but instead I saw a scaffold pole embedded in my windscreen. I drove almost blind for about 100 yards, pulled up and dislodged the pole.

The guard hadn't given up his pursuit of me, so I jumped back into the car and sped off. I made my way to Southend where I parked the vehicle in a friend's garage before lying down on the back seat and going to sleep. I knew that I would be unable to continue using the vehicle as the super-efficient guard would undoubtedly have written down the registration number. I also knew that he wouldn't have been able to wait to tell the police about the guns he had seen, so they would undoubtedly be keen to find the car and its owner.

The following morning I took a drainage rod from my friend's garage, purchased a silver toy gun from Toys 'R' Us and drove to a bus stop on the A13, just outside Southend. I put the drainage rod on the passenger seat, covered most of it with a coat and put the toy gun in the glove compartment. After checking that I had not left any personal effects in the car I left the keys in the ignition and got on the first bus back into town.

As every motorist knows, few traffic violations go unnoticed by the police and so I knew it wouldn't be long before they swooped on a car parked at a bus stop. After checking the vehicle registration the police would discover that it was wanted in connection with an alleged firearms incident. The subsequent search would unearth a drainage rod that looked like the barrel of a shotgun and a toy gun. The security guard could have only told the police what he thought he might have seen, not if the weapons were real.

I know what you're thinking, 'fucking wise guy', but sadly no plan in history has ever been perfect. When I had purchased the vehicle, I had failed to re-register it in my name. Maybe it was a long queue at the post office that prevented me from completing the necessary forms, or the fact that three drug-crazed arseholes were trying to murder me, which made me forget. Regardless of the reason, the vehicle had remained registered in the name of the friend that I had bought it off.

When the police found the vehicle and linked it to the incident with the security guard, they assembled a small army of their finest armed officers and surrounded my friend's house. Just as they had been given the order to kick his door in and make an arrest I drove into his road in my BMW. As soon as I saw a white police Range Rover full of officers in boiler suits I knew that something was amiss, so I turned into the first side road I reached. Before I could breathe a sigh of relief, I found myself facing yet another police Range Rover, and so I fixed my gaze on the road ahead and continued driving.

When I was safely out of the area, I rang my friend to warn him about what I had seen but a police officer answered his phone. My friend told me sometime later that he had been underneath his Land Rover working on the gear box when the police had arrived.

'All I could see and hear were about 20 pairs of heavy boots surrounding my car and some guy screaming, "Keep your hands where we can see them."'

As he raised his hands he was grabbed by officers from both sides of the vehicle and a brief but almost comical tug of war ensued.

'For fuck's sake, lads, can you please decide which side of the car you want me to appear from,' my friend had shouted.

At the rear of his house armed officers were scaling the garden wall. My friend's father lived next door to him and he had been in the kitchen washing up when the officers arrived He recalled that his son had left a book of forged MOTs in his house and so he set fire to the incriminating evidence and put it into the sink. Attracted by the plumes of black smoke pouring out of the kitchen window police officers had knocked on his door and insisted he tell them what he had been burning.

'Photos of the wife. She left me last night,' he lied.

The police demanded to examine the ashes but he refused to let them into his house before he had flushed them down the toilet. A lot of time and public money had gone into this raid, which threatened to prove fruitless and so a decision was made to trawl through both homes for 'anything' incriminating.

After several hours of meticulous searching, the police struck lucky and found a small amount of cannabis. My friend was questioned about the incident with the security guard and the toy gun that was found in the car but he quite rightly explained that he had sold the car to a stranger and knew nothing about such matters. The police had to justify arresting him and so he was charged with possession of cannabis. My friend and his family were not pleased about the trouble that I had unintentionally brought to their door and for that I publicly apologise. Thankfully, they forgave me because of the situation that I had found myself in with Tucker and his firm. It goes without saying that they are good, decent people.

Tucker, without his henchman, was suddenly not so brave. He told everybody that would listen, and particularly those that knew me, that Tate had been planning to lure me to the hospital so that he could shoot me. According to Tucker it was Tate who had stolen everything from my home so that he could furnish a house where his prostitutes were living, and it was Tate who had goaded me into trying to murder Ron Redding.

'Tell Nipper, Tate's been locked up and he is now safe. I won't forget that he tried to shoot me, but I can understand why. If he leaves Essex, I'll forget it,' Tucker said.

My gut instinct was to go and shoot the bastard because I knew that he was feeling vulnerable without Tate, but I had to think of my family, who were still in hiding in Ipswich.

I asked Jason Smythe to tell Tucker that I would leave Essex on the condition that my family could return unhindered.

'If anybody so much as looks at them, I will return and Tucker's family will be the first to go,' I said. That night, my father and my sisters returned home and after a brief reconciliation I left Essex to live in Chichester where I rented a bedsit from a man who was the double of actor John Cleese.

It was my sister's birthday that week and so I went into a local jeweller and bought her a pair of diamond earrings.

As I counted the cash the lady behind the counter happened to mention that there were forged banknotes circulating in the area. I told her that I had been given a dodgy £50 recently and had since become more vigilant when accepting notes from strangers. After gift-wrapping the earrings the lady asked for my name and address. I told her that my name was Steven Stephens and gave a false address, which was then written on the receipt.

I left the shop and after checking the cash that I had on me, realised that I had paid with counterfeit notes. I still had a wad of Tate's forged banknotes. Normally, I would have kept the counterfeit notes separate from any genuine cash and slipped the odd one or two into a bundle when settling a large bill. Because of everything that had gone on, my money had been thrown into a bag and the first wad I grabbed had all been dodgy notes. I couldn't return to the shop and admit my guilt and I knew that it would only be a matter of time before the police were called. The shop had CCTV and I assumed that my image would have been recorded, so it would only be a matter of time before I was identified and I would be arrested not only for the forged notes but also for the three attempted murders.

The following morning, I was in town when I became aware of two people following me, one male, and the other female. I stopped to look in a shop window to see if they would walk past me but they both grabbed one of my arms and informed me that they were police officers and I was under arrest. When I enquired what for, I was told that I was suspected of paying for jewellery with counterfeit money. The officers radioed for a vehicle and when it arrived I was placed in the back.

Fortunately for me, I had not taken my handgun with me that day and I had left all but one of the forged banknotes at home. Opening my wallet I showed the officers my cash and invited them to check that all of the notes were genuine. As I did so I let all of the notes fall to the floor of the vehicle. The officers were keen to help me pick them up as they may have been of evidential value and while they did this I put the forged note into my mouth, chewed it up and swallowed it.

At the police station the officers wrote down all the serial numbers of my genuine notes and checked their validity with an ultra-violet light. When they were satisfied that they were not forged, they asked me where I was living as they wished to search my home. I gave my father's address in Essex and said that I was visiting the area because I had recently split from my girlfriend.

'I rowed with her and drove off. I ended up here and slept in my car,' I said.

The police knew that I was lying but they couldn't prove anything and so I was released with a stark warning. 'Leave town as soon as possible or we will be paying you another visit.'

I didn't need telling twice. If the police had bothered to check me out properly, I could have been languishing in a cell for several years.

The festive season really made me feel homesick. I had spent Christmas alone before, in prison, but this was different. I was being forced to spend it away from my family because of three bullies. In the early hours of Christmas Eve, I decided that I would throw caution to the wind and return to Essex to give Christmas cards to family and friends. After a fleeting visit to family members and a five-minute performance given for the benefit of my girlfriend, I drove to my friend's house who had sold me the Volvo. I reasoned that I had caused him and his family enough trouble and so decided to just post a card through his door rather than deliver my seasons greetings personally. As I pushed the envelope through his letterbox, I was unaware that two police officers, in an unmarked vehicle parked across the street, were watching me. One of the officers later told me that he had nearly choked on his coffee when he saw me.

'That's Steve Ellis, the guy who's wanted for shooting Pat Tate,' he had told his colleague.

They had been waiting for a man who lived in the street, who was wanted for non-payment of fines. Lady Luck must have shone on them because into their sights I waltzed, a man who was wanted for three attempted murders and numerous firearm offences. Merry bloody Christmas!

Unaware that the police were now watching me, I prepared myself for the long drive back to my place of exile. I put a cassette on, turned the music up loud in order to keep me awake and headed for the motorway. Glancing occasionally in my mirrors, I noticed that a white police Range Rover was following three or four cars behind in the traffic. At first, I thought the vehicle was just heading the same way as me but when I pulled up at a set of traffic lights and it started racing towards me on the wrong side of the road I knew that I was about to be arrested. In desperation rather than hope, I pulled my seat belt across my chest just in case I was going to be spoken to about not wearing it, rather than attempting to blow away three of my former friends.

As I looked up I saw that the Range Rover had screeched to a halt beside me and at least ten armed officers were running towards the front of my car. It had obviously been a well-executed plan to snare me as I had no idea where the officers on foot had come from.

'Keep your hands up high where we can see them,' one of the officers barked at me.

His colleagues began shouting things at me too. I am told that this is a deliberate ploy to confuse and disorientate a person so that they cannot focus on aiming a weapon or committing any other heinous crime that they may have had in mind. It worked. However hard I tried, my trembling fingers could not put the seat belt clasp into the buckle. The loud music was adding to the chaos in my head and so I leaned forward to turn it down. This simple movement incited the mob outside my car and they began screaming even louder and hammering on the windows.

I was wearing the bullet-proof vest I had purchased for any meetings that I may have had with Tate, Tucker and Rolfe and this gave me a degree of confidence.

'If you shoot me, you bastards, I will sue you,' I shouted back at the growling faces at my window.

With the benefit of hindsight I am not sure how a bullet-proof vest would have protected my head, the obvious target to those outside my car, but I clearly was not thinking straight at that time. When the car door was eventually opened, I was thrown to the floor and a large boot placed firmly in the small of my back to keep me in position. I was wearing a bum bag but the bag, which contained a revolver, ammunition, forged banknotes and a forged driving licence, was hanging near my groin rather than the recommended bum area. As the officer's boot pushed me in place against the tarmac the revolver dug deep into my reproductive organs and my eyes began to water.

When the police were satisfied that I posed no immediate threat to them, I was hauled to my feet and two officers began searching me. One patted down the right side of me, the other my left. When they reached the waistband of my trousers, one of the officers found the belt of my bum bag. He pulled it around to my hip, saw the butt of the revolver sticking out of the bag and began shouting, 'Gun, gun, gun.'

Returned to the tarmac at lightning speed, I was shouted and screamed at once more and forced to stare down the barrels of several guns. After a second meticulous search, I was taken to Grays police station, where, I have to say, I was treated really well. The officers were more than aware what type of people Tate, Tucker and Rolfe were, so they seemed to understand but not condone why I had felt the need to arm myself. When I was interviewed, I was surprised to learn that the police knew every sordid detail of the attacks on me and my home. Only Tucker, Rolfe and Cuthbert had been present at the initial attack but the officers knew so much it was as if they had been there too. Somebody who had been in my flat that day had been feeding them information and it certainly was not me. At the conclusion of the interview I was charged with several firearm offences and three attempted murders.

The following day, I appeared in court and because of death threats being made by Tucker and his cronies, members of the public were excluded from attending. My father was allowed to sit in the public gallery, as was my friend Malcolm Walsh, but only because my father had lied and said that Malcolm was my brother. I had warned Malcolm, in a telephone conversation the night before, that evidence relating to Tucker and possibly the others being informants might be revealed during the hearing and so he had come prepared with a dictaphone to record it.

As the prosecution outlined the case against me to the magistrates, they said that Tate had said that I had been the man who had shot him, and Tucker and Rolfe were in no doubt that it was me who had opened fire on them. All three were willing to assist the police and attend identification parades if necessary and all three said that they were confident that they would be able to pick me out. After hearing such damning evidence the magistrate had no hesitation in remanding me to HMP Chelmsford to await trial.

I must admit, I was rather apprehensive about arriving in the prison where I had first met Tate, because he also happened to be incarcerated there, on the hospital wing. As soon as I entered the reception area I was separated from the other prisoners and led into an office.

'You will have to be placed under close protection because we know that Tate will try to kill you,' a stern-faced officer told me.

'I am not being put in a cell next to sex cases and grasses, so you can forget protection,' I replied.

The vast majority of inmates requiring protection were inevitably such 'people' and the very thought of living side by side with them horrified me. I would much rather have faced Tate than have a sex offender as my neighbour.

The officer could not force me to accept protection and so he said that I could be housed on D Wing where most of the trusties were housed. When I arrived on D Wing, I met a man I knew named Billy Archer.

I was telling Billy about the problems that I had involving Tate, Tucker and Rolfe and my attempts to shoot them, when suddenly Billy started to laugh and said, 'Fucking hell, Nipper. That was me you were planning to kill at the Esso garage in Lakeside. Tucker contacted me and said that you had tried to shoot him. He was aware that you knew what car he drove and that you would probably try to target him in it, so he asked me to garage it. In an effort to outwit you, Tucker then started using another motor. On the day you saw his Porsche parked near the Sandmartin pub roundabout I had picked it up from his house and was in a mate's house sorting out somewhere to store it. Thank fuck you never did blast the windscreen and shoot the driver.'

I apologised to Billy as I would never have done the guy any harm. My only excuse was that I had not been thinking straight. Fortunately for the trio, I had not been shooting straight that week either.

Despite the countless intrusions into my life, I had remained a keen bodybuilder and so I applied for, and was given, a job as a gym orderly. After a game of baseball one day, I had been walking back across the sports field towards the wing with a baseball bat resting on my shoulder. I had hung a bag containing the ball, gloves and various other items we had been using to play on the end of the bat.

As we reached the door to the wing somebody had said, 'I will see you later, Steve,' and another voice behind me added, 'Yes, and I will see you too, Steve.'

It sounded like a veiled threat to me, so I turned around and said to the person behind me, 'Who the fuck are you?'

'I'm Mickey, Pat Tate's mate,' he replied. When I raised the baseball bat in readiness to launch Mickey's head across the prison yard, the bag of accessories slid down the shaft of the bat and onto my wrist. Feeling somewhat foolish, I threw the bag onto the floor and swung the bat backwards in readiness to strike.

Billy Archer grabbed me and began shouting, 'Whoa, whoa, Nipper. Leave it out. He's all right.'

Mickey raised his open hands to indicate that there was no threat of violence and so I lowered the bat. Mickey introduced himself as 'Mad Mickey' Bowman from south London and said that he had only been joking about being a friend of Pat Tate.

'Me and Billy Archer are in here because of a bit of business we were going to do with Tate and his mate Tucker. I don't trust the geezers,' Mickey said.

He told me that he and Billy had arranged to meet Tate and Tucker at the Happy Eater restaurant in Basildon, the fast-food outlet that Tate had robbed many years earlier. I have no idea what Billy and Mickey were planning to do that involved Tate and Tucker but Mickey did tell me that when they arrived for the meeting he instinctively smelt a rat.

'Call it intuition, a sixth sense, whatever. It didn't feel right and so I said to Billy, let's get the fuck out of here.' Billy thought that Mickey was just being paranoid and tried to reassure him that everything would be OK. Billy reversed his vehicle into a parking bay and the two men then waited for the arrival of Tucker and Tate.

When there was no sign of them after 30 minutes, Billy looked across at Mickey in the passenger seat and said, 'You're right, mate, something stinks. Let's get out of here.'

As Billy started up the engine and prepared to drive out of the car park several armed police officers jumped out of the back of a nearby van and surrounded his car. I have no idea what – if anything – the police found in the vehicle, but Billy and Mickey found themselves on remand in HMP Chelmsford awaiting trial. They certainly didn't need to employ the services of the security guard that had pursued me, aka Sherlock fucking Holmes, to work out that they had been set up and neither man was very happy about it.

While in HMP Chelmsford, Billy and Mickey were reliably informed by none other than Pat Tate that it had been Tucker who was responsible for their arrest. According to Tate, Tucker had heard that Billy and Mickey were intent on taking part of his business over and so decided to have them removed. I cannot say if Tate was simply blaming Tucker to deflect blame from himself. Alone and in prison it can be dangerous if the other inmates think you're an informant. Billy and Mickey chose to believe Tate and good relations between the men were restored. When Tate found out that they had been talking to me, he offered them £10,000 to have me 'done' in my cell but, to their credit, they refused point-blank to get involved. 'Watch your back. Tate is trying to get you murdered,' Billy warned me. 'If you do have any further problems with him or those other mugs, let me and Mickey know and we will back you. Tate's an OK guy but he does need putting in his place occasionally.'

Apart from Tate's effort to have a contract taken out on my life, nobody said anything offensive or threatening to me about my differences with the trio while I was in HMP Chelmsford. There was one minor incident. One morning the prison was locked down and specially trained dogs were brought in to search for a gun. This came about after the prison had received an anonymous tip-off about a firearm being smuggled in to shoot somebody. I was in no doubt that the story had been invented by my enemies to un-nerve me but it hadn't worked. I was angry, not afraid. The more I thought about what Tate, Tucker and Rolfe had done to me, and the fact that I now faced life imprisonment for defending myself against them, the more it made me want to kill them. I knew that if I did survive any attack from their associates while in prison, I still might have to face the prospect of a lifetime behind bars for trying to shoot them, so I began to think of a story that would minimise my sentence.

Being caught in possession of a loaded gun is a very serious offence, particularly when the authorities believe that it is your intention to endanger another person's life with it. I decided, therefore, to say that I had no intention of shooting anybody but myself with the weapon. Nobody would disagree that if Tucker and his firm had caught me, I would have faced a slow and very painful death. I decided, therefore, to say that I had the gun in my possession so that I could shoot myself if I was captured rather than face being tortured.

To my surprise, the prosecution accepted my explanation and dropped the possession of a firearm with intent to endanger life charge. Around the same time, Tate, Tucker and Rolfe also withdrew their statements and told police that they were no longer prepared to attend court. They were not showing remorse or attempting to assist me in any way, as usual they were merely looking after themselves. Malcolm Walsh had made a copy of the tape of the court proceedings during which Tate, Tucker and Rolfe had been exposed as grasses. He had given a copy of the tape to one of Tucker's firm and advised him to contact Tucker after he had listened to the contents.

'Tell them to withdraw their statements, and only when they have done so will we give them the original tape. I am sure the matter can be forgotten, they wouldn't want this tape finding its way onto the streets,' Malcolm had said.

The very same day, Tate telephoned the police from prison and Rolfe drove Tucker to Grays police station and, after making brief statements withdrawing their evidence, the three attempted murder charges I faced were dropped. When I attended Chelmsford Crown Court for sentencing, I still thought that I would receive a five-year sentence for possessing a firearm and ammunition.

All prisoners who have been sentenced to three months' imprisonment or more have to sign a document prior to being released stating that they will not have a firearm or ammunition in their possession for a period of five years after their release. If they are sentenced to three years' imprisonment or more, then the ban is for life. The maximum sentence for breaking this law is five years; you then get an additional sentence for possessing the firearm. I prepared myself mentally for a very rough ride.

Rocking gently back and forth on my heels in the dock I dared not look at the judge as he began to sum up the case. 'Please no more than five, please no more than five,' I kept saying over and over again to myself. The judge paused momentarily before addressing me directly.

'Steven Ellis, I am in no doubt that you feared for your life and for the lives of your family members. The men who sought to harm you are undoubtedly vicious thugs, cowards and bullies, but that does not give you the right to arm yourself and roam the streets of Essex. This is England, not the Wild West. You will go to prison for 15 months.'

Turning to my family in the public gallery I raised both hands above my head and began shouting, 'Yes, yes, yes.' I thanked the judge and almost skipped down the steps to the holding cells to begin my sentence.

CHAPTER SIX

While serving my prison sentence, I was approached by a man who introduced himself as Tony. I had noticed him staring intently at me earlier in the day, not in a sexual way I hasten to add, although you do get a few of those in jail. His face was unfamiliar and so he had begun to unnerve me. Forever cautious but always polite, I had asked the man who he was and why he thought that he knew me.

'I am Steve Darrow's brother,' he replied.

I shook Tony's hand and said that I had known Steve for several years but was unaware that he had a brother. Steve had been one of the very few kids at my school that had never tormented or bullied me. Tony told me that he hated his prison job cleaning toilets and would do anything to work alongside me as a gym orderly. Feeling obliged to repay his brother's kindness, I did what I could to make Tony's stay in prison carefree by putting him in touch with those that sold contraband, and I also put his name forward for a job in the gym. Less than a week later, Tony was given a job working with me.

Since gym orderlies spend longer periods of time out of their cells than many other inmates do, prison staff insist that they reside together; it simply saves prison officers the trouble of having to open up or lock several cells at irregular times rather than just one or two. For the next three months, Tony and I co-existed rather than lived together in my cell. I say that because Tony found it hard to cope with his loss of liberty and my never-ending practical jokes. I tended to forget the world that we had left behind but Tony was always pining for it. He would be sitting on a chair looking morose

101

and gazing into space and I would bounce a healthy portion of my dinner off his head or douse him in water. He never did see the funny side of my pranks, but they always made me laugh.

The day I was discharged from prison was undoubtedly the happiest that I had ever seen him. Two days before that magical day, when I was to walk to freedom, my father had been confronted in the street by Tucker. The fact that my youngest sister was also present meant nothing to the bully as he shouted obscenities and warned that I would be murdered as soon as I set foot outside the prison gates. When I was told about Tucker's threats, I applied to the prison governor to be released at a different time from any of the other inmates. I wanted to foil any plot that Tucker may have planned to attack me, but my plea for common sense was denied.

With no help forthcoming from the prison service, I arranged for a friend to pull up outside the prison in his car. As soon as the gates were opened, I ran out, jumped into the car and we raced away. Fortunately, Tucker had been making more empty threats and was nowhere to be seen. I felt an obligation to visit my friend who had sold me the Volvo. The very least that I owed him was an apology for all the trouble that my actions had caused. Looking genuinely pleased to see me, he thanked me for the Christmas card that I had posted through his door on the day of my arrest but added that he wished I had never bothered. Puzzled, I asked him what he meant.

'The police officers who saw you that day had no idea what was in the envelope you put through my letterbox, so they raided my house again. They found a small amount of cannabis and as it was my second offence within a few months I was imprisoned for six weeks.'

Mumbling yet another apology, I walked sheepishly to my friend's car and we drove off. It's fair to say that I am no longer on his family's Christmas card list and they are most definitely not on mine. God forbid that I ever darken the poor man's door again.

I knew that I could not remain in Essex because Tate and Tucker were still threatening to have me killed. I had no idea where to go, so I simply laid out a road atlas, closed my eyes and pointed my finger at the map. When I opened my eyes, I saw that I had selected Bournemouth as the place for my new life to begin. After collecting my car and my personal belongings I said goodbye to my family and headed for the south coast.

Leaving prison and then moving to a completely new area is difficult enough, but when you have little or no money it is nigh on impossible. Landlords demanded references and two months' rent in advance and potential employers snubbed me as soon as they learned of my most recent address. I ended up 'living' in a tiny dingy bedsit. During daylight I would look for work and at night I would sit in a local bar sipping lemonade, as the very thought of spending an evening lying on my bed watching the damp climb the walls of my 'tomb', as I called it, horrified me. While standing in a queue at a petrol station one morning, I noticed that the till was crammed with cash and there did not appear to be an alarm system. During my numerous lemonade-sipping sessions, I had become acquainted with a local criminal and that night I mentioned the garage and the contents of its till to him.

When the pub closed, we drove to the garage and after looking around agreed that we would break into it the following night. The easiest point of access appeared to be the roof and so after climbing up onto it, we removed a section of tiles, cut through the roof felt and dropped down into the loft. After working out roughly where the till would be below, we sawed through the joists and removed the foam tiles from the false ceiling. Unbeknown to my accomplice and I, the garage proprietor had installed a sophisticated listening device that was connected to a control centre. As we hacked and sawed away at the joists a silent alarm was activated and the police were notified that intruders were on the premises. When we heard a car drive onto the forecourt, we assumed that it was somebody checking to see if the garage was open, so I advised my friend to stop sawing until the car had gone. After a few minutes, the car remained on the forecourt with its engine running and my friend began to panic. He urged me to make a run for it with him.

'It's the police, Steve, I just know it. Let's get out of here,' he said.

I honestly didn't think it was the police, so I told him to shut up and be quiet. Five minutes later, I began to wonder if my accomplice's concerns were founded and the car outside might belong to the local constabulary. Lowering my head through the hole in the ceiling I glanced towards the forecourt and saw a policeman staring straight back at me.

'Fucking run. Get out of here,' I shouted to my friend.

I managed to get out of the loft and onto the roof quite quickly but my accomplice, who clearly enjoyed his food, struggled to fit his large frame through the small hole that we had made. Leaping almost cat-like from the roof, I landed on the other side of a large fence in somebody's garden. As my friend continued to struggle to haul himself out onto the roof, a police officer grabbed both of his legs and hung on to him. Moments later, both men ended up on the shop floor buried beneath a heap of plasterboard and ceiling tiles.

Nobody appeared to be pursuing me, so I walked briskly down the road and hid among some bushes under a large conifer tree. I must admit I felt pretty pleased with myself having escaped the long arm of the law with such ease. 'In half an hour everybody will have gone and I can take a leisurely walk home,' I told myself as I lay under the tree staring up at the stars. I tried to scream as I was suddenly dragged backwards from the bushes. The pain in my left leg was excruciating but I was in total shock and so no noise came out.

Two large police Alsatian dogs had gripped my legs in their jaws and were running back towards their handler as if I were a stick he had thrown for them to fetch. Just when I thought that it couldn't get any worse, a full-figured policeman landed on my chest and informed me that I was under arrest. When he asked if I wished to make any reply to his caution, I shook my head, not because I wanted to remain silent, but simply because I was barely able to breathe.

The dogs had been a tad overenthusiastic when removing me from my hiding place, so I was taken directly to hospital rather than the police station as I needed to have the gaping wounds in my arse and legs sewn up. As well as a fistful of powerful painkillers and a clean pair of pants, I was in desperate need of a decent solicitor. I was still on parole from prison and any conviction could have led to me being returned to complete the remainder of my sentence. When I raised my concerns with a solicitor, I was advised that because I had suffered such serious injuries during my arrest it would be unlikely that I would be treated too harshly. Despite a plethora of damning evidence against us, both my friend and I refused to accept our guilt and so we were bailed pending further enquiries. Now that the police knew I was in town and that I was facing a prison sentence, I decided that it would be a good idea to leave. Aiming the finger of fate once more at my atlas, I closed my eyes and prayed for a destination awash with opportunities.

I had never even heard of the town of Swanage in Dorset, but it turned out to be a place of outstanding beauty in more ways than one. I met Rhiannon while she was working as a part-time barmaid in a pub next door to where I lived. Her family were law-abiding God-fearing folk, who frowned upon the long-term unemployed, criminals and other types of social misfit. By day, Rhiannon studied at college, at night she worked for a pittance behind a bar and, when she wasn't sleeping, she attended to her horses. I have no idea what she saw in me. Perhaps she was feeling charitable; perhaps I was a bit of an enigma, a welcome distraction from her Groundhog Day-type life. I had several reasons for wanting to be with her: she had her own flat, she had the means to serve me free meals at the pub and she looked pretty amazing. What more could a man who was out on his arse want? Within a few days I had moved out of my bedsit and into Rhiannon's flat, which she shared with her dog, Bleep.

Rhiannon rang me one morning to say that one of her horses was ill and would I give her a lift to the vet's as she needed to pick up some medication? When we arrived, Rhiannon began giving an in-depth explanation of the animal's condition to a woman at the counter, so I sat down in anticipation of a very long wait. As the pair rambled on about the joys of horse riding my eyes roamed the room and came to rest upon an open till stuffed with money. Unfortunately for the vet, there was no known cure for my craving for cash and so that night I returned to the premises and broke in through the roof. As I emptied the contents of the till into a bag, a girl walked into the room. We looked at each other momentarily before turning and running in opposite directions. I clambered through a window and she headed for the front door.

Once outside, I fought my way through a hedge and thorn bushes before making good my escape across a field. Among the £1,500 in cash that I had stolen I found receipts, invoices and various other pieces of paper. I was going to put them out with the rubbish for the bin man to collect but I remembered that he had called earlier that very day. Not wanting to have any incriminating evidence at my home, I threw the bin liner containing the papers and my household rubbish into an empty builder's skip that had been left in our road. Mid-way through *EastEnders* the following night my front door was kicked off its hinges by two very unhappy-looking police officers.

'Get your shoes on, Ellis. You're under arrest for burglary,' they said.

I was still on bail for the burglary at the garage and knew that, if charged with any other offence, the chances of me being returned to prison were extremely high. I decided that I would refuse to answer any questions during interview because the only evidence they could possibly have was from the girl who had caught just a fleeting glimpse of me. Even if she said that she could identify me, it would be her word against mine. My confidence boosted, I sat opposite the officers in the interview room with a broad grin on my face. However, my grin soon turned into a grimace as one of the officers produced an evidence bag that contained a bin liner.

The spectres of Tate and Tucker and the threat that they posed had never left me. For insurance purposes only, I had broken a shotgun down into three sections, put them in bin liners and stored the pieces around my car battery. If the police had found the shotgun while searching my home and vehicle in connection with the burglary, I was going back to prison for a very long time.

'Can you explain this, Ellis?' the officer said holding the evidence bag aloft above his head.

'It looks like a bin liner,' I replied. My heart was in my mouth as he opened the evidence bag and tipped the contents onto the table.

'Well done, Mr Ellis, correct answer,' the officer said. 'Can you now explain how your household rubbish came to contain paperwork that was stolen from a vet last night?'

As the story unfolded I sank deeper and deeper into my seat. The man who had hired the builder's skip was outraged that somebody had the audacity to throw a rubbish bag into it. So, after retrieving the offending bag, he had gone through the contents, found the vet's paperwork and driven to the surgery. When he arrived, he had emptied the contents onto the reception desk and warned the vet about his future conduct. Anger soon turned to laughter as the irate skip owner discovered that he had not only snared a litter lout but he had also caught a burglar.

I am not sure if I laughed with relief because the police hadn't found the gun, or if I laughed at my own stupidity for putting the bin bag in the skip but laugh I did.

'It's a fair cop, hang me now,' I said. I was, of course, only joking but when I later sought the advice of a solicitor she told me that the police had been concerned about comments I had made and my general demeanour.

'What do you mean "concerned"?' I asked.

'They think you may have mental health issues. Apparently you were laughing when you found out that you had been caught red-handed and you also talked about wanting to be hanged,' she replied.

With a prison sentence looming, I needed some form of defence, so I decided to milk the situation. I told my solicitor that I had suffered some sort of mental breakdown following the campaign of attacks by Tate and Tucker.

'I break into places so that I will get caught and sent to prison. It's the only place I feel safe,' I lied.

I was sent for a mental assessment and all the experts concluded that I needed help rather than punishment, so when I appeared in court for the burglary at the vet's I was given probation. I knew that I had used up all of the chances the courts were going to give me, so I made a concerted effort to go straight. There was still a chance that I might be charged and imprisoned for the garage burglary, but I knew that I had to stop offending, regardless. If I didn't go to prison for that burglary, I knew that I would eventually be imprisoned for some other offence in the future.

Apart from Malcolm teaching me how to break into other people's premises, I had not received any form of specialist training and so my skills were, at best, limited. I could hardly make an honest living employing the only trade that I knew and so I began to look at alternative ideas. Bodybuilding had given me a fine physique and Tate had provided me with a fairly comprehensive knowledge of body-training techniques and fitness regimes and so I decided to apply for vacancies at local gymnasiums.

When that failed, I paid £3,500 for a three-month course to become a qualified fitness instructor. Once I had successfully completed the course, I set up my own company, providing personal training for large businessmen and -women with equally large bank balances. The business was extremely successful, so much so I was forced to appoint a partner in order to cope with the demand. We hired out a gymnasium for evening classes and purchased two vehicles, which were used to make home visits. When a local newspaper published a story about our success, we were contacted by a production company that asked us to appear on a TV show. I was concerned that Tucker and Tate might see me on the programme and learn where I was living, so I declined the offer. My partner agreed and after appearing on the show and flexing his muscles he was contacted by a healthcare company in London who offered him a full-time and well-paid job in Harley Street, where some of the most prestigious medical practitioners in the world are based.

I couldn't blame him for accepting the job offer, but I did when he set up a rival company and took most of my clients from me. Within weeks the bills from the gymnasium had mounted, forcing me to fold the business. I had built up a fairly good credit rating with the banks and so, rather than lose the roof over my head as well as the business, I applied for numerous cheque books and credit cards. Armed with these cards, I would spend a day visiting chain stores along the south coast where I would purchase goods using my cheque books and cheque guarantee cards. The following day, I would visit the same name brand stores in different towns and claim cash refunds. Since I had the goods still boxed or unwrapped and a receipt, my request for a full cash refund was never denied.

Like most criminals who stumble upon a good thing, I got greedy. Instead of taking back one item at a time I started walking up to counters buried beneath piles of boxes and bags. In Bournemouth, a member of the security staff became suspicious of me and called the police. As I attempted to walk out of the store two police officers blocked my path and advised me that I was under arrest for suspicion of theft. I was then taken to a police station where I was searched and my property taken from me. Among my personal effects the police found my car keys and a car park ticket. When they located and searched my car, they found that the boot and back seats were crammed with goods waiting to be returned to the shops for cash refunds.

In total the police recovered £11,000 worth of goods and £3,000 in cash. I told the police that I had done no wrong; the cheque books and credit cards were in my name and I had every intention of paying the banks back. The goods were bought legally from the shops and had been returned simply because they were unwanted. I was interviewed and then bailed to reappear at the police station in 14 days, as the officers said that they wished to consult the Crown Prosecution Service regarding charging me. When I returned to the police station, I was told that all my accounts had been closed and the banks did not want to press charges and so I was free to go. I was naturally pleased to escape prosecution but I did think that the banks would pursue me for the debts. However, for reasons known only to themselves, not one of them bothered.

As I stumbled from one problem to another, back in Essex Tate, Tucker and Rolfe continued to live as before, creating problem after problem for everybody that they encountered. Sarah Saunders had waited both patiently and faithfully when Tate had been imprisoned after his arrest in Gibraltar for the Happy Eater robbery. The prospect of ten years' imprisonment had made Tate realise that he was not only going to forfeit his liberty but he might also lose the woman he loved. In an effort to salvage his relationship, Tate had promised Sarah that he would change his ways when he was released and begged her to give him a second chance. Against her better judgement, Sarah had eventually given in to Tate's pleas and the relationship had staggered on, albeit via prison letters and monthly one-hour visits. After four years, Tate had been granted weekend leave and Sarah had fallen pregnant, an event that appeared to have galvanised their faltering relationship for a short time. However, Sarah confided in me some time later that deep down she knew that she didn't want to be with Tate, but felt obliged to allow the relationship to run its course, if only for the sake of their then unborn child. When Tate first came to live with me, he had talked excitedly about his plans to start up a legitimate car business, buy a family home and, more importantly, give up drugs. I had believed Tate and tried to help him as I was genuinely pleased that he had found happiness, but Sarah knew him better than me and was under no illusion. She knew from past painful experience that his promises were more often than not just empty gestures.

One of Sarah's closest friends was a former neighbour named Pauline Squires. Her partner, Angus Fletcher, was an astute businessman who was always on the look-out for new ventures where he could invest his hard-earned cash. During general conversation when Tate was still in prison, Sarah had mentioned Tate's plans to launch a car sales business and Angus had expressed an interest in meeting him when he was released. Angus said that if Tate produced a viable business plan he would be more than happy to make funds available so that the stock that would be needed could be purchased.

When Tate was released, he met Angus at the Five Bells public house in Basildon to discuss the loan for his business. Tate explained that he had found vacant business premises opposite Westcliff-on-Sea police station, which he thought he could develop as a good place from which to sell cars. Bill Baxter, a friend of Tate's, had offered to remain on-site selling vehicles, while Tate went in search of stock to sell. Angus said that it sounded straightforward enough and asked Tate how much money he would need. Tate initially asked for £20,000 but after two hours of negotiations he was offered just £5,000, with a promise that further funds would be made available if the business went well. The two men shook hands and agreed that Angus would be a partner in the business and receive a percentage of each vehicle sold.

Within a month, the business flourished and Tate returned to the negotiating table to ask Angus to increase his investment. Tate explained that if he was able to purchase better-quality cars he could make higher profits on each sale. Angus agreed and, later that day, he handed over £10,000 in cash to Tate. Having honoured his promise to Sarah to set up a legitimate business, Tate began looking for a family home to purchase. The property that Tate eventually found was in need of renovation, so he telephoned a man named Mick Steele to look over it for him.

Tate and Steele had met and become friends a few years earlier, while incarcerated at HMP Swaleside in Kent. The bond between the two men had been reinforced when they discovered that their partners were old friends. Sarah had once owned a horse, which she kept at Longwood riding stables in Basildon. These stables had been owned by Steele's partner, Jackie Street. Sarah and Jackie had not seen each other for some time and so they were pleasantly surprised to meet by chance one afternoon in a prison visitors' waiting room. The two women were even more surprised when they learned that their imprisoned partners had also become friends.

After that initial meeting, Sarah and Jackie would travel to the prison together and go shopping once their visits were over. The couples became very close and when Steele was released, prior to Tate, both he and Jackie did all they could to support Sarah. Steele was an intelligent man, who had outwitted Custom and Excise officers for years by single-handedly flying large consignments of cannabis into the country. He was eventually caught quite by chance and sentenced to serve nine years' imprisonment, during which time he met Tate.

When Steele looked over the property that Tate wished to purchase, he found that there were a multitude of defects and concluded that his friend should look elsewhere. When Tate had found a vacant bungalow in Gordon Road, Basildon, he had been able to provide a substantial deposit but was unable to secure a mortgage. The deposit was in fact the £60,000 proceeds from the cannabis robbery that we had carried out together at the house in Kent. I find it rather ironic that the property I assisted him in purchasing is the very same one in which I tried to shoot him dead. Friendship is undoubtedly fickle.

Prior to his incarceration Tate had always been able to earn large amounts of cash but all of his business ventures had been illegal, so he had no checkable credit history. Rather than risk losing the property to another buyer, Tate agreed to allow the mortgage to be solely in Sarah's name. Having built up a business and secured a family home, Sarah could be forgiven for believing that Tate really was going to fulfil his promise and settle down. Unfortunately for Sarah, her son and the good people of Essex, Tate had met and become involved with Tony Tucker.

After I attempted to murder Tate, I had telephoned Sarah to ask her what he had been saying about the incident and she had agreed to meet me at the Lakeside shopping centre near Tucker's home. I didn't fear meeting Sarah as we had always got on well and I knew that she would never betray me to her bullying boyfriend. Sarah told me that she didn't blame me for shooting Tate. Since meeting Tucker, he had turned into a drug-crazed monster. He had pleaded with his brother Russell not to tell Sarah about his drug addiction and threatened others with death if they revealed his sordid secret. Inevitably, Sarah had found out and confronted Tate, who broke down, admitted he had a problem and asked her to help him.

At first, she refused to have anything further to do with him but he begged and cried for her to give him another chance. Out of pity more than anything else, Sarah agreed. Together they visited a drug rehabilitation centre in Southend, where Tate spent an hour with a counsellor. At the end of the session, Sarah had asked Tate if he had found the advice helpful. Tate began laughing and said that it had been a waste of time; he had spent the session discussing how to take various drugs and the counsellor had actually been impressed by his knowledge. Sarah said that she then tried socialising with Tate to help him resist the temptation of using drugs, but that too had been a fruitless exercise. Tucker and his minions were simply not the sort of people whose company she enjoyed. They would flaunt other females in front of their partners, openly take drugs and intimidate everybody else around them. Sarah told me, 'It's horrible, and it's just not the type of behaviour Pat would previously have condoned. The drugs have ruined him. I really cannot believe that the man I first met is the same man who has trashed your home and attacked you after all you have done for him. He is vile, just vile.'

I was not the only friend that Tate had turned on. Angus, his partner in the car sales business, had been complaining to Sarah that her boyfriend had become moody and temperamental and the repayments on his investment had ceased.

'I am going to tell him that our relationship is over,' Sarah had told me. 'All he is bothered about these days is Tucker and drugs. I will probably have to leave the country because he will never let another man near me but I can't continue living like this.'

When Tate was safely back behind bars, following the discovery of a gun in his hospital bed, Sarah had plucked up the courage to tell him that she didn't want anything more to do with him. His broken promises, mood swings, stories about intravenous drug use and infidelity with his harem of prostitutes had finally proved too much for her to take. Tate reluctantly accepted all Sarah had to say, but he had made her promise that she would not tell a soul that she had dumped him because he didn't want his already bruised ego damaged further. Tate insisted that he would continue to provide for his son so long as she pretended to be with him and, when she agreed, he arranged for Tucker to continue paying his mortgage. Tucker happened to be holding £20,000 of Tate's drug money for him while he was in prison and this was used to pay Sarah a weekly allowance.

Approximately six months later, Tate asked Steele to attend HMP Whitemoor, as he said that he had a problem that he wished to discuss. Tate had become so paranoid as a result of his drug abuse that he asked Steele to visit him using the pseudonym 'Mr Still'. Confused but always willing to assist a friend in need, Steele obliged. Tate explained to Steele that Tucker was holding £20,000 of his money, which was supposed to be used solely for maintaining Sarah and their son. However, Tate had heard, or possibly imagined in his paranoid state, that Tucker was using his money to finance drug deals.

'I want you to visit Tucker and tell him that I need the money for something,' Tate said. 'I don't care what excuse you use. I want my money back from him and I want you to hold it and pay Sarah her weekly allowance.'

Steele could see that Tate was losing his grip on reality and didn't really want to get involved, but Sarah and her son Jordan were in need and so he agreed solely for their sake.

When Steele had been sentenced to nine years' imprisonment for importing cannabis, the judge had further ordered that he must hand over £120,000 to the court. This amount was estimated to be the profit that he had earned from his crimes. Steele had failed to pay the balance in full and so he had told Tucker that Tate had agreed to lend him the £20,000 as the courts were now threatening to return him to custody if he didn't make a substantial payment soon. After looking at the documentation that Steele provided, Tucker agreed to hand over the money. It was the first time that the two men had met and Steele had been less than impressed. Tucker had been 'doped up to his eyeballs' and rambled incoherently about pressure he said he was under. Tucker had told Steele that he thought I was going to shoot him and so he had sold his home and purchased a bungalow complete with the latest security gadgets.

'It has high walls and fences around it, an electronic entry system at the main gate, security cameras and a sophisticated burglar alarm,' Tucker said. 'I have also applied for a firearms certificate so even if that little fucker does get near me I will blow his fucking head off.'

Steele was aware that Tate had been shot but he had no idea who I was and so he just nodded and pretended to be interested in all Tucker had to say. Before parting, Steele managed to sell Tucker several lawnmowers and a van full of surveyor's equipment for his new fortress. No doubt Steele had convinced the gibbering, paranoid Tucker that he needed to keep his grass kept short just in case I tried to crawl through it unnoticed. Only Tucker would know why he might have wanted surveyor's equipment. If he ever did come down from his drug-induced high, he was probably asking himself the very same question. Fool!

Later the same day, what was left of Tate's £20,000 was handed over by Tucker to Steele in a bag at Longwood Stables. When Steele counted the money, he found that it was £400 short. Rather than question Tucker about the missing money, Steele told himself that the profit from the lawnmowers and junk that he had sold him more than covered the shortfall. Steele paid Sarah's allowance into a bank account each week and ensured that he kept a record of all transactions so that Tate would not be able to accuse him of siphoning of any of the money for himself.

Pat Tate was released from HMP Whitemoor in Cambridgeshire on 31 October 1995. As he bounded through the gates to freedom the driver of a stretch limousine sounded his horn and the passengers in the back began to call out Tate's name. Tucker, Rolfe and four scantily clad prostitutes had come to welcome Tate home. Before the prison gates had even disappeared from the driver's rear-view mirror, Tate had snorted a huge line of cocaine, injected himself with a cocktail of drugs and was beginning to have intercourse with one of the prostitutes while Tucker and Rolfe laughed and egged him on.

Not everybody who knew Tate was pleased that he had been released from custody. Sarah Saunders sat in the bungalow she had once shared with him dreading what state of mind he might be in when he arrived. Fortunately, Tucker had organised a party for Tate at a snooker hall in Dagenham, called Chequers, and so he had only visited Sarah's home briefly as he was in a rush to get changed and go out. Steele had also called at Sarah's home to welcome his friend home and brought along £1,000 of Tate's money just in case he was in need of some pocket money. To Steele's surprise, Tate had refused the money but added that he would sit down with him in a few days and work out what was left from the £20,000.

Tate's home-coming party was a monumental flop. Apart from the prostitutes, who were on a wage, and a few of the wannabes that hung around Tucker's firm, only a handful of his former friends attended. Parties such as these, which were held regularly by Tucker and members of his firm, would generally go on for two or three days. On one occasion, Tucker had hired the top floor of the Hilton Hotel, in Park Lane, London. The evening proved to be boisterous and a little noisy, which was tolerated by the hotel staff. However, in the early hours of the morning, the police were called to eject the revellers after the lift doors had opened on the ground floor to reveal a group of naked, fornicating guests. The drugged participants had been too engrossed in their activities to notice that somebody had pushed the descend button and sent the lift to the reception area where both staff and guests were horrified by what they saw.

Sarah knew that Tate could be at his most volatile after days of taking drugs, so she had arranged to go on holiday to Portugal with her son and her sister the morning after Tate was released. To her horror and surprise, Tate arrived home in the early hours of the morning and demanded to be let in. When Sarah enquired why Tate had not stayed at the party, he claimed that he was ill and climbed into her bed. Sarah was in no doubt that Tate was hoping to rekindle their relationship but she was no longer interested in him or his promises. Sarah went to sleep in the lounge but Tate kept getting up, making snide comments and slamming doors. Fearing the situation could become volatile, Sarah telephoned her sister, grabbed her son and suitcase and headed for the airport in a taxi.

Four days later, on 5 November 1995, Tate met Steele at the services on the A12 where Tucker had attempted to trap Joel. Steele gave Tate a record of all the payments that he had made to Sarah and returned the outstanding balance from the £20,000. The pair spent approximately 30 minutes together, during which time Tate mentioned that he had been offered 50 kilos of cannabis at £1,100 per kilo from a man named Darren Nicholls. Steele was well aware who Darren Nicholls was. In fact, Steele had introduced Tate to Nicholls initially. While serving his nine-year prison sentence, Steele had become involved in a sit-down protest about the quality of food at HMP Hollesley Bay in Suffolk. Nicholls, who was serving a three-year sentence for possession of counterfeit banknotes, had joined Steele and refused to return to his cell. The prison governor had called for the men to leave the dining area, but they had refused to do so until he had tasted the food for himself. When the governor had obliged the protestors, he had agreed that the food was sub-standard and ordered the kitchen staff to prepare Steele and Nicholls a fresh meal.

The two men had become friends following their victory and, when Tate had been transferred to the same prison, Steele had introduced him to his fellow protestor. Tate told Steele that he was interested in purchasing the 50 kilos of cannabis from Nicholls, but he was even more interested in knowing who his supplier was so that he could cut Nicholls, the middle man, out.

'I know exactly who Nicholls's supplier is,' Steele replied. 'It's himself. He imports the cannabis from Holland.'

Tate did purchase the 50 kilos of cannabis from Nicholls but it turned out to be of very poor quality and he demanded his money back. Knowing just how unpredictable and volatile Tate could be Nicholls, rather wisely, went into hiding. Tate did everything he could to locate Nicholls but when he had exhausted every line of enquiry he asked Steele to find him and act as a mediator. Reluctantly, and rather foolishly, Steele agreed. When Steele informed Tate that he had managed to contact Nicholls, Tate demanded his telephone number but Steele refused.

'Leave it to me. Nicholls doesn't want trouble. I will sort this out for you,' Steele had said.

Tate confided in Steele that it wasn't just himself who Nicholls had upset: the total price that Nicholls had asked for the shipment of cannabis had been £55,000 but Tate had told Tucker, Rolfe and a consortium of their friends that the cost was, in fact, £70,000. They had paid Tate the full amount. He had pocketed £15,000 and given Nicholls the asking price.

'If any of the consortium get hold of Nicholls, they will know that I have had them over,' Tate said. 'Please help me find him first.'

Tate begged Steele for Nicholls's address but he refused and warned him, 'If you start hurting the man, you will not get your money back and all you will end up with is someone who is rattled black and blue.' Steele assured Tate that he would resolve the matter for him but he had to stop making threats about Nicholls. 'If you put him in a corner, he may get tooled up and do something stupid. He has talked about shooting people before,' Steele said.

Tate, as usual, refused to listen to common sense and told Steele that Nicholls had seven days to return the amount in full. The money was eventually returned to Tate and he did repay the consortium but what he failed to tell them was that approximately £22,000 worth of the cannabis had been of good quality and he had sold it. Tate had already pocketed £15,000 and therefore he ended up walking away with a total of £37,000 from the deal. He had also put the life of Darren Nicholls, who had supplied the drugs, in extreme danger.

When Sarah returned from Portugal, Tate was extremely spiteful and vindictive towards her. He ordered her to leave the bungalow immediately and find somewhere else to live. With nowhere to go or anybody to turn to, Sarah and her son ended up living in a women's refuge in Basildon. Financially embarrassed, Sarah did ring Tate occasionally and ask him for money to support his son but he refused to do so until Sarah agreed to sign the bungalow over to him. Tate told Sarah that when the bungalow was in his name he would give her £900, which was the amount she needed for the deposit on a privately rented flat in Basildon. Sarah had little choice but to agree. After taking the bungalow off Sarah, Tate's aggressive attitude towards her appears to have thawed. Her flat was some distance from her family and friends, so Tate, who had numerous contacts in the used car trade, agreed to buy her a vehicle.

At the time, Tate was driving a Mercedes that he had purchased on finance using Sarah's name and bank details. He hadn't bothered to ask her permission, he just explained, after the event, that because of his poor credit history it had been necessary. On the day Tate offered to purchase Sarah a vehicle, he left with Rolfe and returned an hour later with an H-registered Volkswagen Golf. He warned that the vehicle wasn't entirely reliable but it would meet Sarah's needs until he could find something more suitable. The car rarely started and often broke down and so Sarah found herself constantly ringing Tate enquiring about when he was going to replace it as promised. Tate continually fobbed her off and so one day in despair she mentioned the fact that the gleaming Mercedes that Tate was driving was actually in her name.

'Why should you drive about in a Mercedes and I have to carry your son along main roads because our car's broken down?' Sarah said.

Tate flew into a rage and arrived at Sarah's parents' home with Tucker and Rolfe moments later. Shouting, swearing and threatening Sarah, Tate took the Golf's keys from her and ordered Rolfe to drive the car away. When Sarah told Rolfe to stay where he was and dared to shout back at Tate, he attacked her and had to be restrained by Tucker and Rolfe, who somehow managed to bundle him out of the front door. Once outside, he continued to scream abuse before taking the keys off Rolfe and speeding away.

* * *

The date that Sarah had her vehicle taken off her was Tuesday, 6 December 1995. It is a date that I shall never forget as a great weight was lifted from my shoulders on that day. Unlike Sarah, the last thing on my mind that cold winter morning was Tate, Tucker and their sidekick Rolfe. My thoughts concerned the bowel movements of Bleep, my girlfriend's Labrador. Throughout the previous night, Bleep had been suffering from a bout of vomiting and diarrhoea. The stench of the dog's liquid faeces was making me gag as I got down onto my hands and knees to clean it up. How our eastern cousins can feast on our four-legged friends is beyond me, especially if they have had the misfortune to do what I was then being forced to do.

Having completed my unsavoury task, I showered, got changed and then gave my girlfriend a lift to college in Dorchester. I was still on bail for the garage burglary and one of the conditions that had been imposed was that I sign on at Swanage police station every morning at 1030 hrs. I couldn't understand the purpose of such an irritating clause in granting me bail; it served no purpose. If I had signed on at 1030 hrs and then went on the run at 1031 hrs, the police wouldn't have had an inkling that I had absconded until I failed to sign on again at 1030 hrs the following day. By that time, I could have been on the other side of the world, sunning myself on some beach. I know the law is the law and it should be obeyed, but that doesn't mean it cannot be an ass.

After signing on at the police station, I washed my car and then lounged around the house watching drivel on daytime television. My life had become an almost painful existence. Boredom reigned. I didn't feel comfortable making too many new friends and acquaintances just yet. Both Tucker and Tate had contacts throughout the country and I had been told that their enquiries concerning my whereabouts were still ongoing. At 1630 hrs, I picked up my girlfriend from college and we returned home. After taking up my now usual position in front of the television, Bleep ran over to me and began to bark and whine. Glancing out of the window I saw that snow had begun to fall.

I didn't relish the thought of walking Bleep in almost arctic conditions and so I began to calculate the risks of remaining at home. Images and the aroma of liquid faeces filled my head and nostrils and so I was up on my feet, lead in hand and heading for the door in seconds. Judging by the amount of times that Bleep squatted during our brief stroll, I concluded that his condition had deteriorated and so I took him to a local vet.

A hundred miles away, in Essex, others were also considering how to rid their lives of shit, but rather than attempt to cure the sick animals responsible for the mess that had been made, they had decided to have them put down.

CHAPTER SEVEN

Tate, Tucker and Rolfe had been told that a million pounds' worth of cocaine was going to be flown into Essex using a small plane. It was due to land in a field near the village of Rettendon, which is situated on the A130, between Basildon and Chelmsford. Once the plane touched down, all the trio had to do was overpower the pilot and anybody else present and steal the cocaine. Veterans of robbing fellow drug dealers, Tate and Tucker had instructed Rolfe that they would administer the required violence and all he would have to do was drive them to and from the scene in his car.

They had been advised that recent bad weather had made it impossible to give a precise time and day when the plane would land but it would be in their interest to visit the landing strip so that they could rehearse the robbery. Blinded by greed, the three men did not hesitate in accepting the advice and unwittingly arranged to meet up with those who were actually planning their murders. The Range Rover containing Tate, Tucker, Rolfe and at least one of the conspirators made its way to Rettendon. Rolfe, who was driving, pushed his favourite cassette into the stereo. *Rhythm Nation 1814* by Janet Jackson began to boom out of the speakers. Ironically, the final song on that album, the last album that the three men were ever going to hear, was titled 'Living in Complete Darkness'. Within the hour Tate, Tucker and Rolfe were all going to die in complete darkness.

As the vehicle made its way along the A130 the occupants were in high spirits. Tate was in the rear of the vehicle boasting about how he intended to use his share of the cash to expand his drug-dealing business and make even more money. Tucker, who was in the front passenger seat, talked about paying off all of his debts and building a gym at the home he had recently purchased. Rolfe said that he was going to pay off his mortgage and buy a flash car because the Range Rover that he was driving was still on finance. The man sitting next to Tate in the back of the vehicle smiled and reassured them that all of their worries would soon be over.

'Just relax, lads. You will all get what's due to you,' he said.

As the vehicle passed through the village of Rettendon, it slowed on a sharp left-hand bend and Rolfe began to indicate. When a gap in the oncoming traffic appeared, Rolfe edged the vehicle into a farm track that was often used as a lovers' lane or dumping ground by fly-tippers. As the Range Rover made its way in the darkness down the uneven track the occupants were tossed from side to side.

'Are you sure about this?' Tate had asked the man sitting beside him.

'Yes, this track leads to the field where the plane's going to land,' the man replied.

The time was 1840 hrs and Tate's phone began to ring. Glancing at his mobile Tate saw that the caller was Sarah. He answered it, apologised for his earlier bad behaviour and agreed to discuss the situation with her, but was unable to do so at that moment as he was with 'some people'. Moments after the call ended, the Range Rover pulled up at a locked gate and the man sitting next to Tate said that he would get out of the car and unlock it. As he opened the rear door of the vehicle the interior light came on preventing those inside from seeing anything outside.

Once clear of the vehicle the man stood back as an accomplice, who had been hiding in a nearby ditch, approached the open door with a pump-action shotgun in each hand. One was given to the man who had been in the Range Rover and the other was raised into a firing position. Leaning into the vehicle, the man shot Rolfe in the back of the head just behind the ear. The lead shot blasted a 5 cm-diameter hole before exiting between his nose and eye, which was left hanging down onto his cheek. Rolfe's facial skeleton was destroyed completely and this caused his features to collapse.

As Tucker flinched with the noise of the explosion, the gun was pointed at him and fired. The shot punched a 6.5 cm hole in his lower jaw before exiting through the left side of his mouth. The jaw and teeth were totally destroyed and pellets were later found lodged in his tongue.

In the rear of the vehicle Tate, on witnessing the bloodbath, had begun to scream and plead with the killers to spare his life. Grinning, the gunman showed no mercy and blasted Tate in the chest rather than the head. Tate had been the catalyst of all of the trouble and so it was deemed essential that he should witness the gruesome murder of his friends before he too was executed. The gunmen had to work quickly because the shot had broken Tate's sixth and ninth ribs and had lacerated his liver. The 6 cm hole in his chest was pouring with blood.

Tucker's injuries, although terrible, had not damaged any vital organs and he had begun to groan loudly so the gunman shot him once more in the face. The hot lead tore a 4.2 cm hole in Tucker's head, just in front of the right ear. This destroyed the right side of his brain, killing him instantly.

Having incapacitated everybody in the vehicle, the gunman turned to his accomplice and invited him to shoot them. Stepping forward the trembling man pointed a shotgun at the back of Rolfe's head, closed his eyes and fired. The blast tore a gaping wound in Rolfe's neck, which left his back teeth and lower jaw exposed. Turning his weapon on Tate, who was by now curled up in a foetal position and crying uncontrollably, the gunman mocked the man that he had grown to hate before opening fire.

Tate ducked instinctively before the trigger was pulled, resulting in the shot causing an 8.5 cm graze across the top of his head before smashing the passenger door window. The gunman who had initially opened fire on the men walked around to the broken window and began taunting Tate.

'Fucking hard man, look at you now. Stop crying like a baby and take what's coming to you like a man.'

Before Tate could reply the gunman blasted him in the back of the head just behind the left ear. This shot caused Tate's skull to splinter, resulting in extensive destruction of the brain. His work almost done, the gunman opened the front passenger door of the Range Rover, pressed the barrel of the shotgun against the base of Tucker's head and fired. The force of that blast snapped Tucker's neck and destroyed the lower part of his skull. The shot was so powerful it blew bone fragments out through his scalp, leaving a hole the size of a fist just above his ear. Their grisly task complete, the gunmen surveyed the carnage before closing the doors of the vehicle and calmly walking away.

Six months later, Darren Nicholls was arrested in possession of a large quantity of cannabis and questioned for hours about his possible involvement in the murders. Initially, he refused to make any comment, but when detectives revealed that mobile phone records could prove that he had been in the area that night, he came up with a story that vindicated him but implicated his friend Mick Steele, and an associate named Jack Whomes.

I am not going to speculate about who may have been responsible for executing Tate, Tucker and Rolfe. However, I would like to publicly thank them as I am of the opinion that they did the world a favour. I am in no doubt that Jack Whomes and Michael Steele, the two men who were later convicted of the crimes, were innocent. They were just two more of Tate, Tucker and Rolfe's countless victims.

The persistent sound of the house phone ringing awoke me from my deep slumber. I had been up most of the night attending to Bleep the Labrador and his incontinent arse. Opening one eye, the face on my bedside clock appeared to be just a blur, but when I managed to focus I saw that it wasn't quite yet ten o'clock in the morning.

'This better be fucking good,' I groaned as I lifted the receiver.

'They're dead. They're fucking dead, Nipper,' my friend shouted down the phone.

'Who's dead? Who's fucking dead?' I asked.

'Tucker and Tate, they have been found in a Range Rover with their heads blown off,' my friend replied laughing.

I refused to believe him and so he urged me to get out of bed and turn on the television. Sitting on the sofa in my pants with my eyes glued to the BBC news channel, I honestly cannot recall a more memorable experience in my entire life.

'The three men found murdered in a Range Rover were known criminals from south Essex and could have been victims of a gangland killing. One of the dead men was Patrick Tate, 37, from Basildon. He had convictions for possessing cocaine with intent to supply and robbery. The others were Craig Rolfe, 26, from Chafford Hundred, and Anthony Tucker, 38, from Fobbing. Tucker was a former bodyguard to boxer Nigel Benn. Murder inquiry detectives were keeping an open mind on the possibility that the men, who were discovered near the village of Rettendon, were shot point-blank by someone from the criminal underworld. Detective Superintendant Dibley, who was leading the murder investigation said, "It is a possibility. But there are a number of other possibilities. This was no ordinary murder. These men were enticed to their deaths."'

Photographs of the deceased and footage of the Range Rover being removed from the crime scene on the back of a lorry were being shown as the news was read. I accept that some people may consider me sick but I honestly burst out laughing and began dancing around the lounge. Despite the fact that I had heard it with my own ears, seen their faces and their vehicle on television, I still found the news hard to believe.

I rang my father and he burst into tears with relief. I could hear my sisters cheering in the background as my father kept repeating,

'They're dead, girls. It's over at last. Those three bastards are dead.'

My father suggested that I should return from exile immediately but I knew that Tucker's firm would think that I had killed them, so I decided to remain where I was until things had calmed down.

Over the next few days, a lot of the people who were connected to Tucker's firm, and several who were not, appeared in newspapers and on television programmes describing their experiences and knowledge of the dead men. Most portrayed Tucker and Tate as Mafia dons. I had to laugh; Tate and Tucker couldn't run a bath, never mind a criminal empire. They were too busy stealing what they could to feed their drug habits and ensuring that number one – themselves – was OK. In my opinion, the vast majority of the people who sold stories to the press in the aftermath of the murders talked complete rubbish: a large percentage of them didn't even know Tucker or his firm, and others told half-truths in order to distance themselves from their own involvement in criminality.

The war that Tucker and Tate had waged against me was finally over but it had cost me dear. I had lost my home, the contents of my home, my car, my girlfriend, regular contact with my family and I had been beaten and imprisoned. It's fair to say that they owed me. It wasn't all doom and gloom. Unlike them, I can hold my head high and say that throughout my ordeal I retained my dignity. My father said that I should jump on the bandwagon and sell my story but, to be honest, the last thing I felt like talking about were the horrors that I had been forced to live through.

It was only when I started reading the usual nonsense that people come out with when talking about the likes of the Krays, that I changed my mind.

'They may have been violent, but they only ever hurt other villains.'

'They were no angels but they were loyal and always looked after their own.'

What complete bullshit! The girl whose car Tucker had crushed, and Sarah Saunders may hold a different opinion.

When Tate's body was released for burial, the fortune that his friends said he had made from drug dealing in these newspaper stories could not be found. There wasn't even enough money to fund a cheap funeral and not one of these so-called friends offered to pay. As in life, it was Sarah, the woman he had bullied and thrown onto the streets, who came to Tate's rescue. Sarah had swallowed her pride and gone cap in hand to one of her friends in Kent to borrow the money to bury him. Frustrated and angered by the praise being heaped on those three bullies, I rang a tabloid newspaper and was offered a substantial fee for what can only be described as a sensational story. I had decided that I wasn't going to tell the truth about the fear and violence that I had endured, because I knew some wannabe reading the story would warm to the perpetrators. Instead, I invented a story that portrayed the trio as cowards who had soiled themselves with fear as they prepared to meet their deaths. The headline read; 'How do you want to die? A single shot, or piece by piece with an axe?'

I told the journalist, 'They were given two options. They could be taken apart with an axe, starting with their fingers, moving on to their hands and then their legs. Or they could opt for the quick way out; an execution shot through the back of the head. They were told, "Either way, you're going to get it. There's no escape." Tucker and Tate messed their trousers first, then took the shots.'

It was, of course, complete nonsense because I had no knowledge of the murders nor who carried them out. It was a sensational case, a sensational story, and I was paid a sensational fee for dispelling a myth that was rapidly growing. I cannot see any harm in that. After interviewing me, the journalist had contacted Essex police for a quote and DS Dibley issued the following statement.

'Because of a previous incident involving the deceased and Steven Ellis, it is in our interest and his to eliminate him from this inquiry. I would like to urge him to come forward.'

I was signing on every day at Swanage police station because of the garage burglary, so I couldn't understand why the police were urging me to come forward. I was hardly hiding from them. I rang Chelmsford police station and after explaining who I was they asked for my location and a contact telephone number and said that they would send somebody to interview me as soon as possible.

When I entered Swanage police station the following morning, I was ushered into a side room and reassured by two Essex detectives that I had nothing to fear. The officers said that they were well aware that I had shot Tate and had tried to murder Tucker and Rolfe, but they did not believe that I was responsible for the executions at Rettendon.

'Keep it simple, Steve. This is just a paper exercise. It's not going anywhere. We just need to officially eliminate you from our inquiries.'

I have been in numerous police stations throughout my colourful criminal career, but I had never before experienced a pre-interview briefing. To be honest it slightly unnerved me, as I began to wonder if they were, in fact, trying to set me up. Why wouldn't the police consider me to be a suspect for the murders of Tate, Tucker and Rolfe if I had shot one of them and attempted to shoot the other two just a few months before their deaths? It was undoubtedly a strange attitude to adopt. Without any consultation, I was informed that I would have to be placed in protective custody.

'It is for your own good. People think you have murdered those three men and they want to avenge their deaths,' one of the detectives said.

'I don't give a fuck about people, dead or living. I am not going into protective custody,' I replied.

It appeared to me as if the police had been reading the newspapers and believed the myth that Tate and Tucker had worked so hard to develop. They had ruled their drug-dealing empire with fear by simply convincing people that they could have anybody killed at any time. The truth was, they were full of shit. I honestly do not believe that they would have had the bottle to walk up to anybody and execute them in cold blood. High on drugs, they may have accidently beaten somebody to death, but the very next day they would have been grassing one another up to the police in order to escape prosecution.

'I didn't fear them when they were alive and I certainly don't fear them now that they are dead,' I told the detective.

Unsure how to proceed, the officers eyed each for answers and when none were forthcoming they simultaneously said, 'We will have to discuss this with our governor, Steve.' Rather than interview me about Tate and Tucker's criminal activities, such as prostitution, possession of firearms and drug dealing – all matters that could have led to them being murdered – I was repeatedly asked 'off the record' about Tate's mobile telephones. Most drug dealers have at least two; one for their 'clients', who are prone to ringing at unsociable hours or inconvenient moments; and one for friends and family. Tate had at least four mobile phones to my knowledge. He was aware that the police could pinpoint a

Bernard O'Mahoney and me walking away from the Range Rover in which our former friends – Tate, Tucker and Rolfe – were murdered

(© Brian Anderson)

My father holding me (Steven Ellis)

Me as a child – no
wonder the other
kids bullied me
(Steven Ellis)

My friend Malcolm Walsh, who was stabbed to death in front of his young children (Steven Ellis)

My beautiful sister and friend Dawn – Tucker threatened to cut her fingers off one by one when she was just five years old (Steven Ellis)

Tucker (left) and Tate (right)
at Epping Country Club six weeks
before their deaths (Bernard O'Mahoney)

Tate's long-suffering partner, Sarah Saunders,
at his funeral (Bernard O'Mahoney)

The murder scene at Rettendon: Rolfe (left) and Tucker (right), while
Tate is unseen, slumped in the rear of the vehicle (Bernard O'Mahoney)

Carlton Leach promoting *Rise of the Foot Soldier*, a film that claims to be based on his life and events in Essex during the 1990s (© Carnaby Films Ltd)

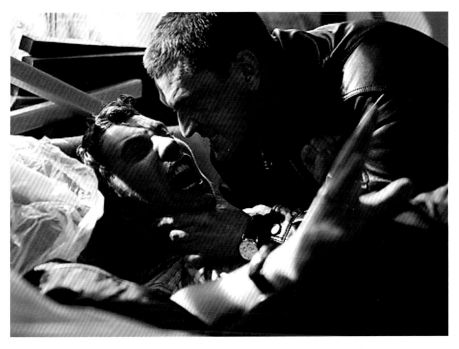

A scene from *Rise of the Foot Soldier*: actor Craig Fairbrass plays Tate, threatening Ian Virgo, who played me (© Carnaby Films Ltd)

Ricky Percival and me on the morning of Essex Boy Chris Wheatley's funeral (Sandy Percival)

This is the picture of Gordon Osborne published on a wanted poster issued by Essex Police

Mick Steele being led into the Magistrates Court at Chelmsford following his arrest for the murders of Tate, Tucker and Rolfe (Bernard O'Mahoney)

Jack Whomes: convicted of the murders of Tate, Tucker and Rolfe (John Whomes)

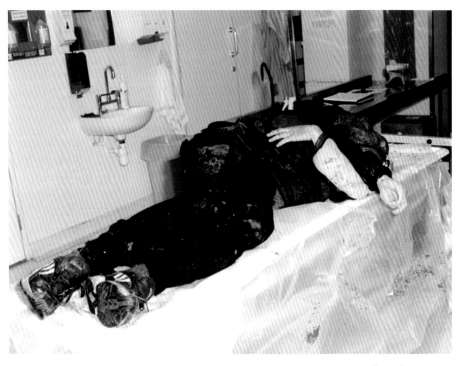

Dean Boshell: he always wanted to be just like Tucker and Tate. Sadly, his wish came true (Beverley Boshell)

Left to right: Danny Percival, me, John Whomes and Bernard O'Mahoney at the Royal Courts of Justice for Ricky Percival's appeal (Bernard O'Mahoney)

person's location by their mobile phone and so when he went to do a 'bit of business' as he called it, he would remove the SIM cards from the 'client' handsets.

A mobile phone is a transmitter and a receiver. It doesn't matter if you are using it or not, the SIM card will still receive or transmit signals to the nearest telephone mast in order to maintain a live line. All contact between a mobile phone and the masts that are now abundant in this country is recorded. As the person moves from place to place so, too, their phone signal moves from mast to mast. It is, therefore, quite easy for the authorities to map exactly where a person has been days, or even months, later.

Whoever murdered Tate also knew this, because the only mobile phone that was found on his body was his 'family phone', which was wrapped tightly in his hand. Perhaps the killers failed to see it, or maybe they were only interested in his 'client' phone because he may have been talking to them on it prior to being shot. I don't suppose we will ever know. The detectives gave me the impression that they knew at least one mobile phone had gone missing because they kept asking me questions about its whereabouts. Had Sarah Saunders rung me from it? Did I have a recent list of all the numbers that Tate used? On and on they went about his bloody mobile phones, but I was unable to assist them.

When I asked the detectives what the significance of Tate's phone was, they would only say that a discrepancy in the evidence had been identified and they needed to clear it up. I later learned, through one of Rolfe's associates, that this 'discrepancy' had come to light after a mechanic named Reynolds had been questioned about work that he had done on Tate's vehicles.

On the morning of his murder, Tate had arrived at the garage where Reynolds worked with a young girl named Lizzie Fletcher in tow. I had met Lizzie several times at Raquel's. Lizzie was a good friend of Donna Garwood, Tucker's teenage mistress, and the pair practically lived at the nightclub. I would describe 'Dizzy Lizzie', as Tate chose to call her, as a typical Essex girl; stunning to look at but challenging to have any sort of intelligent conversation with. Tate and Lizzie had arrived at the garage in separate vehicles, Tate in a black Mercedes 190 and Lizzie in a black Volkswagen Polo. The Polo was left at the garage for repair and arrangements were made that if Tate had not returned by 1800 hrs, when the garage was due to close, then the keys were to be left in the glove box. When Reynolds finished work that night, Tate had not collected the Polo and so he left the keys in the vehicle as agreed.

As Reynolds drove away from the garage and onto a dual carriageway he noticed a blue Range Rover on the opposite side of the road. Rolfe was driving, Tucker was in the passenger seat and a man, that Reynolds assumed was Tate, was in the back. Reynolds guessed that Tate was on his way to collect the Polo. Later that night, between 2100 hrs and 2200 hrs, Reynolds had cause to drive past his place of work and noticed that the Polo had gone. According to the police, Tate, Tucker and Rolfe were murdered at 1845 hrs, just 45 minutes after Reynolds had seen them.

I think it's highly unlikely that they could have picked up the Polo, driven it to wherever and then met their killers, before heading to Rettendon to meet their deaths in such a short space of time. Regardless of how improbable meeting that 45-minute timescale may have been, the police had to present it as feasible because the only phone of Tate's that they had recovered had stopped receiving or making calls at around 1845 hrs. The cessation of mobile traffic to and from Tate's phone at that time proved, the police said, that the murders had taken place shortly afterwards. The phone he had been found with had not linked up with another transmitter after that time and, therefore, they were satisfied that he had not moved from the spot where he was later found dead. What the police failed to take into account is that Tate had several mobile phones and, although he was undoubtedly in the Rettendon area at 1845 hrs, there is no guarantee that he had stopped making calls or was dead at the time they said because his 'business phones' were missing.

The day after the murders, Reynolds telephoned one of Tate's mobile phones and Lizzie Fletcher answered. The slayings had made headline news and Reynolds, one of the last people to have seen the trio alive, was naturally keen to question Lizzie about them. To his dismay, Lizzie said that she had no idea why the men had been murdered. When the police questioned Reynolds about calls that Tate, Tucker and Rolfe had made to him in the days leading up to their deaths, he told them about the work that he had done on various cars they owned and about the conversation that he had with Lizzie when he 'rang one of Tate's phones'. Those five words tipped the entire murder inquiry upon its head because the police had always assumed that Tate only had one phone. Those words meant that they could no longer say, with any real certainty, that the murders had taken place at 1845 hrs.

After quizzing me about Tate's absent mobile phones, detectives were dispatched to interview Sarah Saunders in the hope that she could cast light upon the missing mobiles. Unfortunately for the police, Sarah's evidence only muddied the waters further. Sarah explained that when Tate had thrown her out of her own home, he had taken her contract mobile phone and given it to Lizzie Fletcher. After the murder, Lizzie had been using the phone excessively, talking about Tate's demise to her friends and Sarah's bill had been mounting. Sarah quite rightly contacted Lizzie and demanded that the phone be returned. The police, for reasons known only to themselves, thought that Sarah's request was very odd and during her interviews they kept asking why she had wanted 'the Orange phone back'.

Midway through the intense questioning, Sarah had realised exactly what the police were saying and replied, 'Lizzie didn't have an Orange phone. Pat had that with him the night he died.'

An officer was briefed to review all of the victim's itemised phone bills and when he did so he made a startling discovery. One of Tate's mobile phones had been used to call Lizzie Fletcher at 2145 hrs on the night of the murders. The record of this call was initially made available to Steele and Whomes's defence teams, but it was buried among thousands of other numbers and calls that were documented, on pages and pages of itemised bills and phone schedules. By the time the case reached court and the calls of non-evidential value had been filtered out of the mountain of paperwork, all traces of Tate's crucial call had been removed and the jury was not made aware of it.

Thankfully, this evidence has now come to light following sterling work by a hard-working and honourable solicitor named Chris Bowen. The police can no longer say that they are not aware of a call that was made from Tate's phone at a time they say he was dead, yet they have not yet bothered to enquire if it was Tate who made it and, if not, who had his phone and why?

There is other evidence, which suggests that the murders took place after 1845 hrs. Tate, Tucker and Rolfe had planned to celebrate 'becoming millionaires' following the robbery at Rettendon by visiting The Globe restaurant in Romford. Tucker was well known to Gary Jackets, the manager of the restaurant, because he used to dine there at least three times a week. He also provided the door staff for the venue. Jackets told the police that Tucker had made a reservation for 2030 hrs for four people on the night that he had died. The table had been booked the day before when Tucker had visited the restaurant with 'a pretty young girl in her 20s'. According to Jacket, 'shortly before 1900 hrs' on the night he died, Tucker had rung him stating that he wished to increase the number of his party from four to six persons. Tucker did not say who the additional diners were, nor indicate that he was going to be late. Who were his two additional guests and how could he have rung the restaurant at around the same time that the police believe he was being murdered?

The time that the victims were shot is not the only contentious issue surrounding their murders. There are many other discrepancies and bizarre happenings concerning this case, the vast majority of which have been covered in books such as *Essex Boys* and *Bonded by Blood* by Bernard O'Mahoney. However, new evidence is emerging all the time. It is an inevitable process because as time moves on people's loyalties change, and once important secrets become everyday idle gossip.

Six years after Steele and Whomes were convicted of the triple murders, former Detective Superintendent David Bright of Essex Police made a statement to Hertfordshire Police, who were reviewing the case following an appeal by the convicted men. David Bright said that at 0630 hrs on 7 December 1995 he had received a telephone call from a detective constable, then serving with the Drug Squad, informing him that three men had been found shot dead in a Range Rover in Rettendon, and that it was a gangland-style killing. However, during the trial the prosecution had claimed that two members of the public had discovered the Range Rover at about 0800 hrs.

The failure of the prosecuting authorities to disclose DS Bright's information prior to the trial (in accordance with their obligations) clearly misled the jury about how the police first learned of the murders. If the three deceased men were not under some sort of police surveillance on 6 and 7 December 1995, how is it that DS Bright had known of the murders approximately one and a half hours prior to the two witnesses who, the jury were told, discovered the Range Rover at about 0800 hrs?

I have, quite naturally, taken a keen interest in the case, which has since become known as the 'Essex Boys' Murders'. Steele and Whomes's convictions hinged solely on the evidence of Darren Nicholls, Tate's former cell mate turned supergrass. All the supporting evidence, which convinced a jury that Nicholls was telling the truth, such as the phone evidence and the time of death, has long since crumbled under scrutiny. However, I have to admit that, although the story Nicholls told the jury at the time was extremely convincing, it rarely touched on the truth.

Nicholls had met Tate, Steele and Whomes while serving a prison sentence at HMP Hollesley Bay in Suffolk. Tate was serving his sentence for the Happy Eater robbery, Steele for importing cannabis by aeroplane and Whomes for stealing cars. When Steele was released from prison on 3 June 1993, he moved into a property at St Mary's Road in Clacton-on-Sea. Having served a nine-year prison sentence, the last thing on his mind was committing further crime and so he had set up an engineering company called M.J.S. Commerce. A resident of the Clacton area for more than 27 years, Steele's former occupation had given him a reputation among some police officers that was hard to shake off. Suspicious of Steele and every commercial enterprise that he launched, the police kept a close eye on him and his activities. So much so, in fact, that Steele felt a need to lodge a complaint against the police for harassment just three months after his release. Nobody took any notice of him or his complaint.

Desperate for peace and privacy, Steele decided to sell his home and began negotiations to purchase a secluded bungalow called Meadow Cottage. Nicholls rang Steele regularly from prison but Steele found conversation with him hard.

'He would sit on the end of the phone in silence; I would have to make conversation. I thought he was very odd,' Steele told the jury at his trial.

When Nicholls was granted home leave from prison, he rang Steele to say that he owned some old engineering equipment he could have. Steele thanked Nicholls and arrangements were made for them to meet at a Braintree pub close to Nicholls's house. The two men passed the time of day together but they had little in common apart from the fact they had both served prison sentences. Nicholls was childish, sly and devious; Steele sharp, mature and friendly, and extremely intelligent. In 1970, Steele had qualified as a pilot. He had achieved the Civil Aviation Authority instrument rating, which was the ultimate test of any pilot who wished to fly.

Describing himself, Steele said, 'I think you can say that I am a detailed man, a precise man. I'm very fussy when I set about a task. If I clean something, I clean it well. If I'm going to build something to a dimension, it is to that dimension. I do not settle for second best.'

Jack Whomes had also maintained contact with Steele since their days in prison together. Whomes, like Steele, was a gifted engineer and the pair got on very well. As well as all things mechanical, they shared a common interest in boats. Whomes and his younger brother John could regularly be found down near the Felixstowe ferry port parascending or jet-skiing from the back of their speedboat. Steele would regularly visit Whomes' home at Barham in Suffolk and, on occasion, they would go out to dinner together with their families.

When Nicholls was released from prison, he would often arrive uninvited at Steele's home with his wife and children. As Nicholls was always claiming to be short of cash, Steele felt sorry for him and found him odd jobs to do at his home, his mother's home and his sister's. Within a very short period of time, Nicholls must have known everything there was to know about Steele's habits, his hobbies and general way of life. Steele was not entirely fooled by Nicholls's pleas of poverty; he knew that he had an array of different vehicles at his disposal and suspected that he was involved in drug dealing.

When Nicholls began turning down work that Steele offered him, he confided in Steele that his suspicions had been true.

'I use suicide jockeys to import cannabis,' Nicholls boasted to Steele. 'I go to Holland on the ferry as a foot passenger with a bag of cash and purchase between ten and fifty kilograms of cannabis at a time. I pay pill heads, junkies and anybody else desperate for cash to drive a car out to Belgium or Amsterdam. I meet them, load the drugs into the car and let them drive it on the ferry back into England. If there are three cars containing drugs and one gets caught, it doesn't matter because I will still make a lot of money from the drugs in the other two cars. In the unlikely event that two cars get stopped, I still get my money back from the profit on the drugs in the third car and if all three get through Customs without being stopped, then I am laughing all the way to the bank.'

Steele pretended to be impressed by the ingenuity of Nicholls's operation, but he knew that it wasn't anywhere near as foolproof as Nicholls imagined. If 'pill heads, junkies or anybody else without morals' were caught, the likelihood was that they would inform on Nicholls, rather than face a lengthy prison sentence.

When I shot Tate, Nicholls had gone to visit him at Basildon hospital, but he left deeply regretting his decision to do so. Tate had ridiculed Nicholls about a confrontation that he had had with one of his gofers, named Ian Spindler, who also happened to be at his bedside. Spindler had been in prison with Tate and Nicholls and following a difference of opinion he had offered to fight him. Nicholls had backed down and Tate had made it clear at the hospital that he was not prepared to forget such an act of cowardice.

Throughout Nicholls's visit Tate kept goading him to fight Spindler, saying, 'If you're a proper man you will have it out with him now.'

Nicholls refused to take Tate's bait and stood with his eyes fixed firmly on the floor, inwardly seething.

Later, Nicholls told Steele, 'I can do that. I can shoot somebody. I often speak to myself about it.'

From that day on Steele, who had been unnerved by Nicholls's ramblings, told everybody that, in his opinion, Nicholls was a schizophrenic. When Tate asked Nicholls to supply him with cannabis, it was hardly surprising that Nicholls would try to rip him off. Tate's ego had probably told him that, despite the fact that he had humiliated Nicholls, his reputation would ensure that the deal would go ahead as planned. Unfortunately for Tate, Nicholls felt that he should be compensated for the embarrassment that he had been caused and sold Tate a shipment of dud cannabis.

Predictably, Tate responded by running around making death threats, which Nicholls and half of Essex got to hear about. In fear of his life, Nicholls had asked a traveller named 'Matty' to supply him with firearms and it is accepted that at least one shotgun was sold to him. Another man from Braintree named Terry has since come forward and said that Nicholls had also asked him to supply a firearm.

Terry claims that Nicholls had said to him, 'I don't mind what the weapon is so long as it is reliable and holds plenty of rounds.'

Terry had criminal connections in south-east London and after making enquiries concerning Nicholls' request he reported back that he could get him almost any type of weapon that he wanted. To his surprise Nicholls told Terry to forget about their conversation because he had already sorted things out himself.

In the weeks leading up to the murders, Steele had been busy working on Meadow Cottage, which he had finally purchased, in the hope of escaping what he claimed had been police harassment since his release from prison. The property had been little more than a shell surrounded by overgrown weeds, shrubs and trees.

On 2 December, Whomes and his son arrived at Meadow Cottage in a Transit van, behind which was a trailer carrying a JCB. The trailer belonged to Steele but Whomes had borrowed it to pick up the digger. Throughout the day Steele, Whomes and his son worked hard, clearing the site. All the rubbish, shrubs and trees were thrown onto a bonfire using the JCB. That night, Steele held a firework party for the children and plied all of his friends, who had helped him to tidy up the property, with food and drink.

The following morning, Steele and a friend used the JCB to strip the remaining grass and shrubs and load the remains of the bonfire into a skip. On Monday, Steele returned the JCB but when he arrived at Whomes' yard nobody was there. Rather than unload the digger, Steele had left it on the trailer because he knew that it had to be taken elsewhere once Whomes returned. The following day, Whomes' Uncle Dennis arrived in his yard because he wanted some work done on his vehicle. Dennis noticed the trailer and asked Whomes if it was for sale. After speaking to Steele, Whomes told Dennis that 'the man who owned it' wanted £400. Whomes wasn't being entirely honest with either man. He had failed to tell Dennis that Steele owned the trailer and was willing to accept £300 and he hadn't told Steele that he had accepted £400, but he saw no harm in making money on the sale for himself. Perhaps he felt a tinge of guilt after accepting the £400 from his uncle, because he agreed to repair his car free of charge.

Whomes was unable to work on the vehicle immediately as he had already stripped down an old Bedford van. He told his uncle to leave the car with him and take his brother John's Astra van to get back home to Essex. Dennis wanted to take the trailer with him straightaway as he said that he needed it, but Whomes had already agreed to pick up a tractor for Steele with it the following day. Dennis suggested, and Whomes agreed, that he could take the trailer but it would be returned the following morning when he came to pick up his car. When Dennis did arrive to collect his car, he didn't have the trailer with him. Whomes was adamant that he needed to pick up the tractor for Steele and so it was agreed that he could collect the trailer himself from Dennis's home in Bulphan, a small village on the outskirts of Basildon.

When Whomes arrived at his uncle's home nobody was in, so he left a note saying, 'Bubby called, back tomorrow'. On his way back to Suffolk, Whomes called in at Steele's home and explained that he had been unable to pick up the trailer, but he did offer to return to his uncle's the following day. On the morning of the murders, Whomes was working hard on the docks, unloading soya beans from a ship. He finished around lunchtime and then busied himself with loading a 'Dextor tractor' onto a trailer that he had acquired to transport the machine to Steele's home.

At approximately 1400 hrs, a friend of Darren Nicholls, named Colin Bridge, drove into the yard in an old Escort van. Bridge asked Whomes if he could borrow his trailer because Nicholls's vehicle, an ageing Passat, had broken down at a pub called the Wheatsheaf in Rettendon. Whomes was apologetic and explained that he was using the trailer himself, but he did not think that Bridge's vehicle would be able to pull it if it was loaded in any event. Realising that Bridge had no other options open to him, Whomes said that he would pick the vehicle up for Nicholls once he had dropped the tractor off at Steele's house. Whomes asked Bridge for the location of the Passat and he had said, 'It's on the Chelmsford to Southend road, at a place called Rettendon. You will see a bright-pink Morris Minor at a pub called the Wheatsheaf. It's there in the car park. It's very visible, a beige Passat. The keys are under the seat.'

Whomes left Suffolk at approximately 1515 hrs and arrived at Steele's home at around 1600 hrs. After unloading the tractor, he explained to Steele that he was going to pick up a vehicle for Darren Nicholls and, therefore, wouldn't be able to collect the trailer as planned from his uncle's. Steele had not yet moved into his almost derelict new home and, therefore, needed the trailer to transport the tractor to and from his home when he wasn't using it to prevent it from being stolen. Steele told Whomes that, as he needed the trailer, he would pick it up himself. After Whomes had left Steele's home, he had travelled to a business associate's address to discuss the hire of machinery.

Brian Wilson, the man he had hoped to speak to, was not in and so Whomes left a message with his son to contact him. By the time that Whomes arrived to collect Nicholls's car from the Wheatsheaf pub in Rettendon, it was approximately 1840 hrs. After pulling in front of the vehicle, Whomes found the keys, unlocked the steering, winched the Passat up onto the trailer and tied it down by its wheels. He then tried to ring Darren Nicholls to inform him that he had picked up his vehicle but all he got was a static noise. The Wheatsheaf pub is located in a natural dip that makes mobile telephone reception poor. It was also snowing heavily and so Whomes didn't bother ringing Nicholls again and headed home.

The following morning, Tate's, Tucker's and Rolfe's bodies were found slumped in the Range Rover just a few hundred yards from where Whomes had picked up Nicholls' car. Unfortunately for Whomes, the call he tried to make to Nicholls was picked up by the nearest mast to the murder scene. If anybody ever accused him of killing his former cell mate and his friends, the police would have scientific evidence that he was near the crime scene at the time the police say that they died. Jack Whomes was doomed, as was Mick Steele because he had travelled to nearby Bulphan to pick the trailer up from Dennis's house. He and Whomes had made several innocent calls to each other throughout the day. If the police analysed these calls, they could have mistaken them for being calls between two men involved in a conspiracy. All the police needed was a man who was aware of all the information, to weave it together with a web of lies and the most infamous gangland murders since the reign of the Krays would be solved. For Whomes, Steele and the three dead men, life ended that night, but for Darren Nicholls, particularly now that Tate was out of the way, it was business as usual.

One afternoon, Nicholls had been drinking in a pub called the Sailing Oak near his home in Braintree, when he heard a voice from behind him say, 'I know that you are a drug dealer.' When Nicholls had turned around, he found himself face to face with Detective Constable Wolfgang Bird. Nicholls had never spoken to DC Bird but he knew who he was because their paths had crossed twice in the past. The first time had been when DC Bird had lent his car to three friends who had been drinking in the Sailing Oak. The car had left the road and one of the occupants had ended up in intensive care. The next time that DC Bird had entered the pub, Nicholls and a group of his friends had mocked the detective. On the second occasion, Nicholls had witnessed DC Bird unloading bottles of spirits from his car and taking them into the pub. Enquiries made by Nicholls among the regulars revealed that DC Bird supplied his friend, the landlord, with cheap booze, which he obtained at police auctions. As Nicholls glared at the policeman, who had just accused him of being a drug dealer, he was trying hard to think of something to say.

Before he had chance to open his mouth, DC Bird said, 'I

suppose that you are going to deny it? Everyone always denies it.'

'I don't know what you're talking about. All of that was a long time ago. You're out of date,' replied Nicholls, before turning and walking away.

Two days later, Nicholls received a call on his mobile from DC Bird. Paul, the boss of an electrical company Nicholls worked for, was a friend of the detective's and he had given him Nicholls's number.

'What do you want?' Nicholls asked.

'I'm only telling you this because you're a friend of Paul's,' DC Bird replied. 'You're about to get spun. The drug squad is planning a raid on your place because they reckon you've got a load of gear stashed there.'

Nicholls laughed. 'I didn't think the drugs squad was that slow. I've told you, mate, that was all in the past.'

DC Bird was persistent. He told Nicholls that he was looking at a note on the CID office wall that had details of a raid that was going to be carried out at Nicholls's home address. 'Tell you what,' DC Bird said. 'If you're telling me the truth and you're not at it any more, I will stop it from happening.'

A few days later, DC Bird telephoned Nicholls again.

'I told you, Darren. I stopped it happening. Your home didn't get searched, did it?'

The detective made it clear from the outset that he wanted Nicholls to be his informant. He knew Nicholls was a major supplier of drugs on his patch and he was offering him the opportunity to ply his trade free from prosecution in exchange for information about others. At first, Nicholls was reluctant to comply, but he soon realised that he could use DC Bird instead of being used himself. If anybody threatened or upset him, he could simply have them removed by setting them up and informing on them to his police handler.

Nicholls was told that in order to become a bona fide registered police informant he would have to have a meeting with a senior officer. It was no more than a formality; the officer would explain what was expected of Nicholls, what he might be paid for his trouble, and then he would sign a document agreeing to the terms.

At the meeting, Nicholls was told that he would be expected to pass on all relevant information and to not commit crime himself, unless it had been sanctioned first by the police. Whenever he had any contact with his police handler, he would always have to use the name Ken Rugby. This was to protect him from people eavesdropping on police conversations or dubious officers seeing his real name on informant sheets at the police station.

Two years before Nicholls had become involved with DC Bird, the sister of his wife Sandra had been going out with a local man named Alan Richards. Sandra, Nicholls and Richards all got on well until one drunken night when Richards gave Sandra a lift home. Instead of taking her to her own home, he took her to his, where she stayed the night. When Nicholls found out, he went berserk. A few days later, he confronted Richards, who told him he had been too drunk to drive Sandra home, so she had slept on his settee. Nicholls refused to believe him. From that day onwards, the atmosphere between the two men was dire. It was obvious that eventually they would come to blows.

That night came in the Sailing Oak pub, where DC Bird was also drinking. Nicholls, who was drunk at the time, began calling Richards names. Eventually, Richards lost his temper, stood up and suggested they both go outside to resolve the matter once and for all. Before Nicholls could reply, Richards sat back down awkwardly and fell off his chair. Everybody in the bar burst out laughing. The landlord quickly appeared on the scene and accused Nicholls of causing the trouble. Nicholls flew into a rage, badmouthed the landlord and walked out of the pub.

Seconds later, DC Bird was at Nicholls's side. He said he had spoken to the landlord and he had apologised. If Nicholls returned to the pub, he could have free drinks all night. At that moment, Nicholls realised DC Bird could be more than his handler, he could be his friend and protector. Instead of returning to the pub, the pair stood on the car park talking about Nicholls importing drugs, selling them, telling DC Bird who had purchased them and DC Bird then arresting them.

'That's a bit strong,' Nicholls replied when DC Bird had first suggested it. 'You are kidding, aren't you?'

DC Bird paused momentarily. 'Of course I'm serious,' he said. 'Of course I am.'

Unbeknown to Nicholls and DC Bird, Alan Richards, still smarting from being humiliated, was watching them from the pub window. It all made sense to him now. When Nicholls started being abusive to him, DC Bird remained in his seat and said nothing. When Nicholls had a go at the landlord, DC Bird had gone out of his way to smooth things over on Nicholls's behalf. Watching them talk in the car park, Richards felt uneasy. A voice in his head told him that they were talking about him. That same voice warned him that Nicholls might be thinking about setting him up.

Early the next morning, Alan Richards presented himself at Essex Police headquarters in Chelmsford and asked to speak to a senior officer.

'I have information about one of your officers, who is involved in criminal activity and I think I can prove it.'

When the police realised who DC Bird was involved with, they had little doubt the allegations needed investigating. A massive surveillance operation, codenamed Operation Apache, was mounted, which involved tailing Nicholls and DC Bird and taping all the phone calls DC Bird made and received. In all, 35 officers were assigned to Operation Apache. It remains the biggest internal investigation ever undertaken by Essex Police.

All Customs officers have some sort of system to relieve the boredom of watching hundreds of cars, then pulling one over at random. George Stephens had several, but his favourite was to add together all of the figures in that day's date and then count off the passing vehicles until he reached that number.

On 14 April 1996, vehicle number 43 happened to be a white Mondeo that was passing through Dover at 0945 hrs. Stephens flagged the car down and asked the driver his name, where he had been and why. The driver, Craig Androliakos, appeared nervous.

'I've been to Paris,' he said. 'I was visiting a girl I met a couple of weeks ago.'

'Is this your car then, sir?' Stephens enquired.

'No, it's hired, a friend of mine hired it,' Androliakos replied.

'Who was that, then?' Stephens asked. 'I need to know the name of your friend.'

Androliakos was visibly sweating. He paused for a long time before answering, 'Nick Reynolds. Nick Reynolds hired it.'

Stephens had been in his job long enough to know that Androliakos was hiding something, so he asked him to get out of the car so that it could be searched. The first place Stephens looked was the glove box, where he found the rental agreement from Budget car hire.

'This car's been hired by somebody called Darren Nicholls,' Stephens said.

When he searched the boot, he found a pair of fisherman's waders. They were still wet and covered in sand. In Androliakos's luggage, Stephens found maps of Holland and Belgium, and scraps of paper with mobile phone numbers on them. Although suspicious, none of the items was illegal and so Stephens had to let him go.

As soon as Androliakos had departed, the Customs officer dashed back to the office and ran a few names through the computer. Darren Nicholls's name flashed up on the screen and below was a memo that asked anybody who came into contact with him to get in touch with Essex Police.

On 30 April, DS Ivan Dibley retired and handed over the Rettendon murder investigation to DS Brian Storey. The latter soon realised that he would not be conducting a lengthy investigation because, shortly after taking charge, the taps on the phones of Nicholls and DC Bird began to reveal some startling conversations.

On 10 May 1996, DC Bird and Nicholls talked about a Jaguar that Nicholls wanted to sell for £3,000. Nicholls told DC Bird that drug dealers were going to use the vehicle to transport a large amount of cash out of the country so that they could purchase drugs on the Continent.

'Righto, oh that's goodo,' DC Bird said. 'Oh, right. So really all I've got to do is steal that car when it goes abroad next time and keep the loot.'

'That wouldn't be a fucking bad idea, would it?' Nicholls replied.

'No.'

'That would be a bloody good idea. Wouldn't that be nice between us?'

'Yes.'

'It would be like a hundred and something-odd thousand pounds. No, it would be more than that, actually . . . no, it wouldn't, it would be about a hundred and fifty grand, I reckon.'

'Mmm.'

'It buys a lot of gear down there where they are going.'

'Yeah, exactly.'

'No, it would be more than that. I reckon they're paying seven and a half this time, they said.'

'How many people go driving abroad with the cash then?'

'Only two.'

'What, they leave it in the car?'

'Yeah, leave it in the car.'

'Good grief. That's very remiss of them, isn't it?'

'They used to carry it on, you know, used to get it out of the boot, and then they decided that it's probably worse walking round with a couple of hundred grand, like a dickhead, in suitcases on a boat than just leaving it in the motor.'

'Yeah.'

'Which is a shame, if you know what I mean.'

'Exactly. It's a shame you haven't kept a spare key.'

'Oh, fuck me, I'd get into it.'

'It would be better with a key because all you would do is drive on with them, make sure you follow somewhere near them, you hang around when they go up on deck.'

'Yeah.'

'Swap from one boot into the other and just drive off with them at the same time.'

Unfortunately the gang didn't think the car Nicholls had for sale was reliable, so they hired a vehicle instead. As well as discussing what drug dealers were up to, DC Bird and Nicholls talked about making amphetamines. Nicholls had told DC Bird that two pints of a chemical known as BMK (benzyl methyl ketone, an essential ingredient in the production of amphetamine sulphate) were available, though DC Bird had said more would be needed.

'Say a gallon, Darren,' he'd said.

The pair were recorded laughing and talking about Nicholls dishing the drugs they planned to make out to people 'like sweets'. Thankfully, this scheme never went ahead.

As the proof of corruption and drug dealing mounted, DS Storey organised a briefing, involving not only Essex Police officers but also Customs officers, so that they could trade information and discuss tactics. When the evidence had been thoroughly looked over, DS Storey was amazed to discover that Craig Androliakos, who had been stopped in the Mondeo hired by Nicholls, was working for a gang headed by none other than Pat Tate's brother, Russell.

Customs' spotter planes were put on standby and dozens of undercover officers were earmarked for duty. Intelligence reports showed that Russell Tate and other members of his gang had just left for Spain. When Nicholls had said to DC Bird, 'It buys a lot of gear down there where they are going,' police officers hadn't initially understood what he had meant. It now dawned on them that 'down there' meant Spain, and the money Nicholls and DC Bird had talked about stealing belonged to Tate's gang. DS Storey decided to have the gang's mobile phones monitored, and when transmissions from those phones showed that they were heading north, back towards England, police and Customs would swoop into action.

On Monday, 13 May, Nicholls was driving along the A120 near Colchester in the blue Jaguar that he had failed to sell to Tate's gang. One of his friends, Colin Bridge, was following behind in Nicholls's Transit van. Always cautious when 'working', Nicholls was convinced that he was being followed.

He picked up his mobile and rang DC Bird. 'Oi, am I under surveillance? Are you lot following me?' he asked.

'Nah, don't be stupid, Darren,' DC Bird replied. 'You're just being paranoid.'

'I don't think so, mate, I'm sure I'm being surveyed. I've been paranoid before and it doesn't feel anything like this.'

'I'm telling you, Darren. You're not being followed. If you were,

I'd tell you, wouldn't I? I mean I'm not going to fuck you up, am I? You're on our side, just relax.'

'All right. Listen, though. The shipment came in last night. I'm just going over to pick up my share.'

'I know. Don't worry, everything's under control. Relax.'

A short while later, Nicholls and Bridge arrived at Steele's house, and Nicholls asked Steele if he could pick up some tools he had left there.

Steele, who was sitting on a deckchair sunning himself, said, 'Sure, help yourself.'

Nicholls took a toolbox from the Jaguar's boot and walked off. A short while later, he returned carrying the toolbox and put it in the back of the van. The Transit, driven by Bridge, then left Steele's home with Nicholls in the Jaguar behind.

At just after 1400 hrs, uniformed police officers stopped the two vehicles on the B1053 at Broad Street, Bocking, near Braintree. When the vehicles came to a halt, Bridge got out and began talking to the officers. However, Nicholls refused to open the door of his car and began talking on a mobile phone. First he telephoned his wife Sandra.

'I won't be home, after all,' he shouted. 'I'm being stopped by the police. I'll try and call you later. Bye.'

By now, officers were hammering on the window, telling him to put the phone down and open the door. Nicholls chose to ignore them because he had one last important call to make.

'DC Bird's message pager,' said a woman's voice. 'Can I take your message, please?'

'Yeah, the message is, "I'm being fucking nicked."'

There was a long silence and then the woman said, 'I'm sorry, sir, I don't think I can send that particular message.'

The officers outside the car had pulled out their truncheons and were threatening to smash the window. Nicholls looked at them, sighed and said to the woman, 'All right. Just tell him that Darren has been arrested.'

As soon as Nicholls stepped out of the car, the officers snatched his mobile phone from him and handcuffed his hands behind his back. As he looked up the road, he could see Bridge, also handcuffed, being put in a police van.

'Do you know why you have been stopped?' asked one of the officers.

Nicholls said nothing. He just shook his head.

'Where have you come from?' asked the officer.

'Colchester,' Nicholls replied.

'Well, there have been a number of burglaries in Colchester and you've been stopped today because we would like to search your van in connection with those burglaries.'

Nicholls nodded, 'OK, fair enough, but everything in that van is mine. Colin is just driving it for me. He has nothing to do with anything. It's all down to me.'

Because the back of the van was empty except for the toolbox, it didn't take the officers long to find the ten kilos of cannabis inside.

'What are these, then?' asked the officer.

'They look like chocolate bars to me,' Nicholls replied. 'What do you think they are?'

A huge grin broke out on the officer's face. 'I think they're drugs and you're under arrest.'

All the way to the police station Nicholls had been expecting his friend DC Bird to appear and tell the officers they had made a terrible mistake.

Nicholls could imagine him saying, 'No, this one's OK, he's on our side.'

But DC Bird was never going to come to his rescue: he, too, was facing some awkward questions. Nicholls realised that the only man who could save him now was himself. He decided he would give 'no comment' answers to all the police questions until he knew exactly how strong their case was. Only then would he decide what path he was going to take. One thing was for sure: saving himself was top priority.

At 2116 hrs, Nicholls asked if he could speak to a nominated police officer who was known to him, but his request was declined. At 2326 hrs Nicholls was interviewed for the first time about the importation of cannabis. He answered 'no comment' to all of the questions.

At the end of the interview, DC Winstone, who was asking Nicholls the questions, said, 'I don't intend to say any more about the possession with intent to supply at the moment. The time by my watch is 2335 hrs and you're now going to be arrested for being involved in the murders of Pat Tate, Craig Rolfe and Tony Tucker. Do you wish to make any comment to the fact you've now been arrested for those murders?'

After a pause, Nicholls replied, 'No comment.'

The following day, as the extent of the evidence against him began to be revealed, Nicholls realised he was in a hopeless position, but he still refused to comment when each question was asked. In addition to all of the Customs and police surveillance records – which now included video footage and still pictures – the police had access to his phone records. Additionally, Nicholls had been caught in possession of drugs. Colin Bridge had been released after just two or three hours because it was clear to police he had played no active part in the drug-smuggling operation. Nicholls had told the officers that everything in the van was his, so prosecuting Bridge would have been impossible.

At the end of his second interview, DC Winstone said to Nicholls, 'Last night you asked if you could speak to a police officer. Would you like to tell me who the police officer was?'

Nicholls looked at DC Winstone and said, 'No comment.'

'All right, I can tell you that at the moment two police officers from Essex have been arrested and are currently in custody.'

Nicholls's mouth dropped. 'Oh, fuck, I don't believe it . . .'

DC Winstone continued, 'The officers have been charged with a number of offences including some linked to the possession of controlled drugs. We have evidence that you have had numerous dealings with one of the officers. Is there any comment you wish to make now?'

'No, no fucking comment,' Nicholls replied.

As soon as the tape had been switched off, Nicholls asked to see a senior police officer. DS Barrington was summoned and Nicholls asked him if he were to give him the name of the police officer who had been arrested, would he confirm it? DS Barrington said that he would.

'Is it DC Bird?' DS Barrington confirmed that it was. Nicholls told him that DC Bird was the reason he had got into all of this trouble. 'I've been set up,' he said.

Nicholls knew that he was now facing the toughest decision of his life. If he managed to escape prosecution by the police, which was extremely unlikely, the fact that he was Ken Rugby, police informant, would come out and if he were sent to prison he would undoubtedly be in extreme danger. Even if he escaped imprisonment, all of the people in Braintree he had grassed on and set up would find out, and he would have to move. There was no way out for him. Whichever path he took, he faced ruin.

The police had already established Nicholls was DC Bird's informant, so they knew he wasn't averse to informing on people, even friends. They also knew he had nowhere safe to turn and so they threw him a lifeline. If Nicholls could tell them who had murdered Tate, Tucker and Rolfe, and tell them about the drug importations they were involved in, they would put him and his family on the Witness Protection Programme. This would give him and his family a new identity, a new home in a new area, a completely fresh start in life. Nicholls didn't hesitate: 'It was Mick Steele and Jack Whomes. They murdered them,' he said.

Nicholls constructed a convincing web of lies based on circumstantial evidence, the jury believed him and two innocent men were jailed for life. However, new evidence is emerging all the time and I am in no doubt that Steele and Whomes will soon be acquitted and freed. Securing convictions using people such as Nicholls, who have nothing to lose by telling the police what they need to hear but everything to gain, is unjust, dangerous and reckless. Sadly, Whomes and Steele are not the only ones who have suffered at the hands of a devious liar and a jury that was misled.

CHAPTER EIGHT

Everybody in the Essex underworld appeared to be experiencing traumatic times and it's fair to say that I wasn't having the best week of my life either. Malcolm Walsh had telephoned me from Essex to say that the police wanted to talk to me about 'a bit of work' we had done in Essex. Apparently, they suspected Malcolm and me of committing an armed robbery near the Lakeside shopping centre more than two years previously. I told Malcolm not to worry.

'It's just pub talk; you know what they're like. Just because I am out of the area every man and his dog assumes that I am responsible for all of the crime committed in the south-east of England,' I said.

Malcolm wasn't so easily convinced. He said that he had already been questioned and if our stories didn't match we could be heading back to prison.

'Stay out of the way until it blows over,' he pleaded. 'I don't need any more shit at the moment.'

My brother-in-law, Steve, had recently been diagnosed with terminal cancer and I was planning to go and visit him in Essex, but Malcolm was keen to point out that I would find the experience upsetting. He said that he had met Steve on Southend seafront recently and he had 'looked awful'.

'I hardly recognised him, he was thin and gaunt, the guy is really ill. He looks like he is going to die soon. You are better off remembering Steve as he was before his illness,' Malcolm said. However, when I indicated that Steve's rapid demise gave me more of a reason to see him urgently, Malcolm's tack changed, 'Don't you worry about Steve, he will outlive us both.'

I knew that Malcolm was trying to prevent me from visiting Essex in case the police arrested me and so for his peace of mind I agreed to stay away. I, of course, had no intention of staying away, particularly after hearing just how ill Steve appeared to be. I knew that my brother-in-law had cancer but I hadn't considered the possibility that he might die just yet, as he had only been diagnosed in the past two weeks, and Steve was a very strong young man.

I asked Malcolm about the problems that he was experiencing and he told me that he had become embroiled in a festering dispute with two brothers, eighteen-year-old Steven Tretton and his twenty-year-old brother Stuart, who he claimed owed him £200 for drugs. For a number of months, the Tretton brothers had been subjected to a catalogue of threats and abuse from Malcolm and when their mother Lydia had been informed, she had confronted him, calling him a scumbag and low life. Not the type of lady to mince her words, Lydia warned Malcolm to leave her boys alone or he would regret not doing so. Thereafter, the opposing parties exchanged abuse and threats every time their paths crossed. This turned out to be an all-too-regular occurrence because Malcolm often visited his ex-wife and their children, who resided in Locksley Close, where the Trettons also lived.

I asked Malcolm if he needed any back-up in sorting out the issue but he declined my offer, saying that Damon Alvin, who he was now 'doing business with', was more than prepared and capable of helping him, if indeed help was ever needed. I knew all about Damon Alvin; few in Essex had been spared the stories of his gratuitous violence and bullying. When Alvin wasn't sleeping, drinking, fornicating or thieving, he was terrorising those who displeased him in the area where he lived. I warned Malcolm to be wary of Alvin but he just laughed and said that I was being paranoid because he considered him to be a 'sound guy'.

Alvin, to me, was a control freak, like Tucker; he would bully or beat senseless weaker people who would not give in to his whims and wishes. One person who did resist Alvin's attempts to control her was his long-term girlfriend Clair Sanders. Weary of Alvin's constant brushes with the law and his empty assurances that he would mend his ways, Sanders had eventually told Alvin that their relationship was over. Embarrassed by the fact that he had been dumped and distraught at the loss of his first love, Alvin immediately left Essex in the hope of starting anew.

Eighteen years of age, homeless and unemployed, Alvin's options were at best limited. He eventually washed up in south-east London, where he set up home with a woman named Barbara Russell, who was several years his senior. Despite the age gap, the couple had a lot in common and knew many of the same people. It wasn't surprising really, because Barbara was Alvin's aunt. By all accounts, Barbara is a thoroughly decent woman, who did all she could to make things work with him. Unfortunately for Barbara, her hopes of happiness were dashed by Alvin's overwhelming desire to become a somebody. The life he chose to lead brought the same sort of trouble to her door that his previous partner Clair had endured.

Bullying the youth of sleepy Leigh-on-Sea is undoubtedly less treacherous than picking on the street urchins that roam the streets of south-east London. Upon his arrival Alvin made a half-hearted attempt to intimidate the locals by declaring that he feared no man, but they punched him around the street, dismissed him as a fool and warned him about his future conduct. Fearing for his safety, Alvin purchased a stun gun, which the police found one evening after he was stopped during a routine spot check. When Alvin appeared in court for possessing the prohibited weapon, he was given a conditional discharge and an order was made regarding the destruction of the stun gun.

Disillusioned and genuinely in fear of the local teenagers, Alvin abandoned his wafer-thin plans of a new life in London and returned to Essex with his Auntie Barbara. The news that awaited Alvin upon his return to Leigh-on-Sea did little to please him. Malcolm Walsh, Alvin's mentor and idol, was having an illicit affair with his beloved Clair. Gritting his teeth, Alvin pretended to accept that both he and Clair had moved on but behind his false smile lurked a cauldron of seething hatred and jealousy. Despite the fact that Alvin was living with Barbara, he was desperate to break up Malcolm and Clair, so he told Malcolm's wife Bernadette about the affair. After confronting Malcolm about his infidelity, Bernadette demanded that he leave her home.

Owing to circumstance rather than choice, Malcolm immediately moved into Clair's flat. When Alvin learned that his mischief-making had resulted in Malcolm moving in with Clair, he was devastated and began telling friends that he wished Malcolm was dead. Despite his apparent loathing of Malcolm, Alvin continued to commit burglaries and share the fruits of their labour equally with him. Three days after I had warned Malcolm about the company that he was keeping, Alvin arrived at Malcolm's flat. After parking his car, Alvin noticed that the back window in Malcolm's new 3 Series BMW had been smashed. The offending house brick that had been used to cause the damage had bounced across the roof and ended up on the bonnet, damaging all of the paintwork it came into contact with along the way. Malcolm flew into a rage when Alvin broke the news to him.

'Bastards, bastards, bastards,' he screamed. 'I will kill those fucking Trettons.'

Before Alvin could say another word Malcolm had run out of his home and disappeared up the street. When he eventually returned, he told Alvin that he had caught Steven Tretton on the stairs at his grandmother's house and beaten him.

'Don't think that this is over yet,' Malcolm screamed. 'That bastard Stuart is going to get it when I see him.'

Malcolm was rarely wrong and this occasion was no different. This particular feud was far from over.

The following week, Malcolm drove to Locksley Close to pick up his children. As he got out of his car several members of the Tretton family and their friends happened to be gathered in the street. As usual, both parties glared at one another and began trading insults. By the time Malcolm had been into his ex-wife's house and collected his children the Trettons had gone and so he got back into his car and drove away. That night, the Tretton family received several threatening and abusive phone calls from Malcolm. He warned them that their home was going to be petrol bombed and their stepfather, Terry Watkins, would soon be a dead man.

The following morning, when Malcolm returned to Locksley Close with Clair Sanders to drop off his children trouble flared again. Lydia, the Trettons' mother, began shouting at Malcolm from her window and when he began hammering on the front door her husband Terry opened it. Enraged by the threatening phone calls that his family had been subjected to the night before, Terry began waving a knife around shouting, 'You're going to get it.'

A friend of Malcolm's named Robert Findlay appealed for calm but he was ignored by both men. As Terry stormed out of his house Malcolm was heard asking him to drop the knife but Terry kept repeating almost robot-like, 'You are going to get it.'

Witnesses later described Terry then thrusting the knife forward in a stabbing motion.

As blood began to pour from a wound in Malcolm's chest he looked at Terry in disbelief and said, 'You want to get yourself a decent knife. That one's blunt.'

He then staggered backwards and fell into the arms of Robert Findlay. Moments later he collapsed, dying just yards from where his young children were standing. Less than an hour later, Malcolm was pronounced dead at Southend General Hospital.

When Alvin heard the news, he had ranted about throwing grenades through Terry Watkins's windows and shooting the Tretton brothers. I did wonder if these were the same grenades that he had offered to give to me to kill Tucker. It was always hard to tell if Alvin was being serious or talking bullshit.

Malcolm's death was not all bad news for Alvin. He realised that Clair Sanders, his true love, was single once more. Alvin pledged that he was going to do everything in his power to win her back, and made himself available day and night to console his grieving ex-girlfriend. Friends of Clair at the time describe him as being 'her rock'.

When the police arrested Terry Watkins for Malcolm's murder, he said that it had been Malcolm who had first pulled out the knife.

'He came over in a right aggressive manner. I wasn't going to be intimidated by him. He came round here tooled up. I saw the glint of the knife. I am very sorry that he is dead, but it isn't down to me.'

Malcolm's death resulted in a barrage of threats and abuse being levelled at the Tretton family. Neighbours stopped talking to them and they began receiving up to 50 nuisance phone calls per week.

It's fair to say that the family was far from popular in the eyes of many of the local community.

Another who had been badly affected by Malcolm's premature death was his close friend Ricky Percival. I knew Ricky reasonably well because I had been friends with his older brother, Danny, a professional boxer who worked as a doorman around Southend. The Percival family hailed from Upton Park, near the West Ham United Football Club ground in the East End of London. David Percival and his wife Sandy had two children, Danny and Ricky. Danny did well at school but Ricky experienced difficulties, which stemmed from him being dyslexic. Teachers, who failed to recognise that Ricky had a problem, wrongly assumed that he was lazy, slow or simply not trying hard enough. This resulted in him being punished, which understandably made him resent everything about school.

When Ricky was eight years old, his parents took the agonising decision to leave the home they loved in London and move to Leigh-on-Sea in Essex. They had found a school there that was prepared to give Ricky some assistance by providing one-hour sessions of one-to-one tuition. The teacher that worked with Ricky regularly has described him as the perfect pupil. Unfortunately, all of the other time that Ricky spent in school was in a normal classroom environment and this led to him becoming frustrated, understandably bored and, as a consequence of that, disruptive. By the time Ricky had reached 15 years, he had tired of school and the school had tired of him. It was agreed by all parties that it would be better if he sought gainful employment rather than struggle on at school.

Shortly afterwards, Ricky started work at a local fresh fish shop. The job involved him getting up in the early hours of the morning and working for long hours in an extremely cold and damp environment. His mother did not like him having to work in such poor conditions but Ricky concluded that anything was preferable to school. Ricky's older brother Danny had attended kick-boxing and martial art lessons since the age of eight. By his mid-teens he was, by all accounts, exceptionally good at both. Like most boys, Ricky looked up to his older brother and wanted to emulate him. With his father's encouragement, Ricky too began training. He was careful about what he ate and attended the gym religiously. It was while training at a local gym that he had become friends with Malcolm. Unfortunately for Ricky, through Malcolm he also became acquainted with Damon Alvin.

Ricky reminded me of Craig Rolfe in many ways; always trying to impress and please those that he considered to be friends. Ricky would adhere to all of Alvin's wishes and try to laugh off his bullying and intimidating behaviour. I can recall one incident when Alvin had handcuffed Ricky to a bridge for a 'joke'. Laughing insanely, he had threatened to burn Ricky, beat him and subject him to all manner of unpleasantries. Nobody ever did manage to see the funny side of this particular prank.

Ricky's desire to look and feel as confident as Malcolm and Alvin was hampered only by his lack of finances. The menial jobs that he attributed to his dyslexia ensured that he was never going to be able to afford their lifestyle and so, rather foolishly, he accepted Alvin's offer to sell drugs in order to boost his income. Unlike Alvin, Ricky's sincere and warm personality made him easy-going and approachable and so he found that he had no shortage of customers who were prepared to do business with him.

In the gym where nightclub bouncers and their ilk went to train, Ricky met and befriended many 'useful' contacts, who were involved in the seedy world of drugs. These people – who not only had influence, but also unhindered access to the pubs and clubs where drugs were sold around Southend, which was extremely valuable – soon helped Ricky's business to boom. Long before his 20th birthday the dyslexic boy, who school teachers had said was destined to fail, was wearing designer clothing, driving executive-class cars and enjoying regular foreign holidays.

Still a teenager at the time of Malcolm's death, Ricky had found it hard to come to terms with and so joined in with the name-calling and idle threats that many who knew Malcolm were making. The Trettons informed the police but said that they did not feel intimidated by the calls at any time. However, because of the sheer number being made, they had become irritating and they wanted the calls stopped. The Trettons' solicitor wrote to Ricky and two females warning them that if their campaign of harassment did not stop, further action would be taken. As soon as the letters landed on Ricky and the females' doormats, the nuisance calls stopped. That was, until Ricky had a chance meeting with Lydia at HMP Chelmsford.

Lydia was there visiting Terry, and Ricky had been visiting a friend. What was later described by the police as 'a bit of a slanging match' took place between the pair and Ricky was arrested under Section 5 of the Public Order Act. When he later appeared in court, he was fined the princely sum of £90 and ordered to pay £150 costs. Terry Watkins was later to claim that the slanging match was, in fact, something far more sinister.

'My wife came to see me in prison just before my trial,' he said. 'She was upset because she had just seen Ricky Percival. He made threats that he was going to shoot my family, including my little girl Laura, who was just four years of age.'

Watkins was, of course, stating something that he had not personally heard and so his account of the incident cannot be given credence. True or false, there was undeniably a growing feeling of intense hostility towards Terry and his family in the Southend area.

Having shed crocodile tears for his former friend on his ex-girlfriend's shoulder and cared attentively for her emotional needs, Alvin had successfully managed to convince Clair to rekindle their teenage romance. The couple did not conduct their relationship openly, but Malcolm's family are in no doubt whatsoever that they had become an item once more, long before Malcolm had been laid to rest. Regardless of the exact timescale, Alvin's partner Barbara learned of his infidelity and asked him to leave her home within weeks of Malcolm's funeral. Within the hour, Alvin had packed his belongings into a suitcase and unpacked them again at the flat Clair had shared with Malcolm.

The anger generated by the untimely death of Malcolm was not going unnoticed by Essex police. In an effort to calm the situation and reassure the Tretton family that they would be unharmed, the police agreed to install personal panic alarms in their home. These alarms, when activated, would have an armed police response unit racing to their location within minutes.

In March 1999, 54-year-old Terry Watkins appeared before

Chelmsford Crown Court charged with the murder of Malcolm Walsh. He pleaded 'not guilty', but after a two-week trial he was convicted of an alternative charge of manslaughter and sentenced to life imprisonment. Manslaughter generally attracts a lighter sentence than one of murder, but in Terry's case the life sentence was imposed after the judge heard that he had been jailed in 1986 by the same court for two offences of wounding with intent. He had forced his way into an ex-girlfriend's home and stabbed both her and her new partner.

Unlike my reaction to the news concerning the demise of Tate, Tucker and Rolfe I had been devastated when I heard that Malcolm had been murdered. He had been a good friend to me. I didn't attend his funeral; I was advised by members of his family that the police were looking for me for the robbery Malcolm and I had allegedly committed near the Lakeside shopping centre. When Essex police had pulled me in over the Rettendon murders, Dorset police had sent me a letter stating that they were not going to take any further action against me for the garage burglary. That was it. I thought that I was trouble free and I could get on with my life, but it was clearly not to be. I didn't want to disrupt my friend's funeral by having police officers haul me out of the church, so I agreed to stay away. I did go to Malcolm's grave once all of the other mourners had left. My feelings as I stood over his grave are personal and I will not, therefore, commit them to paper. All I will say is that I am proud to have called Malcolm my friend.

Three days after Malcolm died, my brother-in-law Steven lost his fight against cancer. Malcolm had been 50 per cent correct when he had said that Steven would outlive us both. Steven's death was tragic. I don't wish to appear disrespectful, but it was more so than Malcolm's in my opinion because the guy never hurt or bothered anybody in his life, yet he was still taken in his prime. It's hard to understand this life sometimes.

Despite being happy living with Rhiannon on the south coast, Essex was never far from my thoughts and I often toyed with the idea of returning home. The gruesome threesome were dead and so I had no fear of reprisals for shooting Tate or for trying to murder Tucker and Rolfe. They thought they had friends but apart from

Leach blowing hot air and talking about avenging their deaths, nobody but their families really gave a fuck about them. The only person I feared in Essex was myself; I knew that if I returned there I would get into trouble. Then again, I was hardly involved in missionary work on the south coast.

I am not sure how I knew but one evening, while talking to my father on the phone, I just sensed that something was wrong.

'What's the matter with you, Dad?' I asked. Laughing, my father dismissed my question as paranoia. 'Don't fuck about, Dad. I know something's wrong,' I said.

'Don't worry. I am going to be OK. The doctors have told me that I have cancer of the throat,' my father replied.

I put the phone down, kissed Rhiannon goodbye, packed my bag and immediately headed home to Essex.

My father had recently moved into a new house and so initially there was plenty for me to get on with, such as decorating and unpacking boxes. But as the weeks and months passed and the workload eased, I found that I got under my father's feet and inevitably we began to argue. Perhaps my father and I were subconsciously angry and upset about his condition, I really don't know, but we rowed so often I thought it best that I move out. I didn't go far. Malcolm's widow, Bernadette, lived locally and she suggested that I move in with her. Not in the biblical sense, of course; I had been a close friend of Malcolm's. Bernadette had lost him in unimaginable circumstances and my presence somehow brought her comfort.

One night I was in Yates' bar, in Southend, when I saw my ex-cell mate Tony walking down the stairs. Before he could cover his face and fade into the crowd I had jumped up from my seat and accosted him. I could sense that he was a little dubious about meeting me again; the scars of the mental torture I had inflicted upon him had clearly not healed.

'I don't mind having a beer with you, Nipper, but for fuck's sake, behave,' he pleaded.

As the night wore on and the beer flowed, Tony relaxed and by the end of it he was laughing and suggesting that we go into partnership together.

'Doing what?' I enquired.

'Pills, coke and weed. We can sell it by the shed load in this town,' Tony replied.

I must admit that I was not initially keen on the idea; I had witnessed first-hand the many downsides of the drug trade. Tate, Tucker and Rolfe's involvement in drugs had led to them ending up as corpses on mortuary slabs long before their mothers could have ever imagined. I didn't relish following suit, but surely I was not like them? Surely I could control the drugs instead of them controlling me? I told Tony that I would take up his offer but I wanted to keep it local, among friends. Unlike my predecessors, I did not suffer delusions of power and grandeur. If people could replicate the demand for drugs in any business, they would all be millionaires and retiring in their early 30s.

I started selling a few pills to people that I knew and, before too long, my phone was on meltdown.

'Sell me ten pills. No, better make that twenty just in case I don't see you next week.'

'I know you have got pills for sale, but can you get me any cocaine?'

Like a house on fire our business blazed its way across Southend. People planning to go out for the evening were ringing me all day asking for drugs. Throughout the night, I was in bars and nightclubs meeting the demand of revellers. Then when the pubs and nightclubs closed, those who wanted to carry on partying were ringing me in the early hours of the morning, demanding drugs. I struggled to get any sleep and so I began snorting the odd line of cocaine in order to give me that little boost of energy that I thought I needed. Before I knew it, the substantial profit that I was making was being hoovered up my nose.

I walked out of Bernadette's house one day and Alvin happened to be leaving his brother's home at the same time (Alvin's brother lived next door). I said 'hello', but I could tell by the expression on his face that he was not interested in exchanging pleasantries.

'What's wrong? You look like somebody has given you the hump,' I said.

'Don't worry about people giving me the hump. They are going to fucking regret it tonight,' Alvin replied as he marched past me.

Alvin crossed the road to a car and began talking to the driver, a man named Dean Boshell, who I knew sold drugs on Alvin's behalf. The pair were in deep conversation but when I walked within earshot they both stopped.

'What is wrong with you?' I asked Alvin.

'It's a year today since Malcolm was murdered and I've been told that the Trettons are having a party to celebrate. I intend to make sure that their party gets going with a bang,' Alvin replied.

I know that it is wrong to talk ill of people but I also know that it is pointless trying to paint a pretty picture if you're not in possession of the necessary materials. Life was never kind to Dean Boshell, but then again I can't recall him doing himself any favours. Boshell's father was an alcoholic bully who beat his mother while he was still in her womb. Six hours after his birth, Boshell's father, who was barely able to stand through drink, took him out into the street in a pushchair. It was a cold, foggy day and the infant became so distressed that a midwife had to be called because he had difficulty breathing. Boshell's mother divorced her husband shortly afterwards and a restraining order was imposed by the court, which prevented him from having any contact with Mrs Boshell and her child.

Nobody can say for certain why Boshell grew up to be the unscrupulous man that he was. Some say he misbehaved because he craved attention. Others think he had no love for anybody and so he didn't care whom his actions hurt. What cannot be disputed is that Boshell had no morals; he was a man who stole from his own mother and brother and betrayed everybody that he met, without exception. By the time he had reached his 13th birthday his mother decided that she could not cope with his bad behaviour any more. Social Services were contacted and Boshell was placed in the care of the local authority. Boshell returned home after just two months, but his behaviour had deteriorated rather than improved, and he continued committing petty crime, which in the main involved the theft of motor vehicles.

When Boshell upset a gang of local hoodlums, he told his mother that he was going to leave Basildon and start his life anew. By chance, a friend of Mrs Boshell's had recently told her that he and his partner were moving to Leeds to run a pub. When Mrs Boshell mentioned the problems that her son was having, the couple agreed to let him move with them. They assured Mrs Boshell that they would teach her wayward son all there was to know about the pub trade if he worked for them in return. Two short weeks after moving to Leeds, Boshell was taken into protective custody by the child protection unit after his mother's friend had tried to strangle him. The man and his partner had been arguing and, rather foolishly, Boshell had tried to intervene.

Rather than return to Basildon to face the hoodlums who had been baying for his blood, Boshell informed Social Services that he wished to remain in West Yorkshire. A week later, Boshell was placed in a foster home. After leaving care, Boshell once more immersed himself in criminality, stealing cars, committing burglaries and any other unsavoury act that helped to line his pockets. Inevitably, he was caught and after accumulating 22 convictions for a variety of offences he was sentenced to 15 months' imprisonment.

After being released from this sentence, Boshell returned to Basildon to live with his mother. Understandably, she wanted to believe that her son had changed and welcomed him into her home. As soon as her back was turned, he stole and sold her brand-new stack-system stereo, which was still in the box. Despite his mother's pleas Boshell refused to return the stereo and so she called the police. Boshell was charged and convicted of the theft and when he appeared at Basildon Crown Court for sentencing he was given a meagre financial penalty. A few months later, Boshell called at his mother's home on the pretext of visiting her and stole a cheque from his brother's cheque book. After forging his brother's signature Boshell withdrew £400 from the account. When the theft came to light, Mrs Boshell confronted her son and a terrible argument ensued. Mrs Boshell shouted at her son for what he had done and uttered the last words that she was ever going to say to him, 'Piss off, Dean. I want nothing more to do with you and, as far as I am concerned, you are not my son.'

Prison became an occupational hazard rather than a punishment for Boshell. He had far more like-minded friends behind bars than he ever had out on the street. He thought of himself as a wide boy, a player and a bit of a gangster. He loved rap music and in particular the artist Eminem. Boshell would often talk to his associates using slang that he heard in songs. He thought that it made him appear cool. Everybody else thought that he sounded ridiculous.

While serving one prison sentence at HMP Chelmsford Boshell found himself in a cell next door to Damon Alvin. Boshell was impressed with the confident, smooth-talking hard man that had become his neighbour. Alvin appeared to be everything that Boshell had dreamed of being one day. As soon as Alvin realised that Boshell admired and looked up to him, he decided to exploit him. At first, Alvin presented himself as an extremely friendly and helpful man; he would read and write letters for Boshell and supply him with any contraband that he required. Once Boshell was securely hooked, he asked Alvin if he could do anything for him in return and, within a few days, he was selling drugs on his hero's behalf.

Another resident at this establishment who befriended Boshell was 45-year-old Christopher Wheatley. He had been sentenced to seven years' imprisonment after police had raided his flat and found 30 grammes of cocaine, 3 grammes of amphetamine, 357 Ecstasy pills and £950 in cash. A further 170 grammes of cocaine were discovered hidden under the seat of his car. The drugs had an estimated street value of between £10,000 and £17,000. Wheatley's solicitor told the court that he had become addicted to drugs after losing his job as a doorman. Five years earlier, Wheatley had been a prominent member of Tony Tucker's Essex Boys firm. When a more 'useful' individual, named Patrick Tate, was released from prison in 1993, Tucker disposed of Wheatley and replaced him with Tate.

The drugs that Wheatley had once sold with ease and relative safety, through his job as head bouncer at one of Tucker's clubs in Southend, suddenly became a commodity he could only offload at great risk. A steady stream of punters knocking on Wheatley's door soon came to the attention of the police and, after a short period of surveillance, they raided his home and caught him red-handed. While in prison, Wheatley continued to deal in drugs and one of the men he employed to distribute them was Dean Boshell. An unlikely friendship developed between the two and Wheatley, a competent and powerful athlete, introduced Boshell to the world of bodybuilding, supplements and steroids.

With his ever-expanding frame and ego, coupled with his new gangster friends, Wheatley and Alvin, Boshell really believed that he had finally fulfilled his dream and become one of the big boys. He told fellow inmates that when he was released he was going to set up a drug-dealing empire and live lavishly off his ill-gotten gains. When the duo were released from prison, Alvin and his new sidekick Boshell immersed themselves in a criminal partnership. Everywhere that Alvin went, Boshell would either be at his side or not too far behind. In the pubs and clubs around Southend, Alvin introduced Boshell as his mate but Boshell would tell people that they were, in fact, brothers. It was Alvin who introduced Ricky Percival to Boshell around this time.

Percival told me that he thought Boshell was a ponce who couldn't keep his dick in his trousers, that he would never buy a drink and that he would not hesitate to sleep with any female so long as she had a purse and a pulse.

Apart from seeing each other occasionally in our local pub, the Woodcutters Arms, there was no other contact between Boshell and Percival during this period, and nobody has ever come forward to dispute that fact.

As the first anniversary of Malcolm Walsh's killing had drawn near, the raw emotion that we all felt and the threats against the Tretton brothers and their family intensified. Two weeks before the anniversary of Malcolm's death, Percival and a few friends had gone on holiday to Cyprus. Dealing with the death of a friend as a teenager is difficult enough, but when that friend has been murdered the entire grieving process is intensified tenfold. Percival had added to his own burden by doing all that he could to help and comfort Malcolm's brother and three sisters. Pamela Walsh had taken Malcolm's death particularly hard, so much so she had been prescribed antidepressants by her GP. Her weight plummeted and her general health became a concern for all those that knew her. Percival had begun visiting Pamela regularly in the hope that he could help her come to terms with her loss. Before he departed for Cyprus, he made a promise to visit Pamela as soon as he returned.

While Percival was enjoying his much-deserved break, a man

who I shall call Gary Baron arrived at Alvin's home and said that he was looking for Dean Boshell.

Describing the incident several years after the event, Alvin said, 'He asked me if he could leave something with me to give to Boshell. I asked him what it was and he answered by opening the boot of his car. I looked in and saw a shotgun wrapped in a jumper. I opened up the boot of my car, he picked up the shotgun and put it in my vehicle. I said to him that I would give it to Boshell when I saw him. Because of all the threats that had been made about attacking the Trettons, I knew what it was going to be used for. Two hours later, Boshell turned up at my house and I told him that Gary Baron had left something in the boot of my car for him. Boshell took my keys, went outside, transferred the shotgun from my car to his and drove home. Five minutes later he reappeared and gave me back my keys.'

On the anniversary of Malcolm Walsh's death, Alvin and Boshell were in the Woodcutters Arms in Leigh-on-Sea. Ricky Percival was also present and telling the bar staff about the holiday in Cyprus from which he had just returned. Alvin and Percival didn't speak that night because Alvin appeared to be preoccupied with 'a problem' that he did not wish to discuss. He was drinking heavily and most people in the pub just thought that he was drowning his sorrows thinking about Malcolm.

At closing time, Alvin and Boshell left the pub and got into a stolen white Vauxhall and drove to a park on the opposite side of which stood the Trettons' family home. After sitting in the car talking for approximately twenty minutes, the two men got out of the vehicle and walked across the park. Both were wearing balaclavas and were armed with shotguns. As they crept up to the Tretton home there was little sign of life but they noticed that a neighbour and close family friend was having a party. Alvin walked to the rear of the neighbour's property to see if he could see who was in the lounge. Peering through the window he saw members of the Tretton family were present and so he went back to the front of the house to inform Boshell.

'Are there any kids in the house?' Boshell asked.

Alvin, who knew the family, replied, 'There are, but it's late and they will be in bed, so don't worry about it.'

Alvin was standing motionless outside the premises and Boshell asked him what he intended doing. Alvin replied that he was waiting for the people to leave. Getting agitated, Alvin began walking from the front of the house to the back trying to see through the windows to establish who was where and doing what. As he did this, he put his shotgun down by a white picket fence. Somebody must have walked into the kitchen because suddenly the light came on. The open kitchen door amplified the sound of music and muffled the voices that were coming from the lounge inside the house. Alvin told Boshell that he thought that it was pretty lively inside. Cold and tired, Boshell had told Alvin that it was late, he had been waiting for ages, nothing was happening, so he was going home.

Alvin replied, 'No, just wait, just wait. I am going to do it. I am going to do it.'

Five minutes later he picked up the shotgun, pulled his balaclava down over his face, ran up and kicked open the front door. The revellers were stunned into silence by the almighty bang as the door frame splintered.

Raymond Tretton jumped to his feet and shouted, 'What the fuck was that?'

Before anybody could answer the lounge door was flung open and balaclava-clad Alvin and Boshell stood before the terrified room full of people, brandishing shotguns. Raymond looked at the gunman nearest to him and, through holes that had been crudely cut in the balaclava, he could see that he was staring straight back at him. The sound of the shotguns' loading mechanisms struck terror in Raymond's heart, but the only words that he managed to mutter were, 'Oh shit.'

The blast that followed threw Raymond's body across the room and into a wall. His left hand, which he had raised in an attempt to protect his face, was shredded and he also suffered pellet wounds to his head, chest and arm. Both Alvin and Boshell unleashed a salvo of shots at their screaming victims. As they did so, Raymond ran into the back garden via the patio doors. Once outside he attempted to grip the garden fence in an attempt to climb over it and escape, but as he did so he called out in pain. Looking down at his hand he saw that he had lost the ring and middle fingers and was bleeding profusely. In shock and excruciating pain, Raymond managed to drag himself over the fence and two further fences before coming to rest on the roof of his sister's garden shed. After catching his breath, he rolled off the roof and lay gasping for air in his sister's garden, wondering what to do next.

Stuart Tretton, who had been relaxing in an armchair when the gunmen had burst in, had also leapt to his feet. Initially, he had been tempted to laugh at the men wearing balaclavas because he thought they were friends of his playing some sort of sick joke. But when the barrel of a shotgun was aimed at his face, Stuart realised in an instant that he was in grave danger. As he raised his hands instinctively to shield his face and head, the gunman laughed and slowly squeezed the trigger. The deafening bang caused Stuart to spring from his seat and follow Raymond out of the patio doors and into the garden where he climbed over a fence to reach his mother's home. Rather than knock at her back door, Stuart began to kick it repeatedly until it eventually burst open. As he staggered up the stairs and into his mother's bedroom Stuart began to shout, 'Help me, Mum, help me. I'm going to die.'

His mother sat up in bed terrified, she could see that her son's hand was hanging from his arm by a thin, shredded piece of flesh and skin and he was losing a lot of blood. He also had a gaping shotgun wound in his chest, which she later learned had punctured his lung. As his mother raced downstairs to call the emergency services, Stuart called out in pain and begged for help.

When his mother reached the foot of the stairs, Raymond entered the hallway via the back door and began shouting, 'Look what they have done to me. Look what they have done.' Drenched in his own blood, his face totally expressionless, Raymond suddenly fell silent as if in shock, turned and walked away.

Jenny Dickinson had looked at her fellow revellers in disbelief when she had heard the front door being kicked open by the gunmen. Curled up in the foetal position and screaming at the top of her voice, Jenny had watched in absolute horror as Raymond and then Stuart were blasted. As the wounded men made good their escape, one of the balaclava-clad gunmen had turned and pointed the smoking barrel of his gun at Christine Tretton, who was sitting next to Jenny. In an act of heroism, Jenny grabbed hold of

Christine's shoulder and pulled her towards her. The gunman fired and the shot punched a huge hole in the top of the settee where moments earlier Christine's head had been. A split second later, there came another deafening explosion. As Jenny leapt to her feet to escape certain death she felt excruciating pain and realised that the some of the lead shot that had been aimed at Christine had struck her. In a blind panic Jenny ran to her nearby home, where her ex-partner was babysitting their children. When she arrived, she saw that part of her left hand was missing and blood was gushing out of the wound. Jenny's daughter attempted to stem the flow of the blood and calm her while they awaited the arrival of the emergency services.

Back at the scene of the carnage, Christine had stopped shaking and was sitting zombie-like on the settee. Blood was splashed across all of the walls and lumps of human skin and flesh were scattered around the floor. A spray of shotgun pellets arced across the lounge wall and large chunks of the seats where the victims had been sitting were missing. Getting slowly to her feet, Christine followed the trails of blood out of the patio doors and into the garden. Dazed and confused, Christine's next clear memory is of running into her sister Lydia's bedroom and screaming, 'We have been shot. We have been shot.' Christine lifted her sweatshirt, which was soaked in blood and saw that she had been hit in the shoulder. Fearing she might die, Christine became hysterical, begging her sister to activate the panic alarm that had been installed in her home following the nuisance calls.

'Calm down. Calm down,' Lydia kept saying as she tried to reassure those that had been wounded.

Locksley Close was soon filled with the sound of wailing sirens and blue flashing lights, which intermittently illuminated the horrified faces of neighbours and other local residents. Exercising caution, the police cordoned off the street and refused to allow anybody near the scene of the house where the bloodbath had occurred. When a fleet of ambulances arrived to take the wounded away they, too, were prevented from entering the police cordon and so the injured were forced to walk up the street in order to get medical assistance. When a police officer noticed the severity of the victims' gunshot wounds, he asked a friend of the Tretton family, who lived nearby, to return to the scene of the incident to search for hands and fingers that had been shot off.

After leaving the carnage that they had created Alvin and Boshell had run back across the park towards the stolen car. As soon as they were both in, Boshell had started up the vehicle and sped away. Alvin had his shotgun with him in the front seat and was trying to unblock it. He told Boshell that they would need it in case they got pulled over. He didn't say that he was going to shoot the police if they were stopped, but Boshell was in no doubt that was exactly what he was implying. Boshell pleaded with him to put the weapon down because it was clearly visible and he was trying to drive. Laughing, Alvin had said that he had enjoyed shooting the Tretton brothers.

'I just stood at the lounge door and opened fire; the first person I shot hit the back wall. I then tried to shoot one of them in the chest and they raised their hand to stop me.'

Alvin had found this particularly amusing. He continued boasting and said that one of the people they had shot on the settee had pulled a girl on top of himself for protection. Alvin told Boshell that he had shot this particular person in the face.

Fearing things had got out of hand and he was in above his depth, Boshell had said, 'I thought you were just going to do them in the legs?'

Alvin looked at Boshell with a smirk and replied, 'Fuck them.'

It was clear to Boshell that Alvin was really hyped up, excited almost, so he concentrated on the road ahead and said no more. When they arrived in Shoeburyness, Boshell parked in a road called Burgess Close, near Pamela Walsh's house.

As he did so, Alvin said, 'There's a drain there. Ditch your gun.' Boshell got the gun out of the car, walked to the back of the vehicle and dropped the weapon down the drain.

Unbeknown to Alvin and Boshell, a man was watching them from his bedroom window. Leonard Spencer, a retired gentleman whose home was on the corner of Burgess Close, had been awoken in the early hours of the morning by loud voices and the sound of car doors slamming. Thinking that this disturbance at such an unsociable hour was somewhat suspicious, Leonard had got out of bed and opened his window. Looking to his right he saw a Vauxhall Belmont and two men, who were running from it. After these men had run a short distance, one of them had stopped and returned to the car. Leonard quite rightly assumed that the vehicle was stolen and that the man had returned to it to retrieve something that he had forgotten. After getting dressed, Leonard made his way downstairs and then out into the street to inspect the vehicle. The doors were not locked and inside Leonard could see that audio tapes and a number of coins had been scattered around the footwell. Returning to his home Leonard had telephoned the police who he recalls 'didn't seem interested'. Later that morning, when the police realised the possible significance of the vehicle, they attended Burgess Close and interviewed Leonard about all that he had seen.

Upon his return from Cyprus, Percival had kept his promise and visited Pamela Walsh at her home in Shoeburyness to check on her well-being. The sight he was greeted with was not pretty; since it was the anniversary of Malcolm's death Pamela had hit rock bottom. Finding Pamela in a terribly emotional state, Percival agreed to sleep over to help her through what was a very traumatic time. He spent the evening talking to Pamela and her children and, when they retired for the night, he made a bed up on the sofa and went to sleep.

Alvin and others concede that it was fairly common practice for those in our circle to borrow one another's cars. Percival worked as a motor mechanic for a local company and as a sideline he would buy second-hand cars, carry out any minor repairs that needed doing and sell them on at a profit. This meant that he often had several vehicles at his disposal; I had often borrowed vehicles from him. Percival has since told me that on the day of the Locksley Close shootings Alvin had asked to borrow a car to do 'a bit of work'. Percival had told Alvin that he could have a 4x4 Sierra which he had used to drive to Pamela's house. He was to leave the keys under the foot mat on the driver's side because he had no idea what time Alvin was going to collect the car, and if it was going to be late, he didn't want Alvin to disturb Pamela or her children.

After talking to Alvin, Percival had telephoned his friend Pete Edwards to ask him if he would give him a lift home the following morning because he knew that he would be going his way. In the early hours, Percival was woken by somebody hammering on Pamela's door. Fearing Pamela and her children would be disturbed, Percival opened the door and saw Alvin standing before him. He realised that he had forgotten to leave the keys to his car under the mat as arranged. Alvin immediately barged his way into Pamela's house and when Percival looked outside to see what, if anything, was causing him to be in such an apparent agitated state, he saw two men who appeared to be searching his car. He assumed that they were looking for the keys that he had forgotten to leave under the mat.

Percival asked Alvin what was going on and he replied, 'If you don't know, you can't be accused of any wrongdoing. Keep your mouth shut and you will be all right.'

Alvin demanded the car keys, which Percival retrieved from inside one of his training shoes and then Alvin left. That morning, as arranged, Pete Edwards picked Percival up from Pamela's house and dropped him off near his home.

At 1010 hrs that morning, a number of officers from Essex Police Force Support Unit set up a roadblock to seal off the road in which Percival lived. Satisfied that all exits and entrances were secured, PC Noel O'Hara knocked on Percival's front door and when he answered it he was formally arrested on suspicion of attempted murder. Only a few hours had elapsed since the blood-letting orgy in Locksley Close, and one would imagine that Percival and his clothing would have been a forensic scientist's paradise. The shootings were common knowledge by this time as BBC Essex Radio had broadcast details of the incident on its 1000 hrs news bulletin. Despite the shootings only happening a few hours earlier, the report was extremely accurate and detailed.

The newsreader said that a woman and two men had been shot and seriously injured by two masked gunmen in the early hours of the morning at a house in Locksley Close, Southend. An update in the following news bulletin stated that the masked gunmen were, in fact, wearing balaclavas. After all the talk and all the threats that had been made about avenging Malcolm Walsh's death, and the fact that the Trettons lived in Locksley Close, Percival didn't have to be a super sleuth to work out that the shootings he had heard about on the radio involved the Tretton family.

He made no reply when arrested by PC O'Hara but when he was being handed over to other officers for transportation to Southend police station he had asked, 'Is this about the Trettons?' One of the officers informed Percival that he was unable to discuss the reason for his arrest, to which Percival replied, 'Are they dead?'

The officer ignored Percival's comments and placed him in a vehicle. As they made their way to Southend, Sergeant Caldwell, who was sitting alongside Percival, asked, 'Are you all right? Are those handcuffs a bit tight?'

Percival replied, 'I'm all right, mate. I have got nothing to worry about.'

The sergeant advised Percival to lean forward in his seat so that he would be more comfortable. When Percival had done this, he said to Sergeant Caldwell, 'What's this all about?'

The officer replied, 'I don't know, we are just the taxi drivers.'

Percival then said, 'I knew that this would happen. How are the Trettons? Trouble is, Malcolm knew so many people. One of your officers had already told me that I would be the first one to be nicked if anything like this happened.'

Sergeant Caldwell reminded Percival that he had been cautioned and therefore anything he said could be used in evidence against him, but Percival didn't appear bothered or guarded.

He asked what the penalty for attempted murder was and when the officer replied, 'Life', Percival said, 'I wouldn't want to be the bloke who did it then. I feel sorry for the bloke who gets caught.'

While Percival was in police custody, officers searching the car that had been dumped outside Leonard Spencer's home in Burgess Close discovered an open bottle of white spirit on the back seat. This information was relayed back to the officers dealing with Percival and they decided that specific forensic tests for traces of white spirit and other materials such as gun residue would be carried out on him. Percival's outer and under clothing was seized, as were various other items from his home, such as a boiler suit and footwear. These were sent to the Forensic Science Service Laboratory for examination. Despite Percival's being arrested within hours of the shootings, not a single shred of forensic evidence linking him to the stolen car, the crime scene or the crime itself was found. After three days of intense questioning, and having been subjected to numerous forensic tests, the police released Percival on bail pending further inquiries.

Percival rang me and told me what had happened to him. We both agreed that it was more than likely that Alvin and Boshell had shot the Trettons, but to us it seemed like justice after Malcolm's murder, not a crime. The weekend after Percival was released we threw a big party for him. Everybody came, including Alvin.

When I asked Alvin about the shootings, he just raised his glass, looked up at the ceiling and shouted at the top of his voice, 'One fucking one, Malcolm, one fucking one!'

I took it that Alvin was telling us that he had settled an outstanding score. Looking at Alvin with a huge deranged grin on his face, I couldn't help but wonder how many more scores he would settle before joining the likes of Tate and Tucker in a graveyard or prison cell. As they had found out, somebody somewhere will always step in and stop the insanity.

CHAPTER NINE

The blood-letting orgy at Locksley Close had a dramatic effect on Percival and all of us that associated with him. He was catapulted overnight from being an 18-year-old petty criminal in the eyes of a few, to being a psychopathic, gun-toting madman in the eyes of many. Foolishly, very foolishly, Percival didn't protest his innocence too loudly, if at all, when rumours of his arrest and assumed guilt began to circulate. He chose instead to let the gossipmongers, and the notoriously inaccurate Southend grapevine, promote the view that he was guilty so that his reputation as a no-nonsense hard man would be enhanced. Percival ended up with a fear factor on the streets of Essex that surpassed Tucker's and Tate's.

While Percival prowled around Southend enjoying his newfound fame, Alvin was worrying himself sick thinking the police were going to unearth evidence that would not only implicate him in the Locksley Close shootings, but his sidekick, gofer and occasional best friend Dean Boshell as well.

Shortly after Percival had been released on bail, Alvin and Boshell returned to Burgess Close to recover the shotgun that had been dropped down the drain. Alvin had kept the shotgun that he had used because he had paid out a considerable fee for it and was too tight to do the sensible thing and hide it or otherwise dispose of it. Alvin told me that he and Boshell had parked some distance from Burgess Close when they returned, because they feared that the police may already have found the gun and put the area under surveillance. Not wanting to put himself at risk, Alvin sent his faithful gofer to retrieve it. Boshell seemed to be taking his time, so when Alvin was confident that they were not being watched, he walked up the road to join him.

Boshell told Alvin that he had taken so much time because he was unable to lift the drain cover alone. Together the two men raised and removed the heavy iron cover and then Alvin put his arm in the drain to see if he could feel the gun beneath the water. Still unable to locate the weapon, Alvin told Boshell that the police had probably retrieved it at the same time that they had found the stolen vehicle.

I don't know how, but Boshell later found out that the stolen car that he had driven to and from the shootings had been returned to its owner. Boshell told Alvin and together they decided that they were going to burn the vehicle just in case the police decided to fingerprint it at a later date. I personally couldn't see the point. If the car had been returned to its owner, it would have already been fingerprinted. Regardless, a few days later the car was fire-bombed outside its owner's house. Alvin advised Boshell that if the police had already lifted his fingerprints from the car and he was arrested, he would have to say that he had attempted to steal the vehicle before the shootings had occurred but failed.

Despite Boshell's futile attempts to destroy evidence that could link him to the shootings, he was arrested a few weeks later for the theft of the vehicle. The police had matched his fingerprints to a partial fingerprint they had found on the steering column prior to the car being burned. As soon as Boshell was bailed by the police, Alvin quizzed him about his time in custody. Had the police questioned him about the shootings? Had they found the gun? And had they asked him about Alvin? Boshell denied being questioned about the Tretton shootings, which Alvin found very suspicious. Alvin told me that he didn't believe Boshell and feared that he may have given information about him to the police.

'I don't even know for sure if he was arrested or if he is just fucking storytelling. You can never tell with him. He's always talking gangster shit,' Alvin said.

A month after the shootings, Alvin was left in no doubt that Boshell had been arrested because, on this occasion, he was handcuffed alongside him when police took him into custody. The arrest had nothing to do with the Locksley Close shootings; Boshell and Alvin had been caught breaking into Jewson's, the builder's merchants. Boshell knew that he had no chance of evading justice this time because he and Alvin had been caught red-handed by the police. It was equally apparent to him that no judge was going to give him anything other than a custodial sentence after taking into account his habitual offending.

Previously, Boshell would have accepted his fate and served his time but recently he had met a girl that he hoped he could settle down with and start a family. Between 1996 and 1998, Boshell had been rewarded by the courts with discounted sentences for snippets of information that he had given to the police about his criminal associates. Desperate to avoid losing his girlfriend, Boshell asked the officers involved in the Jewson's case if he could once more trade information for a reduced sentence. No promises were made, but Boshell was told that any assistance he did offer would be made known to the judge who was going to sentence him.

This bargaining process by criminals with police is a fairly common practice, but anybody who agrees to become an informant has to adhere to strict rules that try to ensure that the information given is genuine and the informant is not encouraging others to commit crime, about which he can then tell the police. Documentation generated by the police at the time describes Boshell as being a 'previously untried source and the authenticity of any information he may give should be doubted'. Rules regarding informants had changed since Boshell had first offered evidence to the police in 1996. All informants now had to be registered, which involved them meeting a senior police officer, having the terms and conditions explained to them and then signing the agreement if deemed suitable.

The officer who dealt with Boshell wrote in his notes: 'The source was told in no uncertain terms that he must tell us everything in relation to crime. He was told that if he was arrested then the fact that he was an informant would not assist him in any way. He was told that there could be, in exceptional circumstances, a situation where he could have a minimal involvement in a crime, but only after he has been given authorisation by us and not before.'

Rules, regulations and the law had never meant much, if anything, to Boshell. He considered himself to be one of life's players, the type of guy who would agree to go through the motions of any agreed scenario so long as it was ultimately beneficial to him. Nobody can deny that some of the information that Boshell went on to give to the police proved to be reasonably accurate. Likewise, nobody can deny that some of the information proved to be entirely false. The problem that exists, in the here and now, is that nobody can say with any certainty which evidence falls into which category.

In order to try and protect Boshell's identity, the police gave him the pseudonym Michael Bridges. Giving informants a false name is standard police practice designed to ensure that their informant's true identity does not become known to their criminal associates. All paperwork, telephone calls and conversations with, and regarding, the informant only ever refer to the informant's pseudonym to prevent them from being identified.

It was clear from the outset that Boshell was never going to give the police his full co-operation as promised. Instead, he decided to cherry-pick crimes that he could tempt the police with, and play some bizarre game that he believed would result in the police needing him more than he needed them. Once Boshell believed he had taken the upper hand, he could then negotiate a better deal when he came to be sentenced. The criminal company that Boshell kept meant that he didn't just have a good hand of cards to play the police with, he had an entire pack. Testing the water, rather than diving in head first, Boshell initially offered the police details of fairly minor crimes and criminals that they were already aware of. He told them that a man was selling stolen tax discs; another, counterfeit designer clothing; and he told them the identity and address of the person who stored Alvin's stolen goods for him.

Boshell's information was received with thanks, but little enthusiasm. The police were told about these sorts of matters more often than time, and their limited resources, permitted them to prosecute people for committing them. Sensing that Boshell was holding back on far more serious criminal activities, his police handler felt the need to remind him 'in no uncertain terms' that he had to tell them everything he knew in relation to crime if he wished to continue being an informant. Keen to appear compliant, within a month Boshell had begun telling the police about a plan of Alvin's to rob a drug dealer from Basildon using guns. He also mentioned rather vague details about the stolen vehicle used in the 'Locksley Close shootings'.

Finally, the police appeared to be sitting up and listening. When asked what else he knew about the Locksley Close incident, Boshell said that Alvin had told him that he could lay his hands on cyanide and hand grenades. Asked what Alvin intended doing with such lethal weapons, Boshell said that Alvin had bragged, 'The Trettons could end up getting a syringe full of cyanide, injected into a milk bottle on their doorstep, or a hand grenade thrown through their letterbox.'

Only Boshell knows why he decided to discuss aspects of the Locksley Close shootings with the police. It was a crime that he had been actively involved in. Although he never went so far as to implicate himself in any serious wrongdoing, Boshell must have known that if the police did arrest Alvin there was a possibility that he would talk about his involvement. As the date for Boshell to appear in court approached, he became noticeably depressed and increasingly desperate. Boshell was painfully aware that if he was given a lengthy prison sentence he would lose his girlfriend and all that the relationship promised. His darkest secrets could, he realised, become his guiding light. If Boshell told the police everything he knew, maybe, just maybe he could escape a custodial sentence and set up home with his girlfriend and live happily ever after.

Seven weeks before Boshell was due to appear at Southend Crown Court for sentencing, he concocted a story for the police that was a mixture of truth and lies about the Locksley Close shootings. He said that he had been the driver of the car on the night of the shootings and his passengers, Alvin and Percival, had been in possession of a double-barrelled shotgun. The inclusion of Percival was an obvious choice for Boshell to make, because most people in the area believed that Percival was guilty, or at least involved, because he had been arrested for the shootings. Boshell told the police that they had been 'spooked' by a police car and 'his bottle had gone', so they had abandoned the vehicle.

'Later the same evening,' Boshell said, 'Alvin asked me to drive to the scene of the shootings, but I refused to do so. Alvin had called me a cunt for not doing as he had asked, but the following day he acted as though nothing had happened.'

The police did their best to convince Boshell to tell them more about the shootings but every time he agreed to discuss the incident, his story seemed to change. On one occasion, he said that Percival and 'a doorman named Dave' were responsible but nobody had heard of 'Doorman Dave'. Beginning to doubt the authenticity of Boshell's information, the police reminded him that he had agreed to be truthful with them at all times. In an effort to prove to them that he was being honest, Boshell offered to take the police to the drain where the shotgun used in the shootings had been dumped. Boshell knew that the gun was not, in fact, there because he had already searched the drain for it with Alvin. Regardless, Boshell needed to prove that he was a trustworthy informant and so decided to act out his part. When Boshell accompanied the police to the drain, he feigned surprise that it was no longer there.

The police had also known that the gun was not in the drain because they had recovered it shortly after finding the stolen car nearby. They had just wanted to test Boshell's knowledge of the crime and ensure that he was telling them the truth. Unwittingly, the police had failed miserably with the second half of their objective. Boshell was now considered to be truthful, but in reality he had only lured the police into trusting him with half-truths. He had shown them where the gun had been, but he hadn't told them that he knew it had already been taken.

The general public are, in the main, of the opinion that if the police know who committed a crime they should lock them up. Fortunately or otherwise, depending on which side of the fence you live your life, the police are not supposed to be able to do this. Thinking that they know who committed a crime is a world away from proving that somebody is guilty. That is why the police are duty-bound to painstakingly gather all the available evidence before charging their suspect and presenting everything to the courts, so that the guilt or innocence of the accused can be ascertained by a jury. Owing to forensic tests and the time it takes to gather and evaluate evidence, it can be months before any arrests are made in a major investigation.

The police had already arrested Percival for the shootings and so arresting him again would have been pointless because Boshell's information was not only contradictory, it was also made up of the same gossip that every villain in Essex had been repeating since the incident first happened. Not wishing to dismiss Boshell's information out of hand, the police told him that they needed to know more details about the incident in Locksley Close and tasked him to find out all that he could. Boshell's court date was now only a few weeks away and his chances of securing a reduced sentence were looking increasingly slim. He had taken the information regarding the shootings as far as he dared. So, in a last-ditch attempt to win favour, Boshell told his handler that the robbery of a drug dealer that Alvin had been talking about for some time was going to take place soon. When asked to find out who was going to be robbed, when and where, Boshell said that he had not managed to discuss the job in any detail with Alvin because he was working away from home in Kent. However, he would be returning shortly.

Boshell told his handler at their next meeting that he had spoken to Alvin and he had been asked to steal a car. Alvin said that he needed a vehicle for use in the robbery and was prepared to pay Boshell between £150 and £300 for stealing one. Boshell claimed that Alvin, Percival and I would be the three carrying out the job and we would be armed with two handguns. The reason that we were going to be armed, according to Boshell, was that our intended target received regular visits from 'trigger-happy niggers'.

I must admit I did laugh when I learned of Boshell's treachery and the lies he told about us all several years later. 'Trigger-happy niggers' sounded like a line out of one of the gangster rap songs he was always trying to sing. I have lived in and around the Southend area all of my life and although I admit it can get lively at times, I haven't encountered the 'trigger-happy' set just yet. Boshell told the police that Alvin and Percival trusted each other '110 per cent', but neither completely trusted me. According to Boshell, this was because they knew that I was 'capable of anything after shooting Pat Tate'. Boshell had recently been disqualified from driving, and so was told by his handler that if Alvin asked him to drive, he was to give an excuse for not being able to do so. However, after a risk assessment of the planned crime, of those allegedly involved and Boshell's driving ban, Boshell's handler was instructed by a senior officer to provide him with a vehicle for use in the robbery.

Boshell was offered an estate car, which he refused, but he did accept a Mondeo after explaining when he did steal cars they were usually Fords. The police plan was that when the would-be robbers had reached the busy A127 arterial road, which runs between Southend and Basildon, an armed response unit would stop the car on the pretence of searching for drugs and the occupants would be arrested. Over the next few days, Boshell was constantly on the phone to his handler giving excuse after excuse about why the robbery hadn't yet taken place. He said that he had visited Alvin's home and saw that Alvin's car had broken down. Alvin had mentioned repairing it later that day, but he had failed to mention the robbery. On another day, Boshell claimed that Alvin's partner had decided against going out and so Alvin had remained at home with her. Running out of excuses, Boshell eventually said that he had waited all evening for a call about the robbery from Alvin, but he had heard nothing. If Boshell was being honest with the police, the possibility of the robbery ever taking place appeared to hinge on the availability of Alvin, rather than me or Percival. For reasons never explained by Boshell, the so-called robbery did not take place. When Alvin was asked about this robbery many years later, he of course blamed me and Percival for being the driving force behind the conspiracy.

He told police, 'The reason we focused on robbing drug dealers was because they were easy targets. They had what we wanted; money and drugs. We also knew that they wouldn't squeal to the police. Who in their right mind would report the theft of their drugs? I think the first one we planned to do was a mixed-race guy in his 30s. He was quite flash and wore expensive clothes. He mainly dealt in heroin and crack cocaine. He lived in Basildon on one of the council estates. I had met him once in the Woodcutters Arms pub some time before we ever discussed robbing him. I was aware that Nipper Ellis or Percival knew one of his runners and he had agreed to give us access to the guy's premises so that we could rob him. Various tactics were discussed regarding the robbery and it was eventually decided that the runner would also have to get a slap, so there was no suspicion raised concerning his involvement. One night, myself, Percival and Nipper went round to the man's address to do a reconnaissance of the area. While I was in the car, Nipper produced a handgun; it was like an old revolver. I don't know why he was carrying it that night but it might have been for his own protection as a price had been put on his head for shooting Pat Tate. We looked around the area where the drug dealer lived. It was near a pub called the Watermill. We left shortly after arriving; Nipper still had the gun on him.

'For some reason, the robbery never did take place, I don't know why. It could have been because we had found another drug dealer who had more money and more drugs than the mixed-race guy. This dealer lived off Pound Lane in Pitsea; we referred to him as J.H. Again, this robbery was organised by Nipper. I had never heard of J.H. but I knew he was an old-time villain in his 50s. There was talk that there would be in the region of £100,000 in his home. We decided that we would watch him and his house for a couple of days so we would get to know his movements. We did this by using different cars and communicating by walkie-talkies.

'Through our surveillance activities we discovered that he drove a Mercedes and he had another property at Westcliff-on-Sea. During the planning stage, Nipper said that if we were going to go ahead with the job we would need to arm ourselves as he believed the guy had firearms in his house. The talk of firearms didn't appeal to me; I thought it was a bit out of my league. I didn't trust Nipper either. I thought he would probably put a bullet in both Percival's and my head if we came out of there with a large amount of cash. I decided not to take part in the crime. I can't recall how I got out of it but there was no further mention of it. It never did take place.'

The reason the robberies never did take place is because they were no more than Alvin's drink- and drug-fuelled fantasies. Boasting to his entourage of impressionable young men such as Boshell, Alvin would regularly talk about 'big-time villains' who he knew or associated with. He was fascinated by the murders of Tate, Tucker and Rolfe and all the things they had done prior to their deaths. A well-thumbed copy of Bernard O'Mahoney's *Essex*

Boys was never far from Alvin's grasp and he would constantly quiz me about my involvement with the trio. Alvin knew that burglary had become a crime of the past; safes were just too secure and alarms were becoming too sophisticated. He had noticed that Percival and I were making a good living out of selling drugs, so he decided that he would hang up his gloves, put away his crowbar and concentrate his efforts in and around the lucrative world of cannabis, Ecstasy and cocaine.

Dealing in drugs is an extremely risky business; if the police do not bring you down, rival dealers or informants most certainly will. Counter-surveillance techniques have to be employed when combating the police, and extreme violence has to be used to deter or destroy rival dealers and informants. Alvin thought that he was well equipped on all fronts to protect the drug-dealing empire that he was hoping to build. What he failed to appreciate is the fact that rival drug dealers will think twice about taking on a powerful man, but drug-dealing informants will have no hesitation whatsoever in passing on information to the police to bring down a man who threatens them.

Somebody else facing up to the problems that a lifestyle change brings was Boshell. The police were losing patience with him. The mountain of information that he had given them had not resulted in a single arrest. Boshell knew that he was going to have to come up with something more than idle gossip soon. He needed to be able to tell the police about a serious crime that he knew was going to be, or had already been, committed. Failure would result in him appearing in court with zero bargaining power. A lengthy prison sentence would undoubtedly be imposed and the future he craved with his girlfriend would slip from his grasp.

A man named Mark Bradford was on police bail in connection with the murder of a 24-year-old heroin addict named Danny Davies. Father-of-one Davies had died ten hours after being stabbed once in the buttock during a fight over a drug deal in Basildon. Mark Bradford was completely innocent of any involvement in this murder and did not face any charges in connection with it. However, Bradford's bail conditions, while the murder was still being investigated, included signing on at a police station every day to ensure that he did not abscond. Waiting to be attended to at the police station reception desk one day, Bradford saw Boshell walk out of an office accompanied by a man dressed in a suit who he assumed was a detective.

Bradford said, 'Boshell and I acknowledged one another before he walked out of the police station. A few days later, I met Alvin to buy some cocaine and I told him about Boshell being with the police. Initially, Alvin didn't seem too concerned, but a few days later he rang me up asking what day and at what time I had seen Boshell, and was the man with Boshell in uniform or plain clothes? Alvin seemed really concerned about Boshell being at the police station. He told me that he had found out that he was a grass.'

When Alvin questioned Boshell about what Bradford had seen, Boshell told him that the police had been trying to obtain information from him. Alvin appeared to accept this and told Boshell that he would get in contact with the officer concerned and offer him money to pass on information about police matters that may be of use to him. It is not known if Alvin did actually contact or try to bribe a police officer. Regardless of what Alvin may say today, the seeds of doubt concerning Boshell's loyalty to him must have been firmly planted by this incident. Seeds grow, so too does animosity, which can fester into feelings of extreme dislike or even hatred. Boshell was living dangerously. He knew what the punishment for being an informant was in the Essex underworld, but to save his dream of starting a family and escaping a lengthy term of imprisonment, he was prepared to take his chances.

Seven days before Boshell was due to appear in court for sentencing, he contacted the police and told them that he would be willing to become a supergrass and turn Queen's evidence against those responsible for the Locksley Close shootings and other matters. In return, he wanted the charges he faced to be dropped. Boshell was advised that the charges he faced could not be dropped, but if he was willing to testify against the gunmen 'things could be done for him'. Undecided which way to fall, because either way, fall he must, Boshell went away to consider his options. Before he could reach a decision, fate struck Boshell a cruel blow. Drunk and behaving in a wholly inappropriate manner, Boshell got involved in an altercation with a police officer. During the struggle that ensued, Boshell damaged a police car and was arrested. Boshell was taken to court the following morning and remanded in custody to HMP Chelmsford.

When he appeared at Southend Crown Court, he was sentenced to two years' imprisonment and, to add insult to injury, his long-suffering girlfriend ended their relationship. Not long after Boshell was sentenced, he was visited in prison by the police, who were hoping that he would continue to provide them with information about his criminal associates. Boshell told them that his 'best friend', Alvin, was importing large amounts of cannabis from Amsterdam and another guy named 'Spanish Frank' was smuggling an ounce of heroin into the prison every week.

It's not known what prompted Boshell to do what he did next. Some say it was guilt, others believe that it was fear. As soon as the police officers had left the visiting room, Boshell rang Alvin and told him that he ought to be extra vigilant because the police had been to the prison and wanted to know all about his business. What Boshell failed to mention was the fact that he had supplied the officers with the information they had requested. Alvin told me that this apparent act of loyalty strengthened his trust in Boshell, because Boshell had warned him about the police making inquiries about him. 'He's a good geezer, Nipper, he looks out for his master,' Alvin joked with me. After asking Boshell the names of the officers who had been to see him, Alvin had immediately telephoned them to ask what it was they wanted to know. He also advised the officers that if they wanted questions answered about his business in the future, they should ask him and not Boshell behind his back. Alvin says that he did not get any sort of satisfactory response from the police and he heard no more about it.

Because of the amount of cocaine that Alvin was abusing he had become increasingly paranoid. When Alvin had time to reflect upon the incident, he concluded that Boshell may have only told him about the visit because he could have been frightened that a fellow inmate might have seen the officers talking to him. This confirmed Alvin's suspicion that Boshell was an informant. That particular meeting with the police certainly had an effect on Boshell, because he refused to talk to them ever again. Today, Alvin claims that, if he had known for sure that Boshell was an informant, he would have told his friends to have nothing more to do with him. Although he would have been angry, Alvin says that he considered Boshell to be 'such a loser' he wouldn't have harmed him.

'Boshell was simply not worth it,' Alvin said. 'None of what he told the police was true as far as I know. I think he lived in a fantasy world.'

Nineteen-year-old Kate Griffiths had been the former girlfriend of Daniel Langley, one of Damon Alvin's closest friends. During their relationship the couple used to go to a local pub, the Woodcutters Arms, to socialise, and it was there that Kate was introduced to Malcolm Walsh's younger brother Kevin. Following the break-up of her relationship with Langley, Kate began dating Kevin. Romance blossomed between the two and before long Kate was living between her mum's house and Kevin's flat in Shannon Close, Leigh-on-Sea.

Life for the couple revolved around regular mundane visits to the Woodcutters Arms and work. Kate managed a launderette that she and her father owned and Kevin was employed on a casual basis in the construction industry. That was, until Boshell washed up at the Woodcutters one night in the company of Alvin and his partner Clair Sanders. Boshell had just been released from prison and Alvin had somehow convinced Sanders to allow him to live at their home until he was able to secure an address of his own. Boshell had initially hoped that he could make up with his girlfriend but when he came out of prison he soon learned that his criminal behaviour had resulted in all bridges being burned. Homeless and unemployed, he had turned to his friend and mentor Alvin for help. Thinking that Alvin had resolved his accommodation problem, Boshell began to celebrate and it wasn't long before he was staggering around the pub, drunk out of his mind. Sanders was outraged when she noticed the state that Boshell had got himself into. Pulling Alvin to one side she told him that under no circumstances was Boshell to go near their home.

Embarrassed, but in agreement, Alvin told Boshell in front of everybody that his invitation to stay had been withdrawn. Despite Kate and Kevin having only been introduced to Boshell earlier that evening, they felt deeply sorry for him.

'Don't be like that,' Kevin said to Alvin. 'He's just got out of jail and has nowhere to go.'

'Fuck the cunt,' Alvin replied. 'If you're so fucking worried about him, you take him home.'

Rather than leave Boshell roaming the streets Kevin invited him to stay at his flat until he found a place of his own. Once installed in Kevin's home, Boshell appeared to have been in no hurry to resolve his housing problem. He would hang around the flat all day and ponce drinks from me, Kevin and our friends in the Woodcutters Arms at night.

It took a month for Boshell to secure his own accommodation, and that was only achieved with the assistance of Alvin. Ever prudent, Alvin had employed jobless Boshell initially as a labourer for the building company that he owned. However, once Boshell had become financially dependent upon Alvin he was easily coaxed back into selling cocaine, Ecstasy and cannabis for him. To avoid any large quantities of these drugs being found at Alvin's home, he had decided it would be a good idea to provide Boshell with his own flat, from where the drugs could be stored and distributed. Alvin paid the £350 deposit required on a flat in Elmsleigh Drive, Leigh-on-Sea, and Alvin's entire stock of drugs moved in later the same day. Every weekend Boshell would visit the pubs and clubs that litter Southend seafront, plying Alvin's illicit substances.

On Friday and Saturday nights, the town was awash with revellers and so Boshell had no shortage of customers, drinking partners or pretty girls to choose from. He would flit from bar to club to bar feeling something that he had never felt before – important. Everybody, it seemed, wanted to be his friend, not because they liked him but because the drugs he was selling were of good quality and reasonably priced. Having experienced hard times himself, Boshell was not unknown to give drugs to people on credit so long as they promised to pay him the next time they met. The chance of a drug debt being honoured, which was agreed in a nightclub when both parties were pissed, is about as likely as world peace.

Boshell didn't help himself or me by acting out his fantasy of being a gangster to impress the steady stream of females he was constantly trying to seduce. He would supply them with free pills, free lines of cocaine or peel off notes from a wad of Alvin's drug money to buy them drinks. Many of my regular customers flocked to him for freebies or, at worst, discounted drugs. I warned Boshell that he was fucking things up for both of our drug businesses but he refused to listen. Before Boshell knew it, he was accumulating numerous small debts that amounted to him owing Alvin one large one. Tensions between the two men were becoming more intense, not only because of Boshell's playboy lifestyle, but also because of Alvin's own excessive cocaine use. He believed that he had become somehow invincible and treated everybody he met with contempt. Alvin's change in character was of great concern to Boshell because he knew what he was capable of when angry. He did his best to please Alvin but stories of Boshell handing out Alvin's drugs and cash did not help to reduce the gulf that was growing between the two men. To be honest, I was pleased that Alvin was having a go at Boshell because the distribution of free drugs ceased and I started making money again. I am not naive, and I am definitely not going to say that things returned to normal because I know more than most that 'normal' does not exist in Essex. Something, somewhere was just waiting to give.

After spending an enjoyable evening at the Chameleon nightclub in Southend, two girls named Lisa and Donna started to make their way home. As they passed TOTS nightclub Lisa was grabbed around the waist by a man who laughed and said, 'Hello, Nicole.' It wasn't a case of mistaken identity; people had often remarked upon how much Lisa resembled the Hollywood actress Nicole Kidman. The person who had accosted Lisa was in the company of another man named Sean Buckley and a female, who walked off as soon as she saw what had happened.

'My name is Dean Boshell,' the man said as he released Lisa's waist and held out his hand. After talking for half an hour in the bitter cold, Boshell invited Lisa and Donna to join him and Sean for a drink at his home.

When they arrived at Elmsleigh Drive, they went up to Sean's flat, which was above Boshell's in a converted house. Boshell began to play Eminem CDs on the stereo and told the girls it was his favourite music because he loved gangster lyrics.

In a statement made later to the police Lisa said: 'After a while

Dean said to me, do you want some Charlie? I didn't really know what he meant by this. He then got up and disappeared down the stairs to his flat. When Dean came back up, he was holding a clear plastic bag, which was about the size of a 2lb bag of sugar. He held it up and said, "That's Charlie. You know, coke?"

'It was then that I realised that he was holding a bag of cocaine. I wasn't at all comfortable with this. He then put a line of powder on the table, rolled up a ten-pound note and snorted it up his nose. Sean did the same but Donna and I refused to have any of it. I also noticed that Dean had a big roll of cash, about £600. I don't know why but he did tell me that this was not his money. Dean asked me if I wanted to go down to his flat. I agreed and left Donna with Sean. There wasn't a lot in the flat; he had a mattress for a bed, a three-piece suite, a TV and a video. Dean did wear nice clothes though; they were all designer labels and he also wore a thick gold chain and a krugerrand sovereign ring. Dean went to have a shower and I went into the kitchen to make a coffee.

'As I looked around, I saw a further three bags full of white powder on top of the freezer. These were the same size as the bag Dean had brought up to Sean's flat earlier. I don't know a lot about drugs, but I do know that the amount of cocaine that Dean had must have been worth a lot of money. When Dean came out of the shower, we both sat on the settee and had a cuddle. Dean was initially stuttering but very soon relaxed as he started to talk normally.

'I asked Dean about the cocaine and he said that while serving a prison sentence for burglary he had been bullied by two men who had forced him to deal drugs for them. He told me that one of these men was called Chris. Dean explained that these people used to smuggle pills into the prison for him hidden in the butts of cigarettes, which he would then have to sell to other inmates.

'Dean said that he wasn't happy with the situation but he didn't have much choice, other than to go along with their demands. When he was released from prison, Dean said that the people he had been forced to work for had tracked him down and made him continue to sell their drugs. That is how he came to be in possession of so much cocaine; it belonged to these people. Dean was under extreme pressure. He said that they were blackmailing him and they had threatened to harm his brother. I remained with Dean until Sunday morning and then I went home to have a shower and get changed. I did return to his flat later that evening. At half-seven I put a pizza in the oven. I remember the time because I had to keep my eye on the clock to make sure that I didn't burn it.

'A moment later there was a knock at the door and two men came in. By this time I had sat down to watch the television. Dean said, "Excuse me for a minute, I've got some business." I got up to go to the toilet and as I did so I noticed one of the men putting a bag of white powder into his pocket. I didn't mention this to Dean when they had gone but he did tell me that he had to do his business because he was £600 in debt to his landlady.

'Later that night, I went home but Dean and I spoke to one another on the phone every night thereafter. The following weekend, Dean picked me up from my home in a cab. We went to Clouseau's pub, had a few drinks and then went back to Dean's flat. When we sat down, Dean really opened up to me. I was quite shocked by how emotional he was. He said that he was stuck in a situation that there was no way out of. He started crying, saying that he was suicidal and that he wanted to get a gun. He kept saying that he had a problem that he desperately needed to sort out and that he was really frightened. "I need to face up to this and get it sorted," Dean said.

'It really upset me to see just how distressed Dean was. Unfortunately, he refused to go into detail about just what his problem was. The following morning, I went home.

'During the next couple of weeks, Dean would text or telephone me at all sorts of silly hours. He would either be stoned, drunk or both. Sometimes he would be fine with me, but other times he would say that he needed help or that he missed me a lot. He would say things such as, "I am stuck in a situation that I want to get out of," or "I am going to have to deal with this problem so that I can settle down with you." The next time that I saw Dean was in the Chameleon nightclub. He was really off with me and moody. I wasn't happy with his attitude at all so I left the club and went home. At about 0300 hrs Dean telephoned me. I told him I was unhappy about the way he had behaved and he apologised. I never saw Dean again. However, he did continue to text and telephone me.

'One text I received said, "Miss you. I am not a liar. You are special. I need to sort business out once and for all. Be in touch." I did try to phone Dean back but he did not answer his phone.'

The story that Boshell told Lisa about being forced to sell drugs for a man he had met in prison named Chris was, in part, true. He was selling drugs for a man he had met in prison but his name was Alvin, not Chris. The only Chris that Boshell had encountered while in prison was ex-Essex Boy Firm member Christopher Wheatley. He had been released from his seven-year sentence for drug dealing around the same time as Boshell. On 14 November 2000, two weeks before Boshell met Lisa, Chris had collapsed with heart failure after a particularly strenuous workout at a Southend gym. He was rushed to Basildon hospital but pronounced dead on arrival. The cause of his death was determined as bronchial asthma. Chris was no angel but he was a good friend of mine and highly respected throughout Essex. Percival and I both attended his funeral, which I don't mind admitting was an extremely emotional event. Boshell had been lying when he told Lisa that he was working for, and being threatened by, Chris, but he was certainly afraid of somebody.

Not long after Boshell had met Lisa, Alvin kicked his front door down in a cocaine-fuelled rage and beat him up. Boshell was admitted to Southend Hospital suffering from a severely swollen testicle, but he refused to say how he had been injured. Alvin later told the police that he was responsible for inflicting the injury during a bit of horseplay while Boshell was working for him as a labourer on a house extension.

'It was lunchtime and my wife had dropped off some sandwiches for me,' Alvin said. 'Dean grabbed a sandwich without asking, so I grabbed him by the bollocks. I took it off him and he ended up in hospital. I was only fucking about. He rang me the next day and said that his bollocks were hurting. He had a couple of days off work and then he admitted himself to Southend Hospital. I remember going up to see him. I took him in a phone and a McDonald's meal. I remember that he stayed in there for a few days and then he rang me and said that he was staying with some girl.'

Excuse the pun, but Alvin was talking bollocks. If the remains of Boshell's front door were not evidence enough for some people,

Alvin's boasts in the Woodcutters Arms about how he had kicked Boshell senseless certainly should have been. If Alvin's explanation is to be believed, then Boshell's behaviour, when he was eventually released from hospital several days later, can only be described as puzzling. Instead of returning to his old haunts and continuing to work alongside Alvin, Boshell moved out of Leigh-on Sea and into Southend.

The thousands of pounds' worth of cocaine and the wad of money that he had shown to Lisa just weeks earlier were suspiciously absent. Boshell had walked into a cafe on Southend seafront and asked the man behind the counter if he could offer him any work.

'I will do anything,' Boshell pleaded. 'I will wash up, clean the tables or cook the food.'

Halil Osman, the man Boshell had spoken to, knew that the cafe proprietor was short of staff because his uncle, who was also employed there, was on holiday and another member of staff had just given his notice. Boshell was hired and given the menial task of washing up. He was told that while he worked his probationary period he would be paid cash in hand. The hours Boshell worked were long and extremely tedious. He would start his shift at 1600 hrs and wash dishes and cutlery until the cafe closed at 0300 hrs or 0400 hrs in the morning. For working five night shifts, Boshell was paid the princely sum of £70; hardly the sort of money a one-time well-to-do drug dealer would toil all night, five times a week, to earn.

It cannot be argued that Dean Boshell was trying to make a completely new life for himself, free of drug dealing and the influence of Damon Alvin. Having received his first pay packet on Saturday morning, Boshell told his work colleagues that he was having dinner with a friend the following day. However, at approximately 1700 hrs on Sunday evening a tired and hungry-looking Boshell entered the cafe with an unknown male companion. The proprietor gave Boshell and his friend a portion of chips and they sat down together to eat them. After ten minutes the pair got up, walked out of the cafe and disappeared along the seafront. Nobody has known who that man was until now. Damon Alvin told me that he had found out quite by chance where Boshell was working and had gone to visit him to discuss the money that Boshell owed him for drugs.

'The little mug was dishing my gear out free to his mates and women in clubs, and making out he was a big shot,' Alvin said. 'He owes me fucking thousands and if he thinks that I am going to forget it he is mistaken. I have told him I either want the cash or he will have to work for me to pay it back.'

I didn't for one moment think that Alvin was going to get Boshell to sweep his drive daily to honour the debt, nor did I think that he would trust him again to handle his stock of drugs, and so I assumed that Boshell was going to be used in some form of crime to recoup the cash that he owed.

Halil Osman worked alongside Boshell at the cafe for just six or seven days and during that time Boshell confided in this relative stranger that he was interested in guns. When Halil asked him what he meant, Boshell claimed that he had recently acquired a gun.

'Dean told me that he and his brother had gone to London to buy the gun,' Halil said. 'He told me that he had purchased two guns because it was cheaper to buy a pair. Dean told me that he had paid £500 for them. "Normally," he said, "a clean gun would cost £300 or £400 but because he had been kept waiting a long time, he had got them cheap." I asked him if he kept them at his home address and he replied, "No, I am not that stupid." Dean said that he would bury them or keep them somewhere else or at someone else's. I couldn't make up my mind if Dean was actually telling the truth.' Boshell did not have a brother but he always referred to Alvin as 'bro' or 'brother'. No doubt he had adopted the terms from some crap rap song.

There is no way of knowing if Boshell did buy a gun in London with 'his brother', but Halil is not the only person who claimed to have had a conversation with Boshell about guns. When Boshell left the Leigh-on-Sea area via Southend Hospital, he had moved into a flat at the rear of the cafe where he worked. Not really knowing anybody in the area, he would occasionally visit his old haunts along Southend seafront, seeking out company. One day he bumped into a man I'll call Paul, who he had originally met while serving one of his many prison sentences. Through Paul, Boshell was introduced to a group of people which included Stacey Harris, her brother C.J. McLaughlin and a man named Jason Spendiff-

Smith. Boshell and Spendiff-Smith got on well and they began to go out drinking together.

Like Boshell, Spendiff-Smith had led a fairly nomadic life. moving from one flat and one disastrous relationship to the next. Stacey Harris, his girlfriend at the time he met Boshell, had recently announced that her previous partner was due for release from prison and so Spendiff-Smith would have to leave her home. Fortunately for Spendiff-Smith, a friend of Harris's named Charlotte Taylor was seeking a lodger and so he moved into her flat. Boshell would often visit Spendiff-Smith at Taylor's address when he had finished work at the cafe. Any pizzas, chips or similar fast food that hadn't been sold was given to Boshell by his employers and he would share it with his friends. According to Spendiff-Smith, not long after he had met Boshell he was invited to go on a job with him and 'earn about £1,000'.

'I cannot remember exactly what his words were,' Spendiff-Smith said, when trying to recall the conversation, 'but he said that he and his brother were going to break into a house in Westcliff and steal a load of drug plants. He said that the house was surrounded by fields and it would have to be done in the dark. He mentioned that the people who owned the house were not very nice and not from around here. I assumed from that description that they were foreigners. Dean told me that he knew that the people were going to be away, or out of the house, at the time. He said that the job was planned to take place the following Thursday and he would be getting paid at least £2,500 for doing it. I didn't have any money or anything to do so I said, "Let me think about it."

'The following day, Dean asked me if I would go out with his brother and him to have a drive past the house where they were going to do the job. I agreed to go with him because I was bored at home, but his brother never turned up. For some reason the job didn't take place the following Thursday, but on the Friday Dean told me that he was going to meet up with one of his mates to pick up a gun. I didn't really think much of it, I just thought it was Dean being all mouth. On Sunday, Dean and I went out drinking. We started off in the Last Post, then visited a bar called Motel's and another called the Green Door, before ending up in the White

Horse. On the way to the White Horse we called in at Dean's flat because he said he wanted to show me something.

'When we entered, Dean asked me to close the door, which I did. He lifted his mattress up and I could see that he had a gun and three bullets hidden underneath it. I would describe the gun as a revolver-type handgun, which was about six or seven inches long, misty black or grey in colour and slightly rusty. The handle was brown and looked like it had been taped up. I was surprised to see a gun, as I thought it had just been all talk from Dean. He said, "Go on. Make a man of yourself and hold it. It's not loaded." I didn't want to touch it and felt a bit uneasy seeing it. I said that I was going, so Dean put the gun back under the mattress.

'After that, we walked to the White Horse pub to have a drink. It's quite a long walk from his flat and on the way I told Dean that I didn't want to get involved in the job that he had planned. He said, "You're such a pussy," and I replied, "I don't care, I don't want to do it. I don't care if it's £1,000 or £1,000,000, I am still not going to get caught for that, or go around killing people." I had automatically thought that Dean was going to use the gun on this job. For all I knew he could have gone out and killed himself, or maybe killed me.

'At some point during the evening Dean received a call on his mobile phone from his brother, the one he always spoke to. He said that he was just popping outside to meet him to get some money and make sure the job was still on. I assumed that Dean was talking about the break-in. When Dean came back five or ten minutes later, he said something like, "I love my brother", and took some money that he had been given out of his pocket. He said that the job was still on and told me to look out of the window at his brother's car, which was a red Audi convertible. When I looked out at the car, I could not see the driver, but there was a blonde female in the passenger seat and I think a little girl in the rear. Dean then told me that the job was going to be done on Tuesday, which was only two days away.'

The following day, Boshell didn't see Spendiff-Smith because he went to work at the cafe. During his shift, Boshell was working with a man named Ishmael Mehmet, who was also employed to wash up in the kitchen. Ishmael later recalled that during the evening

Dean received a number of calls on his mobile phone, but he did not know who they were from. At 2000 hrs Dean received a phone call and, when he had identified the caller, he walked out of the cafe to continue his conversation. This was the only call that Boshell felt he needed to take out of earshot of Ishmael and others.

Analysis of phone records by the police, following Boshell's murder, has proven that this call was made from Alvin's girlfriend's phone. Following this call, Boshell asked Ishmael if he thought it would be OK for him to have a couple of hours off the following night. Ishmael told Boshell that it wasn't up to him, but he didn't think their employer would mind if he asked. Out of curiosity Ishmael asked Boshell why he needed the time off.

'I need to do a job,' Boshell replied. 'I am going to rob some drugs in Chelmsford which are worth around £100,000.' Without prompting from Ishmael, Boshell began to elaborate. 'Me and my brother are going to rob a house in Chelmsford. It's in a little village. There's a barn at the back. It's full of skunk and me and my brother are going to take the plants.'

Ishmael, not wishing to become in any way involved in criminal activity, didn't press Boshell for any further information and quickly changed the subject. At 0400 hrs, Dean's employer closed up the cafe and called out 'goodbye' to Boshell as he left. Turning, Boshell raised his hand and shouted out, 'I'll see you tomorrow, mate,' but Dean Boshell never did return to work.

CHAPTER TEN

Looking back on my past, there is not much that I am truly ashamed of; we all have regrets but shame is something deeper. The only thing that I can honestly say that I am ashamed of is the fact that I sold drugs. It is a vile occupation because it spawns animals like Tate, Tucker, Rolfe and Alvin. They operate without morals, limits or regard for any other individual. Hand on heart, I came close to becoming one of them; cocaine made me think I was fucking Superman. Thankfully, Ricky Percival pulled me from the mouth of the abyss by sitting me down one evening and telling me a few home truths about myself. He shouted at me 'to fucking wise up' and explained that Alvin was encouraging my customers to turn against me by saying that I could not be trusted, that I was violent and I had shot Pat Tate and I would not hesitate to shoot anybody else that got in my way. 'Be careful,' Percival had warned, 'if Alvin fails to remove you with gossip or by grassing, he will probably shoot you.' If only Percival had listened to his own advice, he wouldn't be sitting in a cell in HMP Full Sutton today with a minimum of 26 years to serve. Ricky, like me, sold drugs. He didn't shoot the Trettons. He didn't execute anybody. In fact, his most heinous crime was to have courted Damon Alvin's friendship.

Four hours after leaving work that fateful morning, Boshell was knocking on the door of his friend's flat.

Spendiff-Smith later told police that when Boshell arrived, 'Charlotte was in one room. Me and Stacey Harris were in another, and Stacey's three kids were sleeping in the spare room. I got up at about 0930 hrs, then Boshell and I went to the Social Security offices. We had no money, so we were going to try and get what

199

they call "a crisis loan". While we were there, Charlotte came in with Stacey and her boyfriend. We only exchanged hellos, because Stacey's boyfriend doesn't really like me. Dean was refused the loan and so we went down to the Abbey National so I could try and get some cash from the hole in the wall machine. This was about 1045 hrs. I had no money in my account, so we went to the Job Centre. I signed on and then we returned to the Social Security offices to see if they would give me any money, but they refused.

'Dean and I went back to the flat and found that Charlotte, her boyfriend, Stacey and her three kids had all returned. I asked Stacey to lend me some money and although she had none herself, she did say that she would get some off her boyfriend to lend me. Stacey left the flat to find him and about ten minutes later Dean and I went to meet her in town. Stacey never did arrive at the place we had agreed to meet, and so we didn't get any money. As we were walking around town, Dean said, "I haven't been to see my probation officer for ages." I didn't think much of this at first and so said nothing as we walked down towards the Probation Service offices. Standing outside, Dean announced that he had a warrant out for his arrest. He had not kept the terms and conditions of his probation, so he could have, and should have, been arrested as soon as he set foot in there. He obviously knew this, but he didn't seem bothered.

'I haven't got a clue if he was trying to get himself arrested on purpose or not. He did say to me, "I want to make sure that I am wanted by the police." I think he was trying to look big in front of me. I would say Dean was in the Probation Office for only a few minutes before coming out. He said that his probation officer had been surprised to see him because he had missed a number of previous appointments. A warrant had been issued recalling him back to prison but, other than that, he said no more about it. We then returned home where we found Charlotte and her boyfriend looking after Stacey's kids. At approximately 1800 hrs, Charlotte and her boyfriend left the flat, leaving me and Dean to babysit. We didn't mind because we were not going anywhere. Two hours later Stacey's brother, C.J. McLaughlin, arrived.

'He said that he had come to pick the kids up for Stacey, which I was pleased about. When they had all gone, Dean said to me that he needed to borrow some dark clothing for doing the break-in and asked me if I could lend him some. I sorted him out my Adidas trainers, a dark-blue Puffa jacket and a pair of blue jogging bottoms. Dean then left the flat saying that he was going home to get changed and get something to eat.

'About 15 minutes later he came back wearing a grey jumper, my Adidas trainers, Puffa jacket and my blue jogging bottoms. He told me that he was expecting his brother to phone and if he fell asleep, not to answer the call but to wake him. We began to watch *The Brit Awards* on TV but Dean soon fell asleep. At about 2045 hrs, Dean's mobile rang and I nudged him awake. I could hear Dean talking; he was asking the caller what time he was going to meet him and 2100 hrs was mentioned. As soon as the conversation ended Charlotte came home and Dean got up, saying that he had to go and meet his brother, who was picking him up at Lidl's supermarket. Just before he left, I was having a laugh with him, saying make sure you bring back loads of fags, loads of food and things, and he replied, "Yes, I will." Dean then left the flat with his phone and I never saw him again.'

Nobody can say for certain what was going through the mind of Dean Boshell that day. What is known is that Boshell appeared to be extremely concerned about something. If Boshell was planning to commit a crime which was going to earn him a substantial wage that night, why would he apply for a £70 crisis loan at 0940 hrs and why would he hand himself in to his probation officer at 1539 hrs, knowing that there was an outstanding warrant for his arrest?

Boshell's behaviour changed dramatically after he was admitted to hospital suffering from the injuries caused by Alvin's beating. He had abandoned his flat in haste shortly after being discharged from the hospital, and he had left Leigh-on-Sea and severed all contact with his friends there. He had given up selling drugs and labouring for Alvin and, to substitute that income, he had taken a menial job washing up at night in a cafe. On 8, 14 and 27 February, he had pleaded with the Social Security Department to grant him crisis loans as he was desperate for cash. Nobody can say what he was going to do with this money, but he had talked about returning to live in Leeds.

Alvin had been in contact with Boshell by phone on a sporadic basis, and Boshell had talked about doing a job with him. However,

Boshell had wept while explaining a situation that he was in to Nicole Kidman lookalike Lisa. He had told her that there was no way out of it and that he wanted to get a gun because he was really frightened. I know for a fact that Boshell had been dealing drugs for Alvin and the large amounts of cocaine seen by Lisa would support what I say.

The fact that his flat was ransacked and he ended up in hospital would, in my opinion, prove that Boshell had been beaten up by Alvin because Alvin couldn't find the drugs or the money that was owed to him in Boshell's flat. Fleeing Leigh-on-Sea and associating with an entirely new circle of friends would add weight to the fact that Boshell was trying to avoid Alvin. No explanation was given by Boshell as to why the theft of the drugs from the barn had been cancelled. Perhaps he had agreed to do it to work off Alvin's debt and then changed his mind at the last moment. Perhaps there was no 'job' and like Tate, Tucker and Rolfe, Boshell was simply being lured to his death.

What is interesting is the fact that Alvin telephoned him using his girlfriend's phone. Boshell took the call out of earshot of his colleagues when he realised who he was speaking to. A friend of Boshell's, who was interviewed during the police investigation, said that Boshell rarely got calls, but a week or two before his death he was receiving several daily. This, to me, indicates that Boshell had been trying to avoid Alvin, who then used his partner's phone to call him. Boshell would have recognised Clair's number, had no reason to fear talking to her and answered it. Realising it was Alvin and not Clair on the phone, Boshell had then taken the call outside the cafe to prevent anybody overhearing what was being said. Once he had spoken to Alvin, Boshell immediately asked his employer for time off to do 'the job'.

When you try to contact people over debts or grievances, they act in exactly the same way as Boshell. They duck, dive and avoid your calls, but when you lure them into talking to you, they become very compliant. Boshell's nervousness and reckless visit to the Probation Office, knowing that he could be arrested and returned to prison, suggests to me that the last thing he wanted to do was meet Alvin that night.

Earlier that day, Alvin had been at work with his brother. He arrived home at about 1400 hrs. He put on old clothes, trainers, a hat and threw a pair of Marigold gloves in his car. Two hours later he drove to Elmsleigh Drive, where Boshell had lived before fleeing to Southend, and telephoned Boshell from a phone kiosk. Alvin had wanted Boshell to know that he was going to pick him up later, unless of course he could make his own way to Leigh-on-Sea. After making the call, Alvin went to visit Kevin Walsh at his flat. When he arrived at approximately 1800 hrs, Alvin found that Kevin was home with Boshell's friend Sean Buckley. About an hour after he arrived, the three men were joined by Percival. At a loose end, they all decided to visit the Woodcutters Arms.

Phone records show that at 2032 hrs Boshell telephoned Alvin from C.J. McLaughlin's mobile phone. He said that he was in Southend and had no way of getting down to Leigh-on-Sea, so Alvin told him not to worry and agreed that he would pick him up. Alvin made and received a number of other calls while in the pub that night. One was from his girlfriend, Clair, who had asked what he would like for dinner. Clair had also mentioned that she would pick Alvin up later as she didn't want him drink-driving. Alvin agreed meekly and suggested that she pick him up from Kevin Walsh's flat when she had finished work. Shortly after Clair's call, Alvin had told Kevin that he had to go home quickly, but he would return. Kevin said that because the pub was quiet he was going to take a few beers back to his flat and Alvin was welcome to join him. Alvin agreed that he would.

While Alvin was in the car park, Percival came out of the pub and Alvin mentioned that he had to go home briefly before going on to Kevin's flat. Alvin asked Percival if he too was going to Kevin's and he replied that he was. Before parting company, Percival offered to pick Alvin up from his home because he knew that Clair didn't like him drink-driving. Alvin agreed and left in his red Audi. Percival drove to his own home, had something to eat and then set off to pick up Alvin.

At 2100 hrs, after leaving Spendiff-Smith at his flat, CCTV cameras recorded Boshell and C.J. McLaughlin walking to Woodgrange Drive, in Southend, and waiting outside the Lidl's store for Alvin to arrive. At 2115 hrs, CCTV at the Woodcutters Arms recorded Alvin leaving the premises. C.J. McLaughlin later told police that at 2126 hrs Boshell had telephoned Alvin's mobile from a public telephone situated on Woodgrange Drive. McLaughlin said that Alvin had turned up not long after Boshell had made the call in a red car. Boshell had then got into the vehicle and called out, 'See you tomorrow,' before being driven away.

The general conversation between the two men surrounded the job Alvin claimed that they were going to carry out that night. Alvin said that a barn was being used to grow the drug skunk in Chelmsford, and if they stole it Boshell could not only clear his debt but also make a few thousand pounds' profit. As they drove away from Southend, Boshell asked Alvin if he could stop off at an off-licence and buy him some cigarettes as he was out of money. Complaining bitterly, Alvin stopped at an off-licence and gave Boshell a handful of change. Moments later, Boshell returned to the car with cigarettes and two bottles of Lucozade.

When they arrived in Leigh-on-Sea, Alvin parked his vehicle in a quiet side street and told Boshell to follow him. They walked along an alleyway, alongside a small brook. Boshell was drinking the Lucozade that he had bought, having left the cigarettes in Alvin's car. Alvin said that the 'tools' that they were going to use to break into the barn had been left on allotments in Manchester Drive. The site is vast, secluded and ideal for storing weapons, burglary tools and any other such items that may be used by criminals. It is also an ideal place to execute somebody. When they arrived at the allotments, Alvin told Boshell that the tools they had gone to retrieve were no longer there.

'You stay here and look for them while I go and fetch a van. I'm not using my car because it will stink of skunk. I won't be long,' Alvin said.

Instead of going to pick up the van, Alvin drove home and awaited the arrival of Percival. Alvin appeared to be cleaning up in the kitchen when Percival arrived. He let his friend in, gave him a dozen or so bottles of beer out of the fridge and told him to put them in his car. The pair then drove to Walsh's flat in Percival's car. They arrived at about 2245 hrs and gained entry by beeping the horn. It was Kate Griffiths who went down the stairs to let them in. Everybody sat around drinking and talking until approximately 2330 hrs when Percival announced that he was going home to bed. An hour later, Clair arrived at the flat and Alvin left with her. When they were alone in the car, Clair mentioned that Boshell had rung her from a call box and wanted to know where Alvin had got to as he was waiting for him. Phone records show that this call was made at 2348 hrs from a phone kiosk close to the allotments. Alvin told Clair that he needed to sort something out with Boshell, which wouldn't take long and so she dropped him off and awaited his return. As Alvin walked along the street towards the allotments he heard somebody call out his name.

The caller sounded unsure who he was. Alvin looked towards where the voice had come from and saw Boshell standing near the entrance to the allotments. Boshell could see from Alvin's facial expression that he was pissed off. Alvin started firing questions at Boshell about his drugs and money going missing. Boshell tried to explain that he hadn't stolen his drugs, they had gone missing from his flat during a party, but Alvin wasn't having any of it. He kept saying that Boshell had squandered the drugs and his money; nobody else had stolen them because he was the only one who knew the drugs were there.

'I am not a fucking idiot. I know what you have done with the drugs. You were giving it the Big I Am and dishing them out to your fucking friends,' Alvin said.

Boshell was extremely worried by this time. He continued to deny any involvement in the disappearance of the drugs and volunteered to go and search for them.

Alvin began to mock Boshell saying, 'Yeah well, you're obviously cleverer than me. I am obviously too much of a fucking idiot to know what you did with them. Why don't you go and have a look?'

At that point, Boshell turned to his left and put both hands up to his face because Alvin had squirted him with ammonia. Boshell, blinded by the noxious substance, started walking away from Alvin, but he had not taken more than a couple of steps when there was a large bang and flash from a gun. Boshell then crumpled to the ground. Smirking, Alvin stepped forward and stood over Boshell, who remained on the floor. Bending down, Alvin placed the barrel of his gun against the left side of Boshell's head and fired twice.

One of the bullets lodged in the soft tissue of his right temple, and the other came to rest in his upper left nostril. Still not content, Alvin, who was seething with anger, picked up a steel rod that was stuck in the ground near Boshell's body and lashed him across the back of the head with it. When Alvin arrived back at Clair's car, he complained about Boshell being a 'fucking nuisance' and asked her to drive him home. When they arrived, Clair had a Chinese meal waiting for them, which they ate before retiring to bed for the evening. Despite the fact that Alvin had executed his friend that night, he slept as normal.

Colin Todd was employed at the Manchester Drive allotments in Leigh-on-Sea as a general maintenance man. Apart from young people fornicating in the bushes, kids breaking into the numerous garden sheds that cover the ten-acre site, and crops being stolen or damaged, very little of interest ever happened on the site. On the morning of Wednesday, 28 February 2001, at approximately 0920 hrs, Colin Todd and a colleague were walking through the allotments when they came across the lifeless body of 24-year-old Dean Fergus Boshell. The blood-soaked corpse was lying with the right side of the face on the ground and the knees slightly drawn up. Colin Todd could see that the person on the ground was clearly dead. He called the police and the paramedics, who arrived amid a deafening chorus of wailing sirens and blue flashing lights. They, too, recognised that the body was lifeless and so summoned a doctor to the scene, who certified Boshell dead at 1128 hrs.

It was clear from the amount of blood that had poured from the victim's head that this death was, at the very least, suspicious, and so the police erected an air tent around the body to contain and preserve any evidence that might have been present. The allotments where Boshell's body was discovered are surrounded by houses and so the police decided to conduct door-to-door inquiries to find out if any of the residents had seen or heard anything of significance the night before. A man named Gordon Osborne lived at 94 Randolph Close, which is approximately 500 metres from where Boshell's body was discovered.

When the police had called at his home, Osborne told them, 'Half of me thinks that I may have heard a bang, but I could not be sure.'

He added that he didn't know what time he may have heard this bang, but it was possibly between 2300 hrs and 2330 hrs.

With so little evidence to work with, detectives turned their attention towards locating and interviewing Boshell's family, friends and associates.

At 0630 hrs the morning after Boshell's body was found, Damon Alvin claims that he was woken by his phone ringing. The caller, Boshell's friend Sean Buckley, said that he had arrived home earlier that morning and found the police standing outside his flat. As he walked towards his front door, he saw that it had been forced open. After asking the police what they were up to, Buckley was told that they were responsible for breaking down his door. Instead of forcing an entry into Boshell's old flat downstairs, they had broken into Buckley's flat in error. Even if the police had entered the correct address, they would have found that Boshell had vacated the premises weeks earlier.

When the police did eventually find and search Boshell's flat in Southend, they didn't find much of significance other than his address book, which contained four different telephone numbers for Alvin and one for Alvin's girlfriend Clair. There was none for Percival. The police hadn't had the greatest start to an investigation and their luck appeared to deteriorate the longer it went on. Officers advised Buckley to go to the police station and inform them of their mistake and the damage that they had caused to his front door. However, Alvin says that Buckley telephoned him en route to the police station and asked him to repair the door instead. Another pressing problem that Buckley faced that morning was that Alvin had left several thousand pounds at his flat in a carrier bag, and he wanted to know what to say if the police discovered it. Buckley was told by Alvin to say that the money was his.

At approximately 1030 hrs, Alvin had arrived at Buckley's flat and saw the front door lying in the garden. As he climbed the stairs to the flat, Alvin was confronted by several police officers who, he claims, recognised him immediately. The officers said that they were investigating the murder of Dean Boshell and asked Alvin for a contact number because he was a known associate of the deceased, and they wanted him to make a witness statement. Alvin explained that he had a new mobile number, of which he couldn't recall the number nor retrieve from his handset, and so he gave them his girlfriend's number. The officers asked Alvin where he had been on the night Boshell had died, and he told them that he had been in the company of Kevin Walsh, Kate Griffiths and Ricky Percival. A brief note was made of this information and an officer advised Alvin that there was no need for him to repair the door as they were going to contact a contractor themselves.

Alvin left the flat with Buckley to go to the pub to discuss what needed to be said if his money was ever discovered. Since Alvin had said that he had been in Ricky Percival's company on the night Boshell died, the police asked Percival to make a formal statement. He felt he had nothing to hide and so he agreed. Percival told the police that he had first met Boshell in 1999. Alvin had introduced Boshell to him as a friend but their acquaintance had been short-lived because Boshell had been sent to prison.

Percival said, 'Damon told me that he was keeping in touch with Dean in the jail. Boshell had asked him if he could get any weight-training supplements because he had started weight training. I was keen on the sport at the time and as a result of my almost daily attendance at the gym I was able to get the supplements at trade price. I didn't know Boshell as such, but I didn't mind getting them for Alvin to give to him because he was the friend of a friend. I was aware that Boshell had been released from prison around the end of 2000. He turned up at a couple of places where I was socialising, such as the Woodcutters Arms. We didn't say a great deal to one another, as we had little or nothing in common. He did thank me for getting the protein supplements for him.

'I would describe Boshell as a bit of a ponce; he was always borrowing, not from me but from others. He would always drink but never buy his round. I referred to him as "Dopey Dean". I must say there was nothing nasty about Boshell. He was never offensive or rude. I last saw him around midday in Victoria Avenue, Southend, about two weeks before his death. I was paying a speeding fine at the court house. He was going into the Social Security office which is next to the gym. He said "All right?" to me and asked me where I had been. After I explained about the speeding fine, he told me that he was sorting out his Social Security claim. I then said "I'll see you later," and left.

'I think it was the morning after his death that I heard about it on the radio. I was driving home from the gym around midday. I was shocked but it didn't sink in really. I immediately phoned Alvin and he said that he knew already. On the night Boshell died, I went to visit my friend Kevin Walsh at his flat. It was around 1900 hrs or 2000 hrs when I arrived. Alvin and a man named Sean Buckley were already there. We all left the flat shortly afterwards and went to the Woodcutters Arms. I went there in my car and the others travelled to the pub in Alvin's red Audi convertible. After an hour or two, Alvin and I left the pub. I went home, had something to eat and then drove to Alvin's house in Rochford, to give him a lift to Kevin Walsh's flat. He had gone home to drop his car off because his partner doesn't like him to drink and drive. I left Kevin's flat alone around 2330 hrs because Alvin said his girlfriend was going to pick him up later.'

The police thanked Percival for his assistance and told him that they would be in touch if they had any further questions. The following day, the police asked Alvin to make his witness statement concerning his knowledge and relationship with Boshell. In it, he claimed that he had first heard that a body had been found on the allotments after it had been reported in the local newspaper and on the radio. It wasn't until Kate Griffiths had telephoned him that he knew the body was Boshell's.

'I was quite upset when I heard this,' Alvin said. 'I know of no reason why someone would want to kill him. I would describe Dean as a friend; he was friendlier towards me than I was to him. He would confide in me if he was in trouble. The last time I spoke to him he was quite happy; he did not appear to be worried about anything. Dean would contact me on my mobile. I can't remember the number as I have misplaced it since the weekend. I have since bought a new phone but I can't remember that number either.

'I have not heard of any reason why Dean should have been killed but I have let it be known in the area that I will pay £500 to any person who can help catch the person responsible.'

After completing his statement Alvin offered the police a possible 'off the record' motive for the murder.

Doing his best to sound concerned, and looking to appear helpful, he said, 'There is a possibility that Dean was having an affair with a married woman or sleeping with someone's under-age daughter; he was like that.'

Percival's and Alvin's statements led officers to the door of Kate Griffiths, who was also asked to detail her knowledge of Boshell and her movements on the night that he had died. Without realising the severity of the situation she was walking into, Kate agreed to make a statement. Griffiths said that she had spent the day of the murder working at a launderette, which she and her father owned. At around 1900 hrs she had locked the premises up and caught a taxi to her mother's house.

'I sat down with my dad and sorted out the paperwork for the launderette's takings for that day,' she said. 'After having my dinner, I went to the Woodcutters Arms where I met Damon Alvin, Ricky Percival, Sean Buckley and my boyfriend, Kevin Walsh. It was really quiet in the pub that night. I can't recall what time it was, perhaps quarter past, half past nine, but Damon and Ricky left the pub before Kevin and me. About 2200 hrs, we decided to buy a few takeaway beers and go home to watch the television because the pub was really quiet. Half an hour after we arrived at the flat, Damon and Ricky turned up in Ricky's car. They came in and we all just sat watching the television and chatting. Everything was really normal as far as I was concerned. Around midnight Ricky went home. Roughly half an hour later, Damon's girlfriend Clair beeped the car horn outside the flat.

'Kevin went to the kitchen window, looked down onto the car park and told Damon that Clair was outside. Clair was driving Damon's red Audi, he got into it and they disappeared. It wasn't unusual for Clair to pick Damon up from our flat. Clair would do it when she had finished work because she didn't like him drinking and driving. At approximately 0100 hrs, Kevin and I went to bed.'

Griffiths, an honest girl of impeccable character, had been really fond of Boshell and she had absolutely no reason whatsoever to lie to the police. Little did she know, her willingness to assist would later result in her facing ruin. Sean Buckley, who the other witnesses had also mentioned, had made his statement after the police raided his flat in error. He had left the group early in the evening and had had no contact with Boshell and so proved to be of little use to the investigation. Walsh had spent the evening in Griffiths' company and so when he made his statement, unsurprisingly it turned out to be almost identical in content to hers.

When officers visited Clair Sanders and asked her to give an account of her movements on the relevant night, she did so and agreed with everything that Alvin had said in his statement. However, for reasons known only to Clair Sanders, she refused to sign the declaration on the statement that stated that her testimony was true to the best of her knowledge.

Within weeks of the murder, Boshell's funeral took place at Pitsea Crematorium near Basildon. The hearse carrying Boshell's coffin passed the last resting places of Patrick Tate and Craig Rolfe, two victims of the infamous Essex Boys murders who were buried as they lived, side by side. Dean Boshell's dream of being just like one of the 'big boys' had finally come true. He was young, dead and being buried full of bullet holes; just like his heroes. Bonded by blood, three young men laid in a cemetery long before their time.

Nearly four months after his initial doorstep interview, Gordon Osborne was asked to make a further witness statement. Unlike his first rather vague recollection of the night of the murder, Osborne was suddenly able to recall events with extreme clarity.

'I went to bed about 2100 hrs,' he said. 'My bedroom is at the rear of my house and this overlooks the allotments. At about 2300 hrs I was awoken by the sound of two or three shots coming from the direction of the allotments. My bedroom window is always open and I got up to look out of the window towards the allotments but could not see anything as it was pitch black. I can say from my experience in the armed forces that the shots I heard were from a handgun and not a shotgun. I did not see anything at all that night. The following day I found out that a person had been found dead on the allotments.'

Osborne claimed he had heard two or three shots, which were consistent with the number of gunshot wounds that Boshell had suffered. Detectives, therefore, assumed that the shots Osborne had heard were the shots being fired into Boshell. They thought it would be unlikely that he would be mistaken after boasting that, because of his military training, he could distinguish the sound of one particular firearm from another. It therefore followed that Boshell must have met his death at around 2300 hrs.

The police had always harboured a niggling doubt about Alvin's story regarding the loss of his mobile phone. It seemed to be too much of a coincidence that he had just happened to lose it on the very day Boshell died. The fact that Alvin had replaced the phone so early the following morning was equally suspicious. Most people would search high and low before accepting their handset was truly lost before replacing it.

Curious as to why Alvin might not wish his phone to be examined, detectives were soon able to discover his number by simply asking his friends for it. Boshell's mobile phone was also missing, but C.J. McLaughlin, who had been in Spendiff-Smith's flat on the evening of the murder, had told the police that Boshell had borrowed his phone at 2032 hrs to call a friend that he was going to meet.

Detectives retrieved the number Boshell had called from McLaughlin's mobile and soon established that it belonged to Alvin's missing phone. This was the first real evidence that linked Alvin to Boshell on the night he died. Officers were extremely encouraged by the breakthrough because Alvin had claimed that he had not seen or spoken to Boshell that day. The icing on the detectives' cake was that CCTV footage, seized from within the Woodcutters Arms, showed Alvin answering his mobile phone at the precise time that Boshell had made his call. The decision by police to gather all of the CCTV footage they thought might be relevant, proved to be an extremely significant and constructive one. At 2100 hrs on the night of the murder, cameras had recorded Boshell and C.J. McLaughlin walking to Woodgrange Drive in Southend, and waiting outside the Lidl store for Boshell's friend to arrive. At 2115 hrs, CCTV at the Woodcutters Arms recorded Alvin leaving the premises.

C.J. McLaughlin had told police that at 2126 hrs Boshell had telephoned his friend's mobile from a public telephone situated on Woodgrange Drive. Telephone records revealed that this call had also been made to Alvin's phone. McLaughlin told the police that Boshell's friend had turned up, not long after Boshell had made the call, in a red car. Boshell had got in the vehicle and called out, 'See you tomorrow,' before being driven away. Detectives knew that Alvin drove a red Audi convertible. There was real excitement among officers involved in the investigation. Alvin appeared to be lying about his whereabouts after leaving the Woodcutters Arms. He said that he had gone home to drop his car off, but the police now had evidence that he had driven to Southend to pick up Boshell.

Osborne's evidence, that he had heard three shots approximately two hours after Boshell had been seen leaving Southend alive, could have put Alvin in a very awkward position had it not been for Griffiths, Percival and Walsh's evidence. They had all made statements in which they had said Alvin was at the flat between approximately 2230 hrs and midnight. If the phone records were correct, Boshell had left Southend at around 2130 hrs, so he would have arrived at the allotments before 2200 hrs. Gordon Osborne had heard the shots around 2300 hrs. Detectives believed that Alvin had to be lying.

Despite their best efforts, detectives could not find any discrepancies in the alibi that Alvin and his friends had given for the time of the shooting and so, for a while, the investigation ground to a shuddering halt.

Six months after Boshell's murder, Alvin married his first love, Clair Sanders. It was a rather lavish affair, funded in part by sections of the local community. That's Alvin's drug clientele. Among the guests were the Percival family, Kevin Walsh and Alvin's good friend Tony Staunton. When he had heard about the wedding and asked Alvin where his invitation was, Alvin had laughed and said, 'You can have Boshell's. He won't be needing it.' Guests at the event have said that they had never seen Alvin looking so happy. Having out-foxed the police, expanded his drug-dealing empire and married the girl of his dreams, Alvin probably never had been. Happiness, as we all know, doesn't last forever.

On April Fool's Day, Alvin was arrested at gunpoint in possession of a kilo of cocaine. The arresting officers were members of the Boshell murder inquiry team rather than regular drug squad officers. Alvin couldn't be sure if the police had followed him from where he had collected the drugs. If they had, he knew that several of his associates would soon be joining him in custody. He did think it highly unlikely that officers investigating Boshell's murder would stop him two years after the event, for a random spot check and just happen to be filming his arrest with a hand-held camcorder, as these officers had done. The likelihood was, therefore, that they had been watching him for some time. Feeling nervous and dreading what questions might lay ahead, Alvin was transported to Basildon police station, from where he immediately contacted his solicitor. Several hours later, when his solicitor had arrived, Alvin, who was unaware if any of his associates were in custody, was interviewed. He refused to answer any questions. Instead, he read out the following prepared statement:

'I would like to confirm that I was in possession of a quantity of cocaine when I was arrested. I had fallen into debt with loan sharks from whom I had borrowed £15,000 to finish refurbishments at my house. I fell behind with the payments and pressure was put on me to pay the money back. Eventually the loan sharks threatened that they would cause physical harm to both myself and my wife, Clair. My wife is pregnant, has a seven-month-old baby and knows nothing about my business activities.

'Eventually, and in fear for our safety, I agreed to collect and deliver what I believed to be a quantity of cocaine on behalf of these loan sharks. I collected the drugs from a contact yesterday morning with directions to deliver it to Canvey Island. I was arrested with the drugs in my possession en route. The scales were with me to check the weight before delivery and were provided to me with the money, which I received the night before.

'I do have a cocaine habit, which I have suffered from for the past two years. Any drug paraphernalia found at my home address relates to my habit. My wife has no knowledge of my habit or of any drugs that may have been found at my home address. The £31,420 found in my washing machine by police officers was cash given to me to pay for the cocaine once I had completed my delivery to Canvey Island. Other amounts of money found at my address relate to my wife's savings, recent employment and monies I kept at home to pay for refurbishment material deliveries. I accept that the taser gun found at my home is mine. I found it in a car I bought a few months ago. I realised it was a prohibited weapon and so I put it on top of my fridge freezer. I had since forgotten about it.'

Alvin knew that the penalty for possessing and conspiring to supply such a large amount of cocaine was likely to attract a sentence of approximately six years' imprisonment. The very thought of losing his liberty after getting married, having a child and another on the way was too much to bear. Whatever it was going to take to get Alvin out of the predicament that he was in, he knew that he was going to have to do it. The problem Alvin had was that the police also knew the state of mind that he was in and the dilemma he faced.

The evidence they had gathered had left them in no doubt whatsoever that Alvin was involved in Boshell's death, but they needed leverage or some sort of trigger mechanism to get him to start talking. They had received intelligence that Alvin was going to be involved in the supply of a kilo of cocaine that morning and they knew that if they caught him with it that would provide the bargaining tool they needed. It was suggested to Alvin that if he was prepared to assist the police with their inquiries, they might be able to assist him with the jail term he now faced.

At 2032 hrs on 2 April 2003, having already been charged with the possession of a kilo of cocaine with intent to supply, Alvin agreed to give an intelligence interview to DS Carter and DC Staff on the condition that the judge sentencing him for the cocaine would credit him for his co-operation. There is absolutely nothing wrong in law or police procedure with these types of agreements. However, the credibility of anybody giving evidence or intelligence in return for any type of reward has to be, I would suggest, at least questionable. It was explained to Alvin that he was not under caution, he was not under arrest and he was not under any obligation to say anything at all. He was then reminded that the charge he faced, in relation to the cocaine, was a serious one and it was likely to be dealt with by means of a lengthy prison sentence when he finally appeared in court. In plain English, Alvin had been told, 'Help us or face six years inside.'

DS Carter told Alvin, 'There are a number of things that we can do to assist you in relation to that prison sentence that are governed by the judiciary. Basically, the judiciary agree that if anybody turns to assist the police and we go along to court and behind closed doors say to the judge, "This person has assisted us," the judge is then duty-bound to reduce the sentence. That is written in the judiciary. Whatever help you give us, a decision will be made on what help we can give you, and there are a number of options open. But again, it's down to you to decide whether you want to speak to us or not.'

Would he serve six years in prison and risk losing everything? Or would he do what Boshell had done and give these people a load of bullshit intelligence? I cannot imagine Alvin agonising over the decision he was going to make for too long. He did refuse to talk initially because he didn't want what he had to say to be recorded. After being reassured by the officers that the tapes would never be used, Alvin agreed to tell his story. Having read the transcripts of the interview tapes, it is apparent to me that Alvin was not concerned about the finer details of his story, his safety or the pursuit of justice. His main concern appears to have been that the authorities were going to try to seize his home under the Proceeds of Crime Act. This act was designed to show criminals that crime really does not pay, even if they are not caught initially. Any money or assets that a criminal cannot prove he has earned or funded legitimately can be seized by the courts at any time.

It would have been fairly clear to the officers who arrested Alvin and found £31,420 in his washing machine, that the vast majority of his sizeable income was anything but legitimate. They could have quite easily claimed that his car and his home were purchased from the proceeds of crime.

'What guarantees can be made that my wife will be able to keep the house?' Alvin had asked.

'No guarantees at the moment,' DS Carter replied, 'because I don't know what you are going to tell us. The bottom line is you will go to court tomorrow and you will be remanded in custody. We can then get you out of prison on a production order so that we can sit down and talk in more depth. I can't give you any promises whatsoever. We can only help you if you help us.'

Before ending the interview, the detectives once more reminded Alvin that the degree of assistance they could offer him depended entirely upon the quality of information that he could give them. They told him to think about it and they would chat again at a later date.

Alvin said that he would try to remember things but he was having difficulty because 'that shit [cocaine] has fucked my head up half the time'.

DS Carter concluded the intelligence interview by telling Alvin, 'What might seem trivial to you might mean something important to us. It might be that we have a lot of intelligence about somebody and something you might say might make it all fall into place.

'While we wouldn't use you in evidence, unless you actually came fully on board and said, "Right, I am going to clear everything up that I have ever been involved in, and I am going to name these people", then obviously you would go down the line of being what is commonly termed a supergrass. You would have to make statements and you would have to be prepared to stand up in court. Obviously, there are advantages to you that can be put in place. It's been done many times; I was involved with Darren Nicholls, who was the supergrass on the Rettendon murder job.

'He still went to prison for his involvement but he became a protected witness and is now living somewhere completely different. I'm not going to press you today because we now have something to work on and we need to check you are not spinning us a line to try to get something. There has got to be a trust thing between us.'

Damon Alvin has never understood the word 'trust'. His mind was already concentrating on how he was going to overcome the next hurdle between himself and the freedom he was prepared to do anything to secure. Alvin knew that he would have to start fabricating evidence that would make the story he had given in mitigation plausible.

On Thursday, 3 April 2003, Alvin was remanded in custody to HMP Belmarsh, in south-east London, to await a hearing at Basildon Crown Court for sentencing.

Two months later, Alvin was taken out of prison and transported to Gravesend police station, in Kent, where he was formally arrested for the murder of Dean Boshell. Alvin underwent two interviews, during which he refused to answer any other questions other than to confirm his name, address and date of birth. During a break between the two no-comment interviews, the officers said to Alvin, in the presence of his solicitor (who made notes on the subject), that they believed that Ricky Percival was responsible for the murder of Dean Boshell.

In a police statement Alvin made later about this incident, he said, 'They called Percival "the shooter" as opposed to "the murderer". They went on to say that if I was prepared to tell them what had happened the night Boshell died, protection would be offered to my family and me. My wife came to the police station and it was explained to her what assistance could be given if I was in a position to confirm what they suspected.

'I was then allowed a period of time alone with my wife in a room divided by a screen. My wife and I discussed our options. I told her that I knew what had happened that night and that I was involved. My wife made it plain that she did not want to be away from her family; she was pregnant at the time and was scared. She left it up to me, however, to make the final decision. I was allowed the night to think about it. The following morning, I decided to remain silent because I was concerned for my safety, the safety of my wife, her family and mine.'

Just before Alvin was returned to HMP Belmarsh, he was asked 'off the record' why Dean Boshell had been murdered. Without any hesitation Alvin had replied, 'Because he was a liability.' Alvin says now that while at Gravesend he was desperate to tell the police the full story regarding Boshell's murder but he was too scared. Of whom, he does not say. Percival was on holiday in Spain and so one can only assume that Alvin feared the drug-dealing loan sharks to whom he supposedly owed £15,000.

Before people are sentenced in these days of equality and justice, they are interviewed by the probation service so that a report detailing their personal circumstances can be presented to the judge. Those who are homeless, unemployed or otherwise in genuine need are generally sent to prison and people who have wives, children, a job and a home are often spared the indignity of incarceration. The thinking is that jailing a family man will cause his innocent wife and children to suffer. Society as a whole allegedly suffers if a taxpayer is jailed because the public purse has to fund his upkeep while he is inside. Those with nothing are decreed to be an existing strain on the limited resources of the welfare state and so sending them to jail apparently affects nobody. The fact that a person from a stable background should have thought long and hard about the consequences of his actions, before risking losing them, is generally ignored.

When Alvin met the probation officer appointed to write his report, he knew exactly what he was required to say in order to attract maximum credit. He was going to have to invent a story backed by fabricated evidence and say that he had acted under duress and any punishment he received for his crime would punish his innocent wife and child more than it would punish him. Alvin told the probation officer that, following the death of his good friend Dean Boshell, he had become very low and depressed.

He claimed that he had been diagnosed as suffering from depression and his condition had become so dire he began to 'self-medicate' with cocaine. Initially, he only used the drug socially but after moving to the Benfleet area of Basildon, he had become increasingly involved with heavy cocaine users. This had resulted in Alvin's habit spiralling out of control, to the point where he was using up to £250 worth of the drug a week. Alvin said that he was able to conceal his drug dependency from his wife but when refurbishments were required at his home he had secured a £10,000 loan from drug dealers that he associated with, and a further £5,000 from them at a later date.

At first, there were no problems with the arrangement but Alvin said that as his drug habit escalated he fell behind with the repayments, and relations between him and his creditors began to sour. In December 2002, matters came to a head when Alvin was confronted by a number of men from this gang, who demanded their money back. Alvin asked them for more time to pay but the men refused to listen. Alvin said that he was stabbed in the leg and then beaten with a hammer. As he lay on the floor bleeding, he was told that if he did not pay or somehow work the debt off, future attacks would involve not only him being hurt, but also members of his family. As he told the shocked probation officer his story Alvin struggled to keep his composure. He said that he had initially refused to comply with the gang's requests, but when they threatened him and demanded the full amount, he reluctantly agreed to work off some of the debt by making a delivery of cocaine. It was while transporting a kilo of cocaine from Leigh-on-Sea to Canvey Island, on behalf of the gang, that Alvin had been arrested.

While in prison, Alvin said that his wife had been accosted by gang members and forced to withdraw £20,000 from their savings in order to repay the debt. Despite handing over this money, his wife had continued to receive menacing phone calls and death threats. These included a funeral wreath being delivered to her address with a card that read, 'With Deepest Sympathy for You. Tell him to keep his trap shut or these will be yours. May it help you to remember that friends are always there.' In a note posted through her letterbox, which had been made using letters cut from a newspaper, the gang had warned, 'We want our fucking money. Sort it, or we will sort you.'

Alvin claimed that these threats against his family were intended to dissuade him from giving information to the police about the gang. That was why he had refused to answer police questions when he had been arrested.

After hearing Alvin's tale of woe, the well-meaning probation officer wrote in his pre-sentence report: 'Given the circumstances surrounding this offence and further information provided within this report, if the court feels that only a custodial sentence can be justified, I would ask that any term of imprisonment imposed be as short as possible in order to limit further pressure upon Mr Alvin's family, who have already suffered significantly as a result of this offence.'

Knowing the importance of shoring up a bullshit story with factual evidence, Alvin produced a medical certificate to 'prove' that he had been stabbed and beaten by the loan sharks he owed money to. This certificate stated that he had attended a doctor's surgery around Christmas 2002 suffering from cuts to his hands and leg. These were, the document said, 'allegedly caused by a knife'. Alvin's wife had already reported the death threats, letters and funeral wreath she had received to the police. It's unlikely that any judge would have doubted the authenticity of Alvin's dreadful plight at the hands of such an evil drug gang.

On 10 July 2003, Alvin appeared at Basildon Crown Court for sentencing. When asked by the judge if he had anything to say in mitigation, Alvin acknowledged that he was aware that the only sentencing option available to the judge for such a serious offence was a custodial sentence. However, he begged the judge to consider how much he had changed in the past few years of his life.

'My past offending is shameful,' he said, 'and I'm far from proud of my previous convictions, but I have changed in the past few years. I have got married to a wonderful caring woman and together we have bought a house. We have a baby and have another on the way. I started my own business three years ago, which has been steadily growing and I normally employ up to six people. I know the offence I committed was both stupid and irresponsible and I have no one else to blame but myself. I know this is no excuse but I got myself into a position I didn't know how to get out of. I now realise I could have, and should have, done things differently. I am now clean from drugs and receiving help with the depression caused by the murder of my friend [Boshell], which led to my habit. I have helped the police to the best of my ability with everything I know. I ask you for one last chance and for you to consider giving me a shorter term of imprisonment. When I'm released, I want to show that I can live a normal, law-abiding life and continue with my business.'

There wasn't a dry eye in the courtroom by the time Alvin had finished delivering his emotionally charged speech. But the 'Damon Alvin Sympathy Show' was not over just yet. Pregnant and dabbing at her eyes with a tissue, his wife Clair listened intently as a letter she had written as an encore to her husband's performance was read out on his behalf.

'I am living between my own home and my parents' house,' Clair had written, 'because I am scared to be at home alone with my son, due to the threats that I have been receiving. I have had an alarm and panic button installed but I still feel unsafe. I have lost my husband, who I love and miss very dearly. We have never been apart before and I'm finding it hard to cope. We are a very close couple and although I don't condone what Damon has done, I do feel that I now understand the reasons why he did it. Both myself and my young son are still suffering as Damon is away from us, and we are still living with the threat that he tried to resolve.'

Taking into account the circumstances that supposedly led to Alvin being forced to courier drugs and the fact that he had been 'beaten, stabbed and his family left traumatised', the judge sentenced Alvin to thirty months' imprisonment, instead of the six years that he had been told to expect.

A confiscation order was also made against him for the £31,420 that had been found in his washing machine and a further £18,000 was seized out of his savings. Justice, it would appear, had prevailed. Damon Alvin had broken the law and Damon Alvin had been made to pay. Proof, if any were ever needed, that there is no correlation between morality and legality. Neither is there any correlation between justice and 'the law'.

Eight brief months after being sentenced to serve two and a half years, Damon Alvin was released from prison on the condition that he agree to wear an electronic tag for a period of four months. These tags are tuned into an electronic box in the offender's home, which sends a warning signal to the police if the person is not within a certain distance of it at designated times. The idea is that, rather than have low-risk inmates inhabiting prison cells that could be used to house more dangerous criminals, they can be tagged and effectively put under house arrest. This allows them to work during the day, but prevents them from roaming the streets at night. After three long, seemingly inactive years, the Boshell murder investigation appeared to be going nowhere. That was until 2004, when the Labour Government announced that they were going to introduce new legislation.

The then Home Secretary, David Blunkett, said that a new strategy to tackle organised crime was needed and this would include a revamp of the supergrass system. Blunkett said that his proposals were aimed at getting a grip on gangs who controlled drug running, people smuggling, prostitution and financial rackets.

'Criminals who "turn Queen's evidence" could win immunity from prosecution, or have their sentence cut by more than two-thirds if they shop their gang bosses,' he said. 'Existing criminals who "turn Queen's evidence" already have their sentences reduced and are often given new identities, but this will be the first time that this approach has been formalised in an Act of Parliament.'

Nobody knows if Essex police already had a strategy for the Boshell case simmering on some back burner, or if news of this new legislation prompted officers to think again. Coincidentally, or otherwise, the police decided to rearrest Damon Alvin. At 0400 hrs on the very morning that Alvin was due to have his electronic tag removed, the police stormed his house and took him into custody for the murder of Dean Boshell. At the same time, Kevin Walsh and Kate Griffiths were arrested for allegedly conspiring to pervert the course of justice. Ricky Percival's address was also raided but he was not home at the time.

Alvin was taken to Harlow police station for questioning, but on the advice of his legal representative he made no comment when interviewed. He did, however, produce a written statement. Alvin said that he had met Boshell in Chelmsford prison and they had become friends. He said that he had liked Boshell and had had no reason to fall out with him and certainly no reason to want to kill him.

Alvin vehemently denied planning to go on any sort of burglary with Boshell at the time of the murder, adding, 'If I was doing something really serious like that, I would not have relied on Dean.'

In an effort to appear helpful, Alvin offered the interviewing officers a second possible motive for the murder. He said that Boshell might have been involved in gun running and drug dealing with immigrants in the Southend area.

'I simply do not know who killed Dean,' he said. 'When I was taken out of prison to Gravesend police station, the officers told me that they knew that I had nothing to do with the murder. They said that they believed it was Ricky Percival who was responsible for the killing. They offered me all sorts of deals, which I refused. I said I did not know anything about Dean's death and so was unable, even if I had wanted to, to do a deal with the police and implicate Ricky. I have heard various rumours about Percival's involvement in criminal matters. I know nothing of these matters and believe that many of these rumours have been put about by the police. Further, I believe that I have only been charged to put pressure upon me to give the police information about Percival's possible involvement in Boshell's murder. Unfortunately, I do not know anything.'

At the end of the interview, Alvin was bailed to reappear at the police station in two months' time pending further inquiries. Walsh and Griffiths were interviewed at separate police stations and both reiterated the accounts that they had given previously, concerning the night Boshell had died. The police had formed the opinion that the couple had either been coerced or threatened by Percival, Alvin or both men to give them an alibi for the time that Boshell had been shot.

The unofficial time of Boshell's death had been calculated by the police after considering the time Boshell had been seen leaving Southend and the second statement of Gordon Osborne, who claimed that he had heard two or three shots coming from the allotments between 2300 hrs and 2330 hrs. Boshell had not been seen alive again after leaving Southend. He had been shot three times and, according to the police, nobody other than the gunman knew this. Osborne, therefore, must have been telling the truth when he said he heard that number of shots being fired between 2300 hrs and 2330 hrs.

Convinced that Alvin, Percival or both were responsible, the police were left in no doubt that Griffiths and Walsh must, therefore, be lying. They had to be, because they had both said that Alvin and Percival were in their flat at the time the police claimed Boshell had been murdered. Kate Griffiths, a hard-working young woman of good character, was seen by the police as the weakest link in the alleged plot to provide Boshell's killers with an alibi, and so she was subjected to intense questioning over two days. Laughing nervously when they accused her of lying during her numerous interviews, Griffiths insisted that she was telling the truth.

Kevin Walsh was undergoing a similar interrogation to Kate Griffiths. He, too, was insisting that he was innocent, but the police officers interviewing him were far from convinced. After two days of relentless questioning, Griffiths and Walsh were bailed to reappear at a police station pending further inquiries. Shortly after the arrests of his three friends, Percival had handed himself in at a police station and was arrested for the murder of Dean Boshell. Later the same day, after giving a no-comment interview on the advice of his solicitor, he too was bailed to return to the police station at a later date.

On 21 October 2004, all four suspects attended Harlow police station where Alvin was formerly charged with the murder of Dean Boshell and Percival, Griffiths and Walsh were charged with conspiracy to pervert the course of justice. Later that afternoon, they appeared in court, Griffiths and Walsh were released on bail to await trial but Percival and Alvin were remanded in custody to my old address, HMP Chelmsford.

CHAPTER ELEVEN

On 2 September 2005, just ten days before Alvin's trial was due to begin, DC Sharp was dispatched to take a more detailed statement from Gordon Osborne. The police were desperate to firm up their theory that the telephone call made at 2348 hrs to Alvin's then-girlfriend, from the payphone near the allotments, was relevant to Osborne's recollection of hearing a gunshot or, as he later said, 'gunshots', between 2300 hrs and 2330 hrs. The police believed that Alvin had murdered Boshell at around 2330 hrs and then walked to the telephone box, which was described as 'a stone's throw away', to ring his partner Clair for a lift home. Rather naively, the police had never considered the possibility that it may have been Boshell who made the call, which is why Clair had initially refused to sign her statement.

Since the murder, Osborne had left the UK for Spain, where he had set up his own bar and restaurant. When DC Sharp travelled to Spain to meet Osborne, Osborne explained that he had emigrated because he was 'fed up of life in England', so much so in fact, he said, that he was never going to return there. Osborne said that he and his family were settled where they were and, in any event, the weather was far better in Spain than in Essex. DC Sharp noted that during their conversation Osborne appeared relaxed; he spoke freely about his business, his plans for the property he was living in and the quality of life that he was enjoying. However, the mood changed when DC Sharp explained that the contact numbers Osborne had given to the police were no longer in use and the address he had provided was incorrect.

'Locating your whereabouts,' DC Sharp said, 'has not been easy.'

Osborne explained that he was not trying to avoid the police, he had merely lost his phone and he had only recently realised what his actual address was.

I have never heard of an adult not knowing his or her home address, but Osborne's explanation was accepted by the officer without further comment. DC Sharp asked Osborne if he would be willing to return to England to attend court and give crucial evidence about the gunshots he claimed to have heard, but Osborne was emphatic when he said 'no' and assured DC Sharp that he would never change his mind because he feared those who had been charged in connection with the murder. That is 'the official police line' in any event, but many would argue that Osborne didn't want to return to England because he knew that there was an outstanding warrant for his arrest in relation to an indecent assault, which might result in him swapping his good life in Spain for an English prison cell.

We are asked to believe that, although disheartened, DC Sharp refused to concede defeat and asked Osborne to make another statement, which he would submit to the prosecution, in the hope it could be read out at the trial in his absence. DC Sharp knew that if a judge was made aware that Osborne feared for his safety, then this method of including his evidence might be ruled as acceptable. Osborne agreed and, despite it being four and a half years since the night Boshell died, he managed to recall even more details than in his previous statements.

'Dealing first with the house-to-house inquiry form,' he said, 'I recall the details I gave were recorded by a detective who called at my door. I will admit that, at the time, I didn't really think about the answers I gave to the officer and I was quite vague about what I said. However, by the time an officer called to take a full statement from me, I had given it more thought. In this statement I said that I went to bed at about 2100 hrs on the night in question. This was probably earlier than the usual time I go, but I'd had a hard day at work. My bedroom was at the rear of the house. I would always have one of the bedroom windows open; the curtains would also have been open because they were never closed. Occasionally I would read in bed, sometimes I would just drift off to sleep. On the night in question, I can't recall what I did or how long I was awake before I went to sleep.

'I woke up at about 2300 hrs that same evening; I'd heard two or three shots coming from the allotment. I can't be more specific about the time now, but I had a digital alarm clock by the bed, which I did look at. I immediately recognised the sounds as coming from a handgun; this type of weapon has a distinctive sound, totally different from a shotgun or rifle. I have had experience of firearms since I was 11 years of age, when I shot rifles with the Sea Cadets. I remained in the cadets until the age of 16. At the age of 17, I joined the Royal Marines, staying with them for 18 months. During my time with the Marines, I was trained on the Browning 9mm semi-automatic pistol, self-loading rifles, Lee Enfield rifles, American M16 rifles, German Mausers and Lugers. Since leaving the Marines, I have not had any dealings with firearms but, like riding a bike, you never forget what you've learned and the sound each weapon makes. I can't say how far away these shots were. All I can say is that the sounds definitely came from the back of my house.

'I have been asked if I will return to the United Kingdom and give evidence. I can state that I will not. While living in the Leigh-on-Sea area, I would frequent the Woodcutters Arms and I am all too aware of the reputation of the people that use this pub, and of those charged in connection with the murder. I would fear not only for my safety, but also for that of my family, should I return as a witness. I have also been asked if I would consider giving evidence by video link. I will not for the reasons already explained.'

It wasn't the result that the police had hoped for, but Osborne's statement was nevertheless encouraging. Here was a man with an excellent knowledge of firearms who had not only heard two or three shots around the time Boshell was believed to have died, but he had also identified them as coming from a handgun. Such knowledge and expertise were bound to impress a jury and confirm to them that Boshell had met his death shortly before the telephone call had been made to Alvin's girlfriend.

When Alvin, Griffiths, Percival and Walsh appeared at Chelmsford Crown Court to stand trial, they all pleaded 'not guilty' to the charges that they faced. During the first week of the proceedings, the jury was sworn in and the opening speeches were made by both the prosecution and the defence. As a result of legal arguments, the jurors were removed from the room during the second week. The prosecution had said that they wished to introduce as evidence the notes that the police had made when Boshell had given information about Alvin. If the judge agreed to let the prosecution use these notes, they would prove to be extremely damaging to Alvin's defence, so he had instructed his legal team to oppose the application.

The defence claimed that Boshell had been a fantasist whose word could not be relied upon and, to highlight this fact, a letter written by Boshell while in prison was read out in which he talked about taking a knife off a fellow inmate and stabbing him repeatedly, after he had been set upon by a gang. It was proven beyond doubt that no such incident had ever occurred. Using Boshell's words to convict a defendant of murder would, they argued, be at best unsafe. The other problem with permitting Boshell's evidence to be used was that the defence would not have an opportunity to cross-examine him. For instance, nobody, including the police, believed that 'Dave the doorman' had shot the Trettons, as Boshell had claimed. Since Boshell was deceased, the defence would, therefore, be unable to question him, in order to find out what other lies he may have told and why.

During the course of these legal arguments, the judge had invited the prosecuting counsel and two police officers involved in the case into his chambers so that he could be made aware of some of the unused material. This unused material included police intelligence surrounding the alleged identity of Boshell's murderer. Defence lawyers were not invited to attend this meeting and so were unable to make representations on behalf of their clients. It is understood that only intelligence accusing Percival of the murder was put before the judge. When the judge ruled that Boshell's evidence could be used as evidence, Alvin was devastated. He immediately announced that he wished to talk to his barrister in private.

'At this stage in the proceedings, I wasn't happy,' Alvin said later. 'I was getting worried about the possible outcome of the trial. I began to realise that my legal team were talking sense; they had informed me that there was a good chance that I would be convicted if I didn't tell the police the full story. They did not know the truth; all they knew was that I was denying the murder. The trial was adjourned and I was given the weekend to contemplate my future.'

Throughout the weekend at Chelmsford prison, Alvin acted as if nothing had changed between himself and Percival but, behind the mask, he was plotting and scheming against his unsuspecting friend. Alvin had decided that Percival could be adapted to fit any missing space in the picture that he needed to paint in order to avoid a murder conviction. The police believed that Percival had shot the Tretton family, and so convincing them that he had also shot Boshell would not be hard. On Monday morning, Alvin discussed his options in an interview room with his legal team. They advised him that the evidence against him was very strong and there was every possibility that he would be convicted and sent to prison for life.

In a corner and out of ideas, Alvin blurted out that he was innocent; it was Percival who was responsible for Boshell's murder and, although present, he had played no part in the shooting. Alvin's defence team made the prosecution aware that their client wanted to make a fresh statement and when the judge was informed of this development, he granted an application by the prosecution to adjourn the case. The jury was discharged and the judge said that Alvin should be given as much time as he needed to make his new statement in full.

Instead of being returned to HMP Chelmsford that evening, Alvin was taken into police custody so that he could give his latest version of events concerning the murder, and other matters such as the Tretton shootings.

In the first of many interviews, DC Sharp told Alvin: 'Through your legal team, you served a further defence statement in which you indicated that you were not actually responsible for the murder of Boshell. You described in some detail how Mr Percival committed the murder. I must inform you that you're not viewed as a witness for the prosecution and you must understand that your co-operation does not mean that the case against you will, or may, be discontinued. Any information you do provide will, together with the results of any subsequent police investigations, be passed to the Crown Prosecution Service for its further consideration of the case against you.'

Alvin breathed an inward sigh of relief because he knew that the murder allegation against him would no longer be pursued. The freedom that he was prepared to stab himself for, steal wreaths from graves for and tell continual bare-faced lies for was ensured. All Alvin had to do was tell a convincing story that blamed Percival for all the crimes that *he* had committed. His was an easy task. Alvin had been locked in a prison cell for a year awaiting trial with copies of every witness statement, every crime scene photograph and every other document relating to the murder and so he knew the case inside out.

In the weeks and months that followed, Alvin was interviewed on an almost daily basis. After contradicting himself, 'forgetting things' and then miraculously remembering them, Alvin came up with a story that eventually resulted in Percival being convicted and sentenced to serve a minimum of 26 years' imprisonment. Kevin Walsh was convicted of conspiring to pervert the course of justice and sentenced to three years' imprisonment, because he allegedly gave Percival a false alibi. His ex-girlfriend, Kate Griffiths, was charged with the same offence, which had allegedly been committed at the same time and in the same circumstances, but she was found not guilty. Damon Alvin was praised for assisting the police, handed a large sum of public money and offered all of the help available to assist him and his family to walk away from the mess that he had created.

Like Tucker's Essex Boys gang, Alvin's firm had fallen apart after an orgy of violence and, when the police began investigating their crimes, it was every man for himself. Like Tucker, Tate and Rolfe, Boshell lay dead; like Nicholls, Alvin ended up in the Witness Protection Programme; and, like Steele and Whomes, Percival was wrongly convicted and sentenced to life imprisonment. I thank God that I remain the last man standing from those two violent, drug-fuelled eras. I certainly won't tempt fate and make the same mistakes again.

Following Boshell's murder and my friends' arrests, I found myself alone, which gave me time to think about my past but, more importantly, about my future. Unnatural thoughts began to fill my head. I imagined myself finding a girl, settling down and doing an honest day's work for a day's pay. Laughing as I lay on my bed I began to warm to the idea of having 2.5 children, a 3-bedroom semi-detached house, a white picket fence and a modest car on the driveway. I hadn't felt such a buzz since the night I had gone to the Epping Country Club to celebrate my birthday when Tate had given me my first ever Ecstasy pill. I had never attempted to dance before, but half an hour after swallowing the small white pill it had suddenly dawned on me that I was, in fact, the best dancer in the building. Prancing about on a raised podium, I had grinned insanely at the crowd, who all appeared to be mesmerised by my unique moves. As I looked down at my adoring fans I could see that Craig Rolfe was laughing, Tucker was glaring at me and Tate was shaking his head in disbelief.

'Fuck them,' I kept thinking to myself, 'this boy was born to dance.'

Fantasising about a trouble-free life actually made me feel better than I had felt that night, so I decided to do an incredibly irrational thing. I tipped £1,500 worth of quality cocaine into my toilet, threw 500 Ecstasy pills in after it and flushed away the lot. I then left the house looking for a job. Let's not get carried away here, this is the real world that I'm talking about. Of course I didn't find a job. Who in their right mind would employ a man who had a reputation for shooting people? The main thing is, I tried, and I kept on trying because I knew that, in the end, my luck would change.

One evening, I was out with a very good friend named Lee 'KO' Mayo, so called because he is a cage fighter who spends more time on his back looking up at the latest opponent to knock him down than he does fighting. Lee introduced me to a beautiful girl named Rachel to whom I was instantly attracted. I don't think Rachel shared my enthusiasm regarding a potential liaison, but after a great deal of persuasion she finally agreed to meet me the following week for a date. Rachel was still uncertain about my intentions when we met, so I joked that I would untie her brother and release him from the boot of my car as soon as she had finished having dinner with me! Sitting in the restaurant I poured my heart out; I told her all about my past and waited for her to flee in terror.

Much to my surprise, Rachel said that if 'those events' were in my past and not part of the present, she would like to see me again. After that night, I met Rachel regularly, a relationship developed and in time we fell in love. I cannot thank Rachel enough for helping me to stick to the path that I had chosen to take. On several occasions, a face from the past has appeared and offered me the chance to take part in a criminal enterprise, but because of Rachel, I have declined. She has supported me through some very dark days and always kept me believing that if I persevere, opportunities other than crime will come my way.

For quite some time, I agonised over whether or not I should tell Rachel about my childhood cancer, which doctors had told me would leave me infertile. When we talked about getting married and Rachel mentioned children, I found myself blurting the whole sorry story out. To my surprise, Rachel said that she too had been diagnosed with cancer at the age of 19 years, and so she totally understood what I had been through. True to form, she remained positive and reassured me that if we couldn't have children naturally, we could always try some form of infertility treatment. On 10 May 2008, Rachel and I married and I can honestly say that it was the happiest day of my life. Our union has not yet produced any children but we continue to enjoy trying, and Rachel has recently started to undergo IVF treatment.

My search for employment had been no more fruitful than my numerous attempts to become a father, so a friend suggested that I should try to learn 'The Knowledge' and become a taxi driver in London. The Knowledge is a term used to describe a test that all London taxi drivers have to pass before being given their licences. They have to memorise the name of every street and know every conceivable route to get from one part of the sprawling city to another. I didn't think the body that licensed cabbies would entertain me, as you are supposed to be of good character and have a clean record, but I decided to take my chances. I couldn't quite believe it when I received a letter stating that, as it had been 11 years since my last custodial sentence, I had passed the police check.

I bought a moped and spent eight to ten hours every day trying to learn the name of every street, road and avenue in London, in the hope that I would one day pass The Knowledge and earn myself a lucrative London taxi-driver's licence. I wasn't making any money while I was doing The Knowledge, and so I accepted a job as an electrician's labourer working permanent nights. After spending eight hours on my moped, I would sleep for four hours and then labour for eight hours at night before sleeping for another four hours. Travelling back and forth to Essex took up half of my sleeping time and so in the end I made a bed up in my car.

One morning, I was driving along Park Lane when an unmarked police car pulled alongside my vehicle in the traffic. I did not know that it was the police at first; all I saw were three burly guys glaring at me. Not wishing to appear intimidated I glared back before continuing on my way. As I reached the roundabout at Hyde Park Corner the car cut in front of me and blue lights previously unseen near its boot began to flash. One of the plain-clothed officers got out, flashed me his warrant card and asked me who I was and where I was going. After answering all his mundane questions I was ordered to get out of my car, which was then thoroughly searched.

Holding a hammer aloft that he had found underneath the driver's seat, the triumphant officer asked me to explain. 'What is this used for?'

I am not sure what level of education people need to get into the police force these days but surely even mentally challenged individuals know what hammers are used for. Not wanting to insult the policeman's intelligence I replied, 'If you want two pieces of wood to be fixed together and remain so, one requires a long thin metal object, which is commonly described as a nail. You then place said nail on top of the two pieces of aforementioned wood and bash it into them using that thing that you have in your hand,' and I pointed at the hammer.

I was immediately pushed onto the bonnet of my car, handcuffed and taken to a police station where I was cautioned for possessing an offensive weapon. I wasn't bothered about the caution but the taxi-licensing authority held a very different view. The police informed them about the 'incident' and they banned me from holding a London taxi-driver's licence after explaining that London cabbies with hammers under their seats was not an image the Tourist Board or they wished to embrace. All the time and effort that I had put into learning The Knowledge had been wasted. I don't mind admitting that I was absolutely gutted; I mean, it wasn't as if I had actually done anything wrong. What workman doesn't have the tools of his trade in his car? Once again, Rachel was there to catch and guide me. She told me to put the episode behind me and continue working as a labourer until something better came along.

Six months after I had married Rachel, I was working at Mile End Underground station one night, loading scaffolding tubes from the platform down onto the track. I failed to see a puddle of water and as I stepped into it I slipped and fell head first down onto the tracks. I stood up feeling dazed and confused and can recall being surrounded by my work colleagues.

'Are you OK, Steve? Are you OK?' one of them kept shouting.

I then recall somebody saying, 'What the fuck have you done to your arm?'

I looked down and saw that my hand was facing the wrong way around and my arm had been snapped in two. I didn't faint but I do not remember much more. I was later informed that I was rushed to the Royal London Hospital in Whitechapel where I underwent emergency surgery. When I awoke, Rachel was at my bedside with tears in her eyes.

'I don't know how to tell you this, Steve, but a nurse has told me that you will never be normal again,' she said.

I am not sure if Rachel was confused, deeply upset or a mixture of both, but her words made me laugh.

'Never be normal again? Who the fuck told you that I was normal in the first place?' I replied.

Thankfully, Rachel laughed too; I hated seeing her so upset. When I looked down at my right arm, I instantly understood what Rachel had meant. I had lost huge amounts of muscle and the bone was broken and twisted out of shape. I instinctively knew that the injury couldn't possible heal fully and that I would lose the use of my arm. I am still undergoing surgery and regular physiotherapy to this day, but my condition has failed to improve. I won't let my disability beat me; I still attend college and hope soon to become a qualified electrician.

My greatest hope is that one day, God willing, Rachel and I will be able to have the children we long for. Cancer took away my ability to become a father in the same way that the accident at Mile End tube station took away the use of my arm. As we go through life we do tend to get knocked down occasionally and our resolve is tested, but one must always rise to any challenge and never back down. It's pointless giving up, taking drugs or drinking in an effort to avoid the reality of day-to-day life because reality, whoever you think you are, will eventually catch up with you.

Tate, Tucker, Rolfe, Boshell and Alvin all immersed themselves in a world of make-believe that they thought they controlled. Had they not been out of their heads on drugs they might have realised just what fools they actually were, but the drugs were part and parcel of the fantasy life that they were living, and so they were unable to grasp reality. I am not going to preach to anybody about how they should, or should not, live their lives because up until I met Rachel I had made a complete mess of my own.

The only advice that I will offer is that you should treat others how you would expect to be treated. I don't care who you think you are, or how hard you think are, somebody some day will tire of your bad behaviour and take you out of the game. It's not other hard men you have to worry about, it's the little ones that you bully. In my experience, the most dangerous person in the world is usually somebody who is scared and in a corner. We all get what we are due in the end.

On 21 May 2009, Ricky Percival got what he was long overdue when his case was referred to the Court of Appeal. The only evidence that had supported Alvin's story at the original trial and, therefore, made him appear credible, was that of Gordon Osborne.

Despite his absence from Chelmsford Crown Court, Osborne's statement had been the most crucial independent evidence produced that the jury had been asked to consider. Without his evidence being heard, the prosecution would have struggled, and probably floundered, in proving their case. Unfortunately, Osborne's time as a Royal Marine and his boasting about his knowledge of firearms had convinced the jury that such a man couldn't possibly be wrong.

After reading the seven pages of Osborne's previous convictions, alarm bells regarding his credibility and the accuracy of his statement should have rung loud and clear in the ears of the police, the Crown Prosecution Service, solicitors, barristers, and everybody else connected with the case. It is a disgrace that despite the significant changes made by Osborne in his statements and, knowing that he was a fugitive from this country, everybody concerned failed to delve further into his background. If they had done, they would have learned that Gordon Osborne had deliberately lied. The reason I say this is simple; he was never in the Royal Marines and knows absolutely nothing about firearms. Therefore his claim that he can distinguish the sounds of various weapons being fired is, at best, ridiculous.

Acting Steward Gordon Osborne, service number P100762, enlisted in the Royal Navy on 30 January 1967. He was discharged less than five months later on 24 June 1967, because he was deemed to be 'unsuitable'. According to the Royal Navy, as an Acting Steward Osborne's duties would have included providing hospitality services and learning 'core skills in the hotel trade' aboard ship. In short, Gordon Osborne was a waiter-cum-hotel porter who simply failed to make the grade.

If it wasn't for the investigative skills of Tony Tucker's former business partner Bernard O'Mahoney, Percival's appeal might never have been possible. For many years, O'Mahoney has campaigned tirelessly on behalf of Steele, Whomes and my friend Percival. It was O'Mahoney who discovered the truth about Osborne's deceit. At Percival's appeal, as I looked along the long wooden bench in the public gallery of the Royal Courts of Justice, my mind was awash with memories. To my left sat Bernard O'Mahoney, once one of the Essex Boys' most feared henchmen. If only I had listened to him the night he had warned me to stay away from Tucker! Beside O'Mahoney sat John Whomes, whose brother Jack was convicted of murdering Tate, Tucker and Rolfe. Even in death the trio were able to heap misery on innocent people. I feel for the Whomes family. God knows that I am painfully aware of what they are going through. To my right sat Percival's brother, Danny, and his heartbroken mother Sandy. Another family torn apart by the lies of a Judas whose only desire was to save himself.

Sitting alone, on a bench in front of me, was a man who represented an organisation that has hindered me for more than 20 years. DC Sharp of Essex Police was clearly finding the judge's words uncomfortable to listen to. Lord Justice Hughes said that the use of Osborne's evidence warranted further investigation and eight points that contributed to Percival's conviction also needed to be reconsidered.

A full hearing to deliberate the findings and decide whether Percival should be released immediately or face a retrial, is scheduled to take place later in 2009. I understand that Whomes and Steele are also due to have their murder convictions reconsidered shortly.

I sincerely hope that all three men are released as soon as possible and this story can then end. There has been too much bloodshed and too much pain. I, for one, would never wish to live through times like that again. Last man standing I am, and last man standing I intend to remain.

ACKNOWLEDGEMENTS

STEVE ELLIS

First and foremost, thank you to my wife Rachel, who has given me a life enriched with love and a reason to live. Thanks to Bernard O'Mahoney for all his great work and help, without which this book would never have happened. His many other worthwhile projects involving prisoners go unnoticed by many, but the few are deeply in his debt. Thanks to all of my sisters, too many to name. My close friend Ricky Percival, I am thinking of you and your long-suffering family constantly. Thanks also to my friend John Whomes; I'm thinking of his brother Jack and co-defendant Mick Steele in their fight for justice. I'm also thinking of a man I loved as a brother – Malcolm Walsh. Much love to his widow Bernardette, daughter Sophie, son Anthony and extremely annoying brother Kevin.

Thanks to two very good friends, Cliff and his wife Heidi. I cannot thank enough my true friend Geordie, without whom I would undoubtedly be dead or still imprisoned now. Thanks to my very good friends Badger and his girlfriend Deb 'lushkins'. Regards to my best little mate Georgia, if only I could be blessed with a daughter like you. Thanks to her family for all you have done for me, words are simply not enough. Thanks to my friend Lee 'KO' Mayo, who has spent more time on his back in the ring than the average working girl spends on her back in a lifetime. Thanks also to KO's girlfriend Charlie and their beautiful daughters, and to Gorgeous George. Thanks to a man I have known and respected forever, Jim the wise man, who owned the gym in Hadleigh. Thanks to Sensei Steve, the mad man on Canvey Island, and to my new friend and gifted surgeon, the wonderful Mr O-J, who can perform miracles.

BERNARD O'MAHONEY

I would like to say a huge thank you to Steve Rowan, who was kind enough to allow us to photograph the Range Rover in which the murders were committed for this book's cover. Thank you to my friend and the Cristiano Ronaldo of photography Brian Anderson for taking those and many other incredible photographs for a book we are working on entitled Faces. A mere thank you seems inadequate to express the gratitude I feel for the love my beautiful fiancée Roshea Tierney has shown me over the last year. I love you, Ro, and eagerly await the birth of our first child (Sinead or Paddy) in January 2010. Much love also to our wise and wonderful children: Adrian, Vinney, Karis, Daine and Lydia. Thanks to my mad mother Anna and the rest of the O'Mahoney clan. Thanks also to the Tierney clan – Malcy, Carolyn and Elric. May your God – whoever or whatever it, they, he or she may be – be good to you.